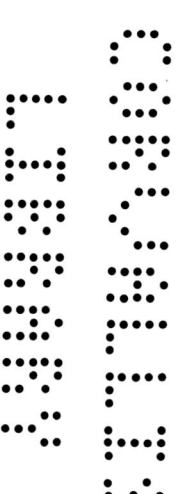

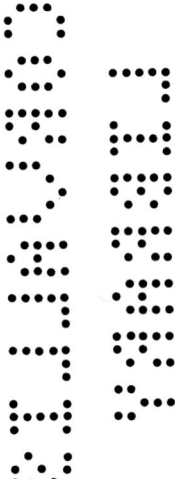

paradise under glass

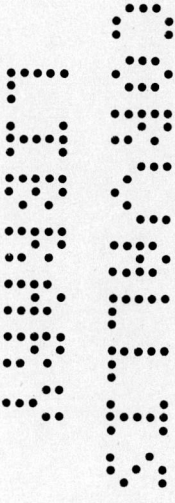

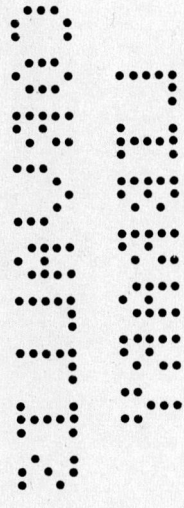

paradise under glass

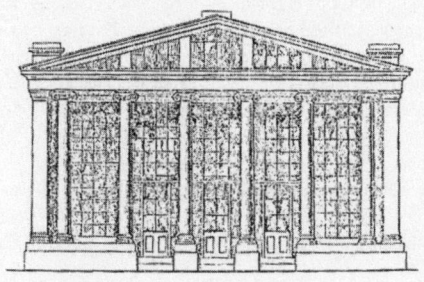

*An Amateur Creates
a Conservatory Garden*

RUTH KASSINGER

wm

WILLIAM MORROW
An Imprint of HarperCollins*Publishers*

HarperCollins books may be purchased for educational, business, or sales promotional use. For information please write: Special Markets Department, HarperCollins Publishers, 10 East 53rd Street, New York, NY 10022.

FIRST EDITION

Designed by Lisa Stokes

Chapter-opener drawings courtesy of Eva-Maria Ruhl.

Library of Congress Cataloging-in-Publication Data

Kassinger, Ruth, 1954–
   Paradise under glass : an amateur creates a conservatory garden / Ruth Kassinger.
     p. cm.
   Includes bibliographical references.
   ISBN 978-0-06-154774-4
   1. Conservatories—Design and construction—Case studies. 2. Conservatories—History. 3. Conservatories—Maryland. 4. Kassinger, Ruth, 1954– 5. Women gardeners—Maryland—Biography. 6. Suburban life—Maryland. 7. Maryland—Biography. I. Title.
   NA8360.K375 2010
   635'.0483—dc22

                                                                2009045875

10 11 12 13 14   OV/RRD   10 9 8 7 6 5 4 3 2 1

For Ted, and in memory of Joan Huber Good

Contents

Introduction

I was sitting at the breakfast table in the conservatory this morning, looking out the window and watching the wind blow puffs of snow off the roof, when a kumquat, deep orange and the size of a large grape, fell off a tree and rolled across the limestone floor. Scotia, our white West Highland terrier, who was lying in a wicker armchair with her head on her paws, saw it, too. Before I could open my mouth, she launched herself off the chair like a swimmer out of the blocks, snapped it up, and swallowed it whole.

Many, many are the pleasures of an indoor garden in a cold climate. Mostly, they are visual ones. I look around me. I have eight hanging baskets: orange, goldfish-shaped *Nematanthus* flowers are brilliant against the mat of their plump, deep green leaves; the Boston ferns sport thick manes of bright green, serrated fronds; and the winter jasmine has a blizzard of starry, white flowers that nod in the light breeze of the overhead fans. My two traveler's palms brush the skylights with their giant canoe-paddle leaves, and *Juncus spiralis,* a wiry marsh grass, corkscrews up from shallow planters on the floor. There are aromatic pleasures, too. The Calamondin orange, 'Meyer' lemon, and key lime trees are in bloom, and the scent of their small, white flowers is sweet and piercing. Still, I have to say, and I assume Scotia would back me up, a kumquat fresh off the tree in February is a delight without compare.

I call this room a conservatory, but others might call it a sunroom or a Florida room. In the nineteenth century, if it had been many times larger, it would have been called a wintergarden. The room is an addition we had built in the angle between the two wings of our old house in suburban Maryland. Its walls and roof are of standard two-by-four construction, and the outside is sheathed in white-painted shingles to match the rest of the house. Glass fills the walls: the windows on the long side are ten feet tall, and the shorter wall is one large bay window. More than half the ceiling is open to light, thanks to twelve skylights in the roof. Two overhead fans keep the air moving. A pale blue wirework dining table with six chairs and the wicker armchair—Scotia's chair—are the only pieces of furniture. For the most part, the space is furnished—Ted, my husband, might say overfurnished—with plants.

Most of my plants are thriving. The tall, green-leafed plants—a dragon tree *Dracaena,* an umbrella tree, four bird-of-paradise, a batwing *Alocasia*, and a cutleaf *Philodendron,* among others—are doing very well. In pots on the floor,

I have a collection of *Anthurium, Dieffenbachia,* and an assortment of begonias whose pink, green, and chocolate leaves are wildly patterned in polka dots, swirls, and rays. Three varieties of *Streptocarpus* with their small and velvety, blue, red, and purple flowers dress the windowsills. Because it is winter, my collection of ten citrus, guava, and other tropical fruit trees and bushes is clustered under two pairs of grow lights. A coffee bush, a fig, a large jade plant, several cactus, and a pineapple plant, which to my astonishment has sent a pineapple skyward, are lodging in the bay window. One wall is completely carpeted in plants. Ted might have a point.

All is not success, though, and I am sorry to see that some plants are looking tired, and some that could have flowers do not. This is because, in part, I am still new to indoor gardening, and I keep experimenting, choosing among the hundreds of tropical and semitropical plants that could, hypothetically, grow indoors. I am still having trouble accepting the fact that my conservatory is north-facing and partially shaded from the best southern sun by the second floor of our house, and so is not well suited to "high-light" plants. Although I have learned to stay away from plants with tags that read "requires full sun," I am fundamentally an optimist, and if a plant promises brilliant flowers and calls for "partial sun," I will take a chance. Sometimes these plants work; sometimes they don't. I wasn't so venturesome when I started out, but I've learned by now to deal with losses.

There is another reason for some of my failures: until I stocked this conservatory, I had no gardening experience of any kind, either outdoors or in. Many of my friends and my family—Ted, an avid outdoor gardener, in particular—are amazed that I set out to create a conservatory and that I have had any success at all. Frankly, so am I.

It isn't that I don't appreciate gardens. I do, and always have. I grew up in Baltimore, and when my sister, Joanie, and I were young, my parents took us to all the public gardens. There was Sherwood Gardens where we went every April to see the tulips, Cylburn Park where we picnicked among blue and yellow wildflowers, and Druid Hill Park, near my grandparents' apartment, where we strolled around the reservoir and admired the flowers and the fountain that at night changed colors. Now, when Ted and I travel, we often visit the local botanical gardens. Our house is just a mile outside Washington, D.C., and we occasionally ride bikes in the National Arboretum and walk through the gardens at Dumbarton Oaks. Longwood Gardens in Kennet Square, Pennsylvania, Winterthur Garden in Delaware, and Ladew Topiary Gardens in Monkton, Maryland, are an easy drive.

Enjoying a garden and creating one, however, have always been completely unrelated activities to my mind. Ted, who will jot down names of shrubs and plants he sees so he can investigate whether they might work in our backyard, has never understood my attitude. I enjoy going to museums and concerts, I tell him, but that doesn't mean I go home and want to pick up a paintbrush or a clarinet. No, I have always been perfectly content to appreciate the expert efforts of others. The urge to pick up a trowel, much less a shovel, or even a pair of clippers never struck me, at least not until recently.

So what inspired me to build a conservatory?

One winter four years ago, I briefly held a consulting job at an office on Capitol Hill. Walking to the Metro station to go home one late afternoon, I was in a gloomy mood. Our oldest daughter, Anna, had left for college on the West Coast, and Austen, a high school senior, was filling out college applications. Our youngest, Alice, was thirteen and seemed especially eager to grow up. She was so busy with school and sports, homework and her social life, we were often reduced to communicating by text message. Where had our little girls gone, the wide-eyed toddlers with their pixie haircuts who tracked my every movement, dripped juice on the kitchen floor and spilled tears when I took their drawings off the refrigerator (only to make room for new drawings!), and told me solemnly, each one, that they would never ever ever leave home? And where was that young mother who failed to get those promises in writing and—how could I have been so foolish?— daydreamed from time to time of the day when her thoughts would not revolve around those little girls?

In a different universe of loss, Joanie had died of a brain tumor in February a year earlier. She had been my best friend and my older girls' special aunt, the looser, cooler version of their mother. She was the brunette with the fierce blue eyes and the traffic-stopping figure who had Roller-bladed around our staid neighborhood dressed in shiny aqua leggings and a leotard, pushing Alice in her stroller. For decades, Joanie and I talked several times a week and, during certain stretches—during one of Joanie's boyfriend crises, for example—every day. We had long ago decided we would always visit our aging parents together. It had all been planned.

I had less than a month to grieve for her, though. In early March, I was diagnosed with breast cancer and was instantly swept from the shore of the present by a riptide of disease. I could only ride it out out there, essentially alone, trying to keep my head above the chop of fear, through the surgeries, the waiting, the radiation, and the gut-twisting chemotherapy. I treaded water, hoping I wouldn't be swept over the horizon, out of view of my family who tracked me, anxiously and steadfastly, from the shores of health. Indeed, a year later, my hair had grown back and my oncologist assured me I would outlive him. But although I seemed to be back on solid ground, I was uneasy. What other treacheries lay in wait in middle age?

So it was into the late afternoon, with change and loss on my mind, that I walked west down Independence Avenue. I didn't usually go this way; another Metro station was closer, but the street had been blocked off—a demonstration maybe or the imminent arrival of a motorcade. Suddenly, I was struck by the view of the U.S. Botanic Garden's Conservatory ahead of me, with its cluster of rounded glass roofs gilded by the setting sun. As I drew closer, I saw that the conservatory had reopened; for years it had been closed and surrounded by a tall, board fence. It had been a very long time, about four decades I realized, since the last, the only, time I'd been inside. Although my watch read 4:30 and the sign on the door said the building closed at 5:00, I decided to take a quick look.

I walked in from the cold and through the anteroom. The glass doors to the largest conservatory, the Palm House, silently parted, and I stepped through. In the instant before a wave of moist warm air fogged my glasses, I was over-whelmed by a view of a vast and dense jungle of greenery. When my glasses cleared, I looked up, following the trunks of the palm trees to the roof, an arching structure of curved glass crisscrossed with metal frames and struts. Several stories above me, through a scrim of palm fronds, I could see pieces of sky. Vapor languished in the air, and the mugginess after the biting cold outside made me feel almost drugged.

I wandered along the sinuous flagstone paths, crossing the stream that wound through the understory. There were so many variations, it struck me, on the theme of Green Leaf: sculpted or feathery; veined in white, gray, or maroon, edged in pink, or backed in a somber purple; shiny or dull; vining, spreading, or gripping the ground; as small as shirt buttons or as big and wrinkled as an elephant's ear. Only a few bright flowers pricked the backdrop of foliage: *Anthurium* with lipstick red flowers that looked as if they were made of plastic, and bromeliads with spiky blooms in garish shades of orange and magenta.

I hiked up an accordion of a metal staircase that led to a catwalk that circled the Palm House. Here was where most of the flowering plants lived, out of the shade of the palms. Tiny yellow orchids, bougainvillea with flowers that shaded from pink to peach, a rainbow of hibiscus, bleeding heart with drops of blood at the end of their white blossoms, and indigo passionflowers clung to tree branches and railings or perched on the ledge that ran around the perimeter.

Too soon it was closing time. My visit stayed with me, though. I thought of the Palm House often, and I stopped there regularly that winter. There were smaller conservatories off the main jungle: a desert garden with cacti and grasses, an orchid collection, and, most appealing to me, a misty "garden primeval" carpeted with mosses and filled with what looked like Jurassic-era tree ferns and strange squat palm trees. It was always hard to leave this place where I felt so thoroughly revived.

I began to notice in newspapers and magazines how many ads there were for sunroom and conservatory additions for homes. How odd that I had never seen any before. The structures came in a range of options, from simple sheds with sliding patio doors to palaces with Palladian windows, carved pilasters, and curving glass roofs. I started tearing out the ads and saved them in a folder.

Gradually, it occurred to me that adding a conservatory onto our house was just what I needed. Warm and humid, beautiful, ever-green, peaceful and still, a conservatory would be the perfect antidote to the losses and changes of middle age. It would be my personal tropical paradise where nothing unexpected lurked in the landscape. I determined to have one.

paradise under glass

The Plant at the Top of the Stairs

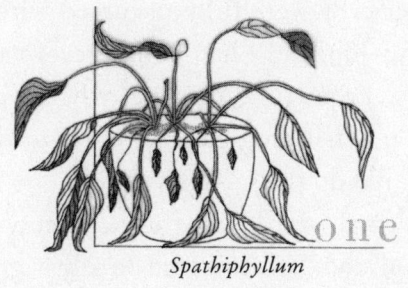

one

Spathiphyllum

Over the years, I have received numerous houseplants as gifts for birthdays and other occasions. I am sure the givers thought they were sending me a better, more lasting token than a bouquet of cut flowers. However, the life span of a houseplant in my care was, if anything, briefer: at least with cut flowers, I knew when to add water.

Anyone who knew me would have given long odds on the life of the plant in the green pot, a gift from my office colleagues that a deliveryman dropped off shortly after Alice was born. Actually, I wasn't certain that what was growing in the pot—a forest of shiny, dark-green, lance-shaped leaves growing straight up from the soil on slender stems—qualified as a plant. I don't recall any blooms, but I was wandering around in a postpartum miasma at the time, so perhaps they were there and I didn't notice them. Someone (was it me?) found a place for the plant at the top of the stairs to the basement and put a white plastic plate under it. A window on the landing, narrow and partly obscured by an overgrown crepe myrtle outside, allowed a little light to filter onto it.

Once settled, the gift faded from my consciousness. All my gray matter cells were fully occupied with three young children and my job, and I had no interest in any additional responsibilities. From time to time, when I passed by the plant, I'd dump a drinking glass of water in the pot. Occasionally, I saw Ted do the same.

Not surprisingly, it did not thrive. Gradually, the leaves lost their sheen and faded—some to olive green, some to yellow—and drooped on their slender stems like pennants on a windless day. Some gave up entirely, and stem and leaf together turned brown and brittle. I accepted the sorry condition of the plant. Like dusty baseboards and unwritten thank-you notes, I figured the plant was an inevitable but minor casualty of my hectic campaign of working and parenting. Besides, I had never had any success with houseplants—I didn't seem to have a knack—so the plant's decline seemed preordained.

Then, one summer afternoon when Alice was three, I noticed that my next-door neighbor had moved several of her potted plants into her backyard. Maybe my plant would also benefit from a little fresh air and sunshine. I took it out to the deck and put it on the glass patio table. When I looked at the plant at eye level and in full sun, the extent of its decline was more apparent. Most of its stems were certainly dead.

I tugged on one of the brown ones and was surprised that it readily came free in my hand. In a minute, I had collected a small pile of dead brush. Already the plant was looking better. Next I gave it a good drink of water from a full watering can Ted had left on the deck and then showered it gently with the remaining water. I stood back and contemplated the scene. A mockingbird sang from a perch on the roof gutter. Planters on the deck railing that Ted and the girls had filled with purple and pink petunias and yellow marigolds were blooming in a cheerful, chromatic chaos. This was like sending my plant to summer camp. It would be inspired and reinvigorated by its surroundings, and by fall it would be healthy again. Thanks to me.

It must have been a good two weeks before I looked at the plant to see how it was faring. We'd taken a short vacation, and then I'd worked extra hours at my office downtown to make for up the time away. A tiny piece of my mind was reserved for the plant, though. I recall sitting at my desk one afternoon, thinking that the afternoon thunderstorm sending hollow rumblings through the canyon of buildings would mean my plant was getting watered, and that it was very convenient of nature to take care of that for me.

So, when I finally checked on my camper, I was shocked. The thing had gone into a complete swoon; its stems were nearly horizontal, splayed like the ribs of a wind-sprung umbrella. Many of the leaves were jaundiced and all had blackened tips. It was obvious, even to me, that my plant had a bad case of sunstroke.

Reproaching myself as well as the plant (how could it fail to take advantage of such an opportunity?), I carried it back inside and put it back on the landing. There I left it for several weeks. I may have been hoping it would make a miraculous recovery, or at least that it would once again melt into the background. Instead, it became a constant, unpleasant reminder of my incompetence, and one evening I resolved to get rid of it. I imagined the pleasing clunk the pot would make when it hit the bottom of the kitchen wastebasket and the satisfying clank of the lid closing. Ugliness banished. Evidence of ineptitude erased. Problem solved.

At the critical moment, however, with the plant poised above the wastebasket, I hesitated. From somewhere deep in my psyche, a worry wriggled its way to my conscious mind. The plant and Alice had arrived together, the plant to celebrate her birth. What if, as in a fairy tale, the two were linked? In the Disney version of *Beauty and the Beast,* which I had watched dozens of times with my daughters, the handsome prince turns away an old beggar woman from his castle door, refusing to give her shelter in exchange for the single rose she offers. As punishment, the old woman, an enchantress, turns him into a beast and links his life to the rose. He will die if no one will see past his ugly exterior and kiss him. No one seems to, and near the end of the movie, as the last petal of the rose drops to the floor, the Beast we have come to love slowly expires. What if Alice's life was connected, like the Beast's to the rose, to this plant? I knew the thought was ridiculously superstitious, but I couldn't quite let go of the pot. I had just tucked Alice into bed in her Pooh-bear pajamas and her last sleepy words to me—the family mantra: "Don't forget I love you"—were still in my ears.

Once again, the plant went back on the landing where, perhaps magically, it survived the next ten years.

————

Before I got serious about a conservatory, I thought I should see first whether I had any aptitude for indoor horticulture. The plant on the landing, I decided, would be a test case. If I could bring it back to life, then there was hope for me.

My first step was to figure out what exactly it was. I bought a book and deduced that I had a *Spathiphyllum,*[1] although the resemblance between my plant and the photograph in the book was only a passing one. Not only did the specimen in the book have a dense crop of dark green and glossy leaves, but rising well above them were several flowers, each a single, elongated, hoodlike petal as white and sleek as a swan's head poised gracefully on a tall green stem. The serenity of these lovely white "spathes" must have given the plant its popular name, peace lily. But although the book provided instructions on how to care for a healthy *Spathiphyllum* (including—no surprise here—keeping it out of direct sunlight), it didn't give me any clues as to how to bring one back from the brink of death. So, on a Saturday afternoon in October, I strapped the pot in the front seat of my minivan and set off for the nearest garden store, Johnson's Flower and Garden Center.

Through the front doors, past the displays of gleaming trowels and clippers and beyond the shelves loaded with pots of all colors and sizes were the houseplants. That section of the store, lit by ranks of fluorescent lights, was crammed with hundreds of houseplants, clustered on the floor, packed pot-to-pot on shelves, and hanging in baskets from bars overhead.

---

[1] See Appendix A for a guide to pronouncing the Latin names of the plants noted in the book.

"Can I help you?" a female voice asked in an accent and tone that was, oddly enough, pure Brooklyn.

I turned to find a small and wiry woman about my age with hazel eyes and dark hair pulled back in a haphazard ponytail. The strands that hadn't made it into her ponytail were corralled under a pair of half-glasses on top of her head.

Could she help me? I wasn't sure. I had someone in mind along the lines of Vita Sackville-West or Virginia Woolf, someone who looked genteel and a little delicate. This woman didn't look in the slightest bit fragile. Her jeans were torn at one knee, her hands were dirty, and she had a black-and-white border collie at her heels. But as I was pondering whether I might find another, more likely-looking employee—say that tall, blond woman with pale skin and a vaguely distracted manner over by the orchids—she focused on the plant in my hands.

"Wow," she said, "that is the worst-looking spath I have *ever* seen. Did you do that? That's an accomplishment."

I was taken aback, and stuttered how it had actually survived a long time, and that I wanted help reviving it. I hope I didn't try to explain how I was thinking about a conservatory, but I may have.

In any case, she looked very dubious.

"You sure you don't want to just start over and buy a new one instead? These over here are twenty bucks," she said, and pointed to a row of *Spathiphyllum* on the concrete floor, all in bloom. They looked even more handsome than the ones in my book.

No, I said, I was determined to save this one.

"Well, okay," she said, raising an eyebrow. "Let's see what you've actually got here."

With that she relieved me of my plant and took it over to the counter by the cash register. She turned it onto its side and gave it a couple of solid whacks on the countertop. I winced, but out popped the plant, complete with its soil in a pot-shaped form. Then she grabbed all the leaves in one hand and shook the whole thing vigorously over a tall black trash can, loosing a shower of dirt. What remained she dropped on the counter. She then pulled her reading glasses down onto her nose, released her hair, and peered at my plant. She began to pull it apart, teasing it into what I could see were its constituent plantlets, each of which had a half dozen or so stems and its own roots.

"You see the root on this one?" she asked, holding up one limp individual. "See how yellow and mushy it is? It's got some sort of root rot. I take it you've been watering it a lot recently? Anyhow, this one's a loser," and she tossed it into the trash can. She picked up the plantlets one after another. "As is this one . . . and this one . . . and this one. And this one," and she flipped them one after another, ruthlessly, into the trash.

This wasn't looking good.

Then she held up a plantlet with a root that I could see was whiter and had a number of trailing fibers.

"Oh, now look at this!" she said, pleased. "Here's one that might make it. And here's another."

At the end of the sorting, three plantlets remained on the table and she said she needed to get a smaller pot. Looking at them naked on the table made me anxious; they reminded me of the little sunfish that we, as children, caught at Loch Raven reservoir and left on the dock while we continued to fish. Out of their element and silently gasping, the fish quickly expired.

"They're okay just exposed like this?" I asked as she turned to leave.

She practically snorted, "Oh, they're fine. They can do without soil for a long time. Water is another matter, but they're good for a couple hours."

She came back with a plastic pot the size of a large coffee mug and a bucket of soil. She dropped a handful of soil in the bottom of the pot, placed the plantlets in it, and then added more soil, pressing it down with her fingers. Finally, she watered the plantlets until water ran out the bottom. She hadn't taken much care to spread the root fibers evenly, and when I asked her a little anxiously about it, she shrugged.

"Not a problem," she said. "Plants are easy. That's why I like them. No moving parts, no delicate psyches, nothing to it. Give them the right amount of water and light, add a little fertilizer, and that's it. Spaths are particularly tough. This plant can survive a lot worse than some twisted roots."

She took up a pair of small scissors and cut off the yellowed leaves and clipped the brown tips off the green ones. The plant wasn't beautiful—the stems were sparse and the leaves were dull—but it looked a lot better than it had, and she assured me the new leaves would look fine.

"Here's some important stuff," she said, taking a sheet titled "Caring for Your Peace Lily" out of a plastic sleeve on the wall. "Spaths can handle all levels of light, just no direct sunlight. They're pretty tolerant of dryness, too. Just don't let the soil stay soggy. After you water it, empty the water in the saucer, otherwise it's going to get root rot, guaranteed."

I guess that had been the problem. I thought leaving the water in the saucer was a good deed, like leaving a glass of water on a child's bedside table at night in case she got thirsty.

She gave me instructions on fertilizer: once a month (but not in winter), a half-teaspoon dissolved in a gallon of lukewarm water. This was another revelation. I thought fertilizer for a plant was like a multivitamin for the average American adult, that is, generally superfluous.

She cautioned me that my biggest problem was going to be paying too much attention to my spath.

"I see it all the time, people who start thinking maybe a little extra food will hurry a plant along or maybe a little more sun would do it good. Plants are not like kids," she said. "They don't benefit from extra enrichment. They need what they need and that's it. They're simple, so just let them be."

Her advice had a great appeal; she made taking care of plants sound easy. But it was far more likely that, after my first rush of enthusiasm, I wouldn't provide enough care; that once I stocked my conservatory, my attention would move elsewhere, to some new unexplored subject, and I'd be left with a roomful of withered memento mori. My plants were more likely to die, not from drowning, but from distraction.

Before I left, I introduced myself, figuring I would be back, and asked her name. Edie April, she said, and she was the buyer for houseplants. I thanked her profusely, paid my bill, and headed to my car.

At home, I put my spath on my desk in front of a north-facing window where I could keep my eye on it and tend it carefully (but not too carefully). Nothing much happened for a month, and I wondered if in fact the thing was dead and just hadn't decayed yet. Then one day in January, I noticed a short, slender, bright green spear rising out of the soil among the old stalks. Life! I wasn't sure what plant part a spear was—I didn't see any spears in the *Spathiphyllum* photographs in my book—but surely this was a positive development.

Every day the spear grew a little taller. When it was about six inches tall, I saw that the top inch or two of it was unfurling: the spear was actually a stem with a leaf so tightly and seamlessly wrapped around it that it had been invisible. How sleek, how high-tech really, a remarkable feat of botanical engineering.

A few days later the leaf, shiny and fresh-green among its more olive, matte companions, was nearly full size. Over the next weeks, more spears emerged and transformed into leaves. Then one day I noticed that there was another miracle to observe. The stem of one of the new leaves, a particularly large one, developed a longitudinal split midway up the stem. Poking out of the slit was what looked like a white, crescent-shaped chrysalis. The chrysalis emerged on its own sturdier stem, finally rising above the leaves, where it slowly opened and expanded. There, above a sea of green leaves, was the graceful spathe of the *Spathiphyllum,* a pure white spinnaker billowed by an imperceptible breeze.

It was at that moment that I began to plan a conservatory.

Oranges

two

Calamondin orange

Ted was skeptical about my plans to become a gardener, in a conservatory or anywhere else. For years, he had tried to interest me in the vegetable garden he plants in a small raised bed in a corner of our eighth-of-an-acre lot. Because he is a lawyer and his work frequently takes him out of town, the watering, weeding, and harvesting periodically fell to me. I have always found vegetable gardening an oppressive business, and I have made no bones about it.

First, I hate to sweat, and there is no time of day in our summers when working outdoors does not mean getting sweaty. (I don't think of waiting until dusk. Mosquitoes have been waiting all day, honing their long and razor-tipped snoots, to dig into me for dinner.) Second, a vegetable garden is relentless. Come July, the plants need watering every day and the vegetables constantly want picking. Miss one day of harvesting and the lettuce has gone to seed and the bean pods are vulcanized. Worst of all, there are bugs everywhere: fat green caterpillars inching up the stalks of the eggplants, bees burrowing in the pea flowers, and gnats determined to ditch themselves in my eyes. When I crouch down to get at the cucumbers, I see awful multilegged things slipping in and out of the dirt around my feet. I slap at every touch of a leaf. In this vegetal clutter, I'm a flurry of twitches.

Our vegetable garden offends my sense of order. The pumpkin vines sprawl onto the lawn, the tomato bushes escape their cages, and peas send their inquisitive tendrils everywhere. It's chaotic and confusing, too: vegetable plants are so unlovely and some weeds are pretty. I once weeded out the watermelon seedlings, and I've been known to water St. John's wort.

It's not just the plants, but the vegetables themselves I dislike. The cherry tomatoes ooze warm juice from split skins; the cucumbers are surprisingly prickly. Yellow squash, lurking beneath huge and hairy leaves, are the worst. I try to pick them while they are still of an edible size, but a few hide so well that I don't see them until they have swelled to the size of tenpins. Sometimes these monsters are partly rotted, which I discover only when my fingers sink into their slimy undersides. I don't need my vegetables shrink-wrapped, but I prefer picking them out of a basket at the Saturday morning farmers' market to excavating them from our garden.

I explained to Ted that my aversion to vegetable gardening would have no bearing on my ability to garden in a conservatory. Indoors, there would be no mosquitoes, and if it got too hot, I'd turn on the air-conditioning. When I had to put my hands in dirt, it would be the nice clean kind that comes packaged in plastic bags, the kind that comes without crawly creatures of any sort. My plants would be tidily contained in pots, not creeping nastily about like creatures from a horror movie. I liked plants, I insisted, just not outdoor vegetable plants.

Ted found my argument less than convincing.

"What about the fuchsias on the front porch last summer?" he wanted to know. "The ones that died when I went to Houston and you forgot to water them? A fuchsia," he reminded me, "is not a vegetable."

I do not like to argue with Ted, both because I naturally shy away from conflict and because although I am most often right, he always seems to prevail. I have never encountered a verbal red herring I didn't want to follow.

"I'm not sure they were in such good shape when you left, and you didn't tell me that I had to water them in the mornings." Really, it had been amazing how by the end of just one afternoon without water—well, maybe it had been two—all their petals had dropped. "Besides, that was just one time."

"There were four fuchsias," he muttered.

Ted, no doubt banking on the fact that a good percentage of my enthusiasms prove to be short-lived, let the subject drop.

I began to consider exactly where we could build a conservatory.

Our house is a 1927, center-hall, two-and-a-half-story colonial clad in cedar shakes and painted white with green shutters. A red brick chimney runs up one side. From the front it looks like a kindergartner's drawing of a house; from the back you can see the two-story addition that makes the house L-shaped. In the angle of the L there was an old wooden deck, a deck that was well along in the process of recycling itself into mulch. A conservatory could replace the deck, I realized, docking with the house on two sides and completing it like a missing puzzle piece.

I bought conservatory books. They were to me what seed catalogs are to Ted: the raw material for midwinter nights' dreams. One volume, Olivier de Vleeschouwer's *Greenhouses and Conservatories,* arrived the day a wet and heavy mid-March snow shut down our power, and I leafed through it at the kitchen counter, zipped up to my chin in a down jacket. Would I prefer a conservatory like Sir Cecil Beaton's, a lacy affair furnished with a chandelier, Chinese stools, and ceramic mermaids? Maybe something along the lines of the working greenhouse in southern France, covered with grapevines and sheltering a rough-hewn wooden farmhouse table and benches? Or how about that one with a black-and-white-checkered floor and a decorative white spiral staircase with red geraniums on the treads? I ordered brochures from sunroom and conservatory companies, too. But with their lists of sizes, options, and, above all, prices, they were no food for fantasy, and I filed them away in a pile under my desk.

Then, one Sunday morning in early April when winter was on the run, I stopped off to browse at Johnson's, and out by its driveway was the most beautiful tree I had ever seen. It was taller than I, with a slender trunk and a nimbus of dark green leaves sprinkled with small, starlike white flowers and dotted with orange and green spheres the size of gumballs. Even amid the odor of exhaust, I caught the light fragrance of its blossoms. A yellow plastic tag dangling from a branch read "*Citrus mitis* (Calamondin orange), full sun, minimum 28°F/–1°C, dry between waterings, flowers and fruits year-round." An orange tree—an orange tree there on an asphalt driveway off Wisconsin Avenue in the middle of Washington, D.C.! I walked around the tree several times, touched the leaves, sniffed the flowers, and tapped the little oranges. Yes, they were real, the tree was real. I was smitten. The price tag said $69, a pittance to my mind for such an exotic beauty.

In a matter of minutes I was on my way with the orange tree recumbent in my minivan, my own Danae in a shower of gold.

I put my tree on the deck where I could see it from both the kitchen and the living room. In order for it to get full sun, I had to drag it from the west side of the deck in the morning to the northeast corner in the afternoon, but I was rewarded for my efforts by flush after flush of small white flowers over the summer. When the petals of the blossoms fell away, tiny green ovoids remained, and while many fell off, others gradually swelled into perfect dark green spheres. As they ripened, they ran through hues like notes on a scale, turning from lime to lemony green to yellow before deepening to gold and finally arriving at the very definition of the color orange. Calamondin oranges, I read, make good marmalade, but I had no intention of picking mine; no more would Zeus have asked Danae to get up off the bed, put some clothes on, and rustle up a little breakfast.

My tree appealed to me in more than a decorative way. Vegetable plants develop leaves, blossom, and then fruit in sequence, according to the season. But Calamondin orange trees manage all seasons at once, defying what seems like a firm rule of nature. It is an entrancing sight, a bit of a miracle, and people have long found it so. The ancient Greeks believed that the goddess Hera had a grove of orange trees that conferred immortality on anyone who ate their fruit. Greeks of the Christian era told the tale of how the Virgin Mary, passing through the valley of Jehoshaphat, was so charmed by the scent of orange and citron trees in bloom that she stopped to bless them, and from that day forward, orange trees have been covered all year with blossoms and fruit. Through the Renaissance, artists often portrayed Mary and her baby with orange trees in the background. How alluring, to have simultaneously the innocence of youth and the wisdom of maturity. No wonder people have always adored orange trees.

Romancing orange trees where the weather is balmy has always been an easy affair. The trees are native to subtropical regions of China, and in prehistoric times their seeds were carried, probably by both people and birds, throughout Southeast Asia. In the pre-Christian era, traders carried the fruit to India, the Middle East, and Rome. Arab gardeners planted citrus trees—oranges, lemons, and citrons—as well as oleander and cypress, along the sides of long reflecting pools and channels and around trickling fountains. The evergreen trees with their vivid fruit were a refreshing contrast to the dry and tawny landscape.

When Moslem warriors conquered Spain in the eighth century and Sicily in the ninth century, they brought along their citrus trees, which became an integral part of the gardens and interiors there. Near Palermo in Sicily at the Villa Fawara, an island in a small lake was entirely planted in orange trees, the fruits of which, wrote an Arab poet, "are like blazing fire among the emerald boughs." At the Alhambra, a thicket of oranges and lemons surrounded the fountain of the Garden of Princess Lindaraja. In Cordova in the garden of the Mosque of the Omayyads, rows of orange trees led up to the arches in the mosque and seemed to continue inside, transformed into rows of interior columns. Orange trees also became a common sight in the general landscape. Granada, one visitor observed, enjoyed "an eternal autumn," so adorned was the city with ever-fruiting orange trees.

In the eleventh century, the Normans invaded Sicily and defeated the Arabs. Instead of eradicating Moslem culture, they embraced it wholeheartedly, dressing in Arab robes, reveling in harems, building Arab-style palaces, and filling their gardens with citrus trees. When they continued their campaign and conquered the southern half of mainland Italy, they took the Arabs' orange trees with them. Naples and Sorrento became centers of citriculture. By the late medieval era, orange trees were so common and oranges so plentiful in southern Italy that in one town, Reggio di Calabria, the annual winter festivities included a daylong battle between two opposing "armies" of young men whose only ammunition was the thousands of oranges, lemons, and citrons that grew in the area. When Charles V, after a long career as Holy Roman Emperor and King of Spain, Naples, and Sicily, abdicated in favor of his son in 1558, he retired to a monastery in San Yuste in southwestern Spain. There he converted two large covered terraces into gardens mainly of citrus trees. A visitor wrote that the king's apartments were "at last entirely surrounded by orange and citron trees whose branches actually creep through the windows of the rooms, cheering him with their scent, with their color, and with their green."

The trees were beautiful, but no medieval gardener planted an orange tree in anticipation of plucking a ripe fruit from a bough and eating it: the oranges of the era were exceedingly bitter. A monk describing a Sicilian orange grouped them with lemons "whose acidity fits them for seasoning food," and noted they were "more apt to please the eye" than the palate. But if medieval oranges were too bitter to eat straight up, chefs used them creatively as a condiment. Fried sparrows with oranges, sturgeon in aspic covered with orange juice, and caviar and oranges fried with sugar and cinnamon graced the archbishop of Milan's table. Oranges, in fact, were more valued for their medicinal than gustatory properties. People believed oranges could cure almost anything, including plague, piles, colic, and cramps, and could counteract "poison of a cold nature" and expel "long intestinal worms." The peel was also popular for scenting wine, and in this era of less than rigorous personal hygiene, orange-flower water was highly valued as a perfume and a cologne. Still, the visual delights of citrus trees were paramount.

Love of orange trees spread northward to Rome and Florence, although January temperatures might dip below freezing. Roman, Florentine, and Milanese gardeners learned to plant the trees in terra-cotta pots, and then, when winter with its killing frosts approached, they moved the pots into any stone outbuilding or grotto that could be marginally heated. The trees went dormant and the leaves fell off, but the branches would leaf out again in spring. This method saved the trees in winter but created a lot of work the rest of the year. Terra-cotta pots release moisture quickly; in the summers, potted trees had to be watered at least once and sometimes twice daily, without the luxury, of course, of hoses and running water. With all this expensive maintenance, a large collection of orange trees became a symbol of wealth, the privilege of popes and princes. In the early 1400s, Cosimo de Medici had his garden at Careggi redesigned and stocked with hundreds of citrus trees grown in giant pots. (The family name, Medici, may owe its origin to the word used for a type of orange, and the five red balls on the Medici coat of arms are said to be oranges.) In Rome, half of the famous garden of the papal villa, the Belvedere, was devoted to flowers, laurel, cypress, and mulberry trees while the other half, paved with terra-cotta slabs, was covered with potted orange trees. Peer into the backgrounds of the paintings of Mantegna, Verocchio, Veronese, and Fra Angelico, and you will often find gardens dotted with potted orange trees.

The preeminence of citrus in late medieval Italian gardens owed much to fifteenth-century architect Leon Battista Alberti. A villa, he opined, should stand on top of a hill and connect physically and visually to an extensive garden below. To make the connection, a line of potted trees sculpted into cones, balls, and lollipops lined the balustrade on the villa's terrace and then proceeded down the stairs and sloping alleys to the garden. In the garden, Alberti called for subdividing the space with wide, intersecting paths that created square, rectangular, and triangular *compartimenti*. Many of these also featured potted citrus, pomegranate, and other flowering trees, either with a single tree surrounded by a carpet of flowers or a number of trees encircling a fountain. The entire garden was often surrounded by a stone wall, which might be lined with green hedges studded at regular intervals with orange trees or even entirely covered with espaliered citrus.

Villa Aldobrandini, c. 1600. *From www.gardenvisit.com.*

In winter in central and northern Italy, the espaliered trees were sheltered from the wind by the wall, and its sun-warmed stones provided a measure of radiant heat. The gardeners also piled the ground around the trunks deep with straw. They protected trees planted in orchards by building a permanent wood frame around them and then, when the weather deteriorated, covering the frame completely with boards. The potted trees, however, exposed to the wind and with their roots above ground, were more vulnerable. So many dozens, even hundreds, of large citrus trees could not be simply distributed, ad hoc, to an unused outbuilding or two or a grotto for the cold season. Instead, they spent the winter in purpose-built, solid-roofed, and usually windowless structures called *arancieras*. Braziers—metal pans of burning charcoal—kept the trees from freezing on the coldest nights.

In February 1495, the young Charles VIII of France, acting on a vague claim to the throne of Naples and a misinformed understanding of international politics, marched his army across the Alps and conquered the city. The king settled in for what he expected would be a long and pleasant occupation. Unfortunately for him, by July other Italian states, Austria, and the pope, concerned about Charles's greater ambitions, gathered together an army and forced him to retreat. During his brief reign, Charles, a romantic fellow, became entranced with the artistic accomplishments of the Italian Renaissance, especially the gardens with their flowering orange and other trees. "You can hardly imagine," he wrote to his brother shortly after his conquest, "what beautiful gardens I own in this town, for, on my faith, it seems as if they lacked only Adam and Eve to make them an earthly paradise." On his way out of Italy, he took with him master gardener Pasello da Mercogliano (as well as some twenty other artists and four tons of art) back to his royal castle in Amboise.

At Amboise, Mercogliano found a small medieval garden whose design was the inheritance of European monasteries. At the heart of a monastery was the cloister garden, a space traversed by paths, with a well or fountain at its center. It was a functional place where the monks tended to medicinal plants, as well as culinary herbs and flowers with religious symbolism, such as the violets that represented Mary's humility or red roses linked to Christian martyrs. The garden was a place for reading and contemplation, so there were turf seats and benches under arbors. Monks might also cultivate pear, plum, and other stone-fruit trees, but they did so in orchards, not in the cloister.

Mercogliano replaced the old garden with a new one based on the geometrical Italian model, with flower and herb beds surrounding or surrounded by trees. Elsewhere on the grounds he built and stocked the first orangerie in France. Charles never saw the completed gardens; he struck his head on a low door frame, went into a coma, and died in 1498. But his successor, Louis XII, saw the work completed and had Mercogliano redesign his garden at Blois.

Louis XII's grandson, Henri II, who came to the throne at the age of seventeen in 1536 also delighted in gardens. He commissioned a garden, an orange grove, and an orangerie for his longtime mistress and power-behind-the-throne, Diane de Poitiers, at her chateau in Anet, and at enormous expense, he had a giant orange tree (known as the "Grand Bourbon") transplanted there. He also installed an Italianate garden at Fountainbleau where a fountain featuring the goddess Diana was surrounded by orange trees. His wife, Catherine de Medici, might have been cheered by the oranges that would have reminded her of her native Florence, but no doubt was less than thrilled with the reference to her rival. Neglected and ignored—except when it came time to generate heirs—Catherine became a great patron of the arts and an avid builder of her own residences and gardens graced with orange trees. Soon many of the French aristocracy were redesigning their gardens à l'Italien, with rectilinear precision and neatly coiffed fruit trees. By midcentury, owners of orange groves in Provence were doing a land office business supplying trees for Parisian nobility and wealthy merchants.

French orangeries evolved from the utilitarian Italian *arancieras* and became more elaborate in order to harmonize with nearby estate buildings. The architects of Anet, Fountainbleau, and other orangeries employed large arched windows, towers, and columns to transform what had originally been simple warehouses into more architectural structures. Advances in understanding of citriculture affected orangerie design, too. In 1600, Olivier de Serres published a groundbreaking text on agriculture that included a chapter on how to best prune, fertilize, water, graft, and overwinter orange trees. He understood that the trees benefited from winter sun and would best make it through the winter if their shelter had windows in its southern façade.

Dutch greenhouse for overwintering orange trees.
From Nederlantze Hesperides *by Jan Heserides, 1683.*

Visitors to France from the even colder climates of England, Holland, and Germany found orange trees equally seductive. The Leyden Botanical Garden had a shedlike orangerie that was filled with trees in rows in the winter. A few English noblemen in the Elizabethan era imported citrus trees from France or Italy. Sir Francis Carew planted an orchard in the early 1600s, which he covered over with a wooden shelter, perhaps with windows, in the winter. In 1609, King James I renovated Somerset House in London for his wife, Anne, and added a permanent "house for orange trees." At his palace in Heidelberg, Frederick V, Elector Palatine from 1610 to 1623, had a permanent stone orangerie for his potted citrus, as well as a wooden one that was constructed around his grove of 430 trees every winter and dismantled every spring. The temporary structure was nearly a hundred yards long, several stories tall, and had windows "to cheer the trees." At Oatlands Palace in Surrey, the English queen Henrietta (whose mother was a Medici and whose husband, Charles I, would be beheaded in 1649) ordered the construction of an orangerie that was more than 250 feet in length. The building, constructed of brick with a blue slate roof, was not inexpensive at £66; the collection of orange trees inside it, however, was valued at £558. The queen had another orangerie built at Wimbledon to shelter sixty tubs of trees.

An orange tree collection became an English royal tradition. Charles II had a royal *greenhouse*—the name the English gave to a building designed to overwinter citrus and other tender green trees—built in St. James's Park. (Samuel Pepys saw his first orange tree there.) The king also had one built for his mistress, Nell Gwyn, a former orange seller. Queen Mary had Christopher Wren build a greenhouse for her at Hampton Court about 1690. Queen Anne used her greenhouse at Kensington Palace, built for her in 1704, for supper parties.

No one approached Louis XIV, however, in passion for orange trees. In August 1661, French finance minister Nicolas Fouquet threw a lavish party—complete with masques, fireworks, expensive gifts, and a new play by Molière—to which he invited the young king who had recently established personal rule after a period of regency. Fouquet, wealthy by inheritance, marriage, and a considerable mixing of his own and the state's business, was celebrating his magnificent new chateau at Vaux-le-Vicomte and thought to impress his sovereign. Louis, however, was facing a bankrupt government and was already highly suspicious of Fouquet. The party was the last straw: three weeks later, he had the finance minister arrested, and he confiscated the chateau, its furnishings, and the 190 century-old orange trees that graced its garden. (Voltaire commented: "On 17 August, at six in the evening Fouquet was the King of France: at two in the morning he was nobody." Fouquet would die in prison nineteen years later.) The trees became the core collection for the first orangerie Louis built at Versailles in 1664. In 1685, he had that building torn down and replaced. The new Versailles orangerie was the largest ever built—its central façade and two galleries were almost a quarter mile in length, forty-two feet wide, nearly five stories high, and had a roof more than six feet thick—and housed thousands of trees during the winter.

Still, the orangerie was essentially a winter tree warehouse, and Louis's beloved trees were packed inside, unseen by anyone but gardeners. This was an unsatisfactory state of affairs, and the king commanded that his orange trees appear in full bloom in the many public halls and private chambers of Versailles, regardless of the calendar. Fortunately, his gardeners learned that if they starved an orange tree of water until its leaves dropped and then flooded it with fertilizer and water and as much sunlight as possible, they could force it into bloom. By applying the treatment to a new group of trees every two weeks, they sustained a constant supply of flowering trees. In the Hall of Mirrors, orange trees in silver tubs were a permanent part of the decor. Lit by the large windows during the day and by the glow of a thousand candles in silver chandeliers and candelabras at night, the images of orange trees were multiplied in the mirrors and on the shining surfaces of silver consoles. Louis was the first person to sit contentedly indoors by his orange trees while snow filtered down on the other side of the windows.

All plants, of course, need water—water transports nutrients up from the roots to the leaves—but citrus trees are particularly finicky about exactly how much they require. Too little and, as Louis's gardeners knew, the leaves fall off or, if water is too long in forthcoming, the tree dies. But overwatering is even more dangerous. Overwater and a tree can get irreversible, fatal root rot. Better too little water, Edie warned me, than too much. So, as I accumulated my own citrus grove—over that summer, I added two four-foot 'Meiwa' kumquats, two five-foot 'Meyer' lemons, a small lime, and a variety of citron called 'Buddha's Hand'—I paid careful attention to the watering instructions that I found in various reference books or on the hang tags on the trees. But the more I read, the more confused I became.

"Gently tip the container," instructed one source. "If it feels light, the plant needs water; if it feels heavy, the plant can probably go a while longer." Probably? What help was that? As for feeling light or heavy—a five-foot lemon tree in a pot, in the view of a small woman who taps computer keys for a living, is always heavy. And in any case, I didn't see how I could assess a container's weight by tipping it, gently or otherwise. Another author advised me to "develop a watering schedule so the tree stays on the dry side of moist." Who would have guessed that there could be *any* dry aspect to moist? I certainly had no idea what it felt like. Even "water when the soil is dry an inch or so down" seemed unclear. Did the inch apply equally to my 'Buddha's Hand' in an eight-inch pot and my Calamondin in a sixteen-inch-diameter planter? I tried poking my finger in at various depths, but wherever I did, I couldn't determine exactly what dry felt like. Was dry desert-dry? Or was pretty dry dry enough? Worse, I discovered that if I waited until the soil felt very dry at one inch, it also felt pretty damn dry at two or even three inches. Moisture in a pot is not like water in a measuring cup; there are no clear demarcations. Or maybe there were and I have a defective finger.

I went back to Edie and laid out the issues.

She looked at me as if I had just told her that I really didn't get this business of walking: how high, exactly, should I raise my foot off the floor and where, exactly, should I put it down?

"Normally," she said, "I wouldn't recommend this, and

frankly, I think you'll eventually get the hang of it, but in the meantime . . ." She led me to a display of garden tools and picked up a plastic-encased device that looked like a giant meat thermometer.

"I think you better try a moisture meter," she said. She opened the package and held out a sheet of printed cardboard. On it was a long list of houseplants. Beside each plant was a number from one to six. "So you stick the meter in the soil, look up the plant on the guide, and only water if it registers that number or lower."

Right off the bat, I liked this alternative, this gardening-by-numbers approach. It was the way I cooked. Pop the frozen plastic package into the microwave, tap in the number of seconds or minutes indicated in the instructions, and push *start*. (The best recipe as far as I'm concerned is the one for microwave popcorn with its wonderfully measurable "continue until no more popping is heard for three seconds.")

"But exactly how far down do I stick the meter?" I asked.

The goal, Edie explained, is to measure moisture where the roots are. In a six-inch pot, the roots would probably be only an inch or two below the surface. In a large planter, I might have to push down the probe six inches or more. It would depend. But, if I wanted to be sure where the roots were, I should tip the pot on its side, slide the plant and dirt out, and look. This sounded unnecessarily risky, like opening a patient's chest just to check his pulse, but I happily bought the moisture meter.

Every morning, I poked the meter's probe into my citrus pots. (It's best, I learned, to water plants in the morning.

Water added in the evening tends to sit in the soil and provide a place for bacteria and fungi to multiply. In daylight, the heat of sunlight turns water in the leaves to vapor. As the vapor evaporates, it pulls more water, with its dissolved nutrients, up through the stems from the roots.) Whenever the meter registered a "2," I watered.

It worked. By September, the Calamondin was laden with little oranges and the lemon trees were full of bright green, fist-size fruit. I also had six limes and two 'Buddha's Hand'—which looked more like the tentacles of a sea creature than any human hand—as well as two dozen or so deep orange kumquats. I was terrifically pleased with myself.

In late October, I noticed that no more new leaves were emerging on my citrus and all of them, even the prolific Calamondin, had ceased to flower. The days had gotten too short. Winter was on its way. I had two choices. I could put the trees in our unused, windowless garage. The garage, tucked under the house, stays frost-free although it is unheated, so it could be my equivalent of a northern Italian grotto. The trees would drop their leaves but ought to leaf out again in spring. Or I could take heroic measures and try to sustain them inside. However, because our neighbor's house is a mere ten feet away and shades all our south-facing windows, I would have to use grow lights at least twelve hours a day.

I opted for heroic measures. When the outdoor temperature dipped below 40 degrees at night, I hauled the trees up two flights of steps to my office. There, an east-facing dormer window created a six-foot-by-six-foot alcove with a seven-foot ceiling. I was going to convert this cube of space into a citrus refuge.

Metal halide lights would have been my first choice for lighting. Unfortunately, while they produce bright light that closely matches the color of sunlight, they also produce a great deal of heat and can't be placed within eight inches of a ceiling or twelve inches of a plant. My trees were too tall and my ceiling too low. My second choice was high-output, T-5 fluorescent grow lights. Although it would take six forty-eight-inch bulbs to produce the same amount of light as two metal halides, the fluorescents would burn cool, and they were considerably more energy efficient. The most efficient light systems use LEDs, but not only were they out of my price range, but because they use only red and blue bulbs (plants don't absorb light in the yellow-green part of the spectrum), they glow an unearthly pink.

I ordered two fluorescent fixtures, and when they arrived I girded myself for the task of installing them. Normally, I would have asked Ted for help. He is not only competent with such projects, he likes to do them. But we weren't seeing eye-to-eye on this business of bringing the tropics to my office. Running lights twelve hours a day, he argued, was wasteful, and he appealed to my environmental consciousness. But there was more to it than that. My project made him uneasy: it seemed eccentric, which is not an adjective a Washington lawyer finds greatly appealing, and, worse, he suspected it was the thin end of the wedge of an even more oddball—and expensive—endeavor. So I drilled four holes in the ceiling in what I hoped was a joist, hammered in two pairs of plastic anchors, got four lengths of chain cut at the hardware store, and hoisted the fixtures into place where, somewhat to my surprise, they stayed put.

Humidity came next. With less than 60 percent humidity, citrus trees are highly susceptible to spider mites that flourish in a dry atmosphere. I bought a room humidifier and set it up in the middle of my office, but the delicate drifts of mist it produced vanished instantly in the Sahara of our forced-air heated house. Even at its highest setting, the humidifier was clearly inadequate to the task. After twenty-four hours, according to a humidistat, the humidity level in the room was only 30 percent, a long way from my goal. So I bought a large piece of clear plastic and closed off the alcove by duct-taping it around the alcove's front edges. I cut a five-foot slit up the center from the floor so I could get in and out, and put the humidifier inside. The humidity climbed steadily through the day, and by evening it seemed to have stabilized at 50 percent. I sat at my desk and marveled at my citrus trees, busily photosynthesizing, oblivious to the fact that the sun had set hours ago.

The next morning, cup of coffee in hand, I opened my office door. Someone, it appeared, was taking a shower in the alcove. The plastic was thoroughly fogged, except for the transparent trails where water droplets had evidently slid down. I poked my head in: the trees were sparkling in the morning light. There was so much humidity, the ceiling was dripping, and the carpet was spotted where drops had fallen. My refuge had turned into a rain forest.

I cut back the plastic to make a wider opening, dialed down the humidifier, and put a small fan on the floor for air circulation. After a few days of making adjustments, I had a working greenhouse, albeit of Lilliputian proportions.

The trees were evidently happy. After a few weeks, they

began putting out little, shiny, fresh green leaves, and even some flowers. I doted on my little greenhouse not only for its vibrant self but because it also made me hopeful about a full-scale incarnation.

There was still the matter of Ted. I had been carefully talking up the idea of a conservatory, striving to sweep him into my enthusiasm while not making him feel railroaded. So far, he had agreed only that we needed to do something about the dissolving deck, and he had made noises about building a screened porch in its place. I pointed out that a conservatory had the advantage of being usable in the winter and could be nearly as open to the outdoors. So far, a "hmmm" was as much of a response as I'd gotten.

One evening I was in my office talking on the phone when Ted, just home from work, walked in. He stood in front of the alcove, tie loosened, looking in on the grove. The window was black with night, a dramatic backdrop for the leaves and fruit that glowed almost surreally under the fluorescent blaze. Ted looked tired, and the lights silvered the gray in his dark hair.

"I ran into John Meisner outside," he said, "staring up at this window, which, by the way, gives off more light than the street lamp. He wondered if it's just oranges we're growing or whether they're just cover—window dressing, so to speak— for a crop of weed."

I laughed. John was not the first neighbor of our generation to make such an insinuation.

"Did he sound wistful, like he was remembering the good old days, or hopeful, like he might score some?"

"Wistful, definitely wistful," he said, and paused. "I feel like we're getting to the age of wistfulness. Or would that be the age of wist?" He shook his head and sighed. "John said Sarah is having a baby in May. I can't believe she's old enough to have a baby." Sarah had babysat our kids. "You know, I see all these children and their young parents in the neighborhood. . . . Somehow I didn't imagine there would be other kids after ours grew up. Like we'd closed the book on that."

"You *are* feeling wistful," I said, and got up from my chair to give him a hug.

"At least," he said with a sigh, "Alice is still at home, and we've got another five years before she leaves. Although sometimes I feel like she's got one foot out the door already." Together we gazed at the trees.

"But how good it is," I said quietly, "just to be thinking five years ahead."

He tightened his arm around my shoulder and turned to rest his chin on the top of my head.

"You're really serious about a conservatory?" he asked.

I nodded, knowing he could feel my answer.

He said nothing for a minute and then turned back toward the trees, his arm still tight around me. "Too bad you're not thinking of growing wheat or corn—we could get some nice federal subsidies for that. Although, how about sugarcane? That's tropical. I bet sugarcane would be happy in a conservatory. There are massive subsidies for sugarcane growers."

"We'd need a lot of subsidies to pay for a conservatory," I said. "It wouldn't be cheap, you know."

"I know," he answered, "but we've got to spend a certain amount to replace the deck. Why don't you at least look into it, maybe call Ben?" Ben was an architect friend. "Let's start with a ballpark number."

Construction

three

Ananas comosus

It was easy to moon over photographs of antique conservatories, those crystalline structures that a Georgian- or Victorian-era home wore like a diamond brooch pinned on an elegant, watered-silk gown. But when Ted and I stood in the backyard and contemplated the back of our house, it was impossible to imagine such a structure joined to our plain-Jane home. Ours is a work shirt sort of a dwelling, its shakes alligatored with eighty years of paint and its shutters hanging slightly askew. No glass bauble was going to look right pinned to its frayed collar, and I could only hope that Ben would come up with an inspired design.

I have no ability to conceive space. Those tests that require you to figure out which two of five geometric shapes are identical just viewed from another perspective? I can't even guess. Years ago, the second-floor toilet overflowed—which is what happens when a toddler sends her plastic fish home to the ocean—and after turning off the water and mopping upstairs, I went downstairs to inspect the damage in the first-floor bathroom. Miraculously, given the flood above, no water had come through the ceiling. Only days later when I opened the hall closet on the first floor and found a collection of sodden coats did I understand how the rooms were spatially related. I'm all right reading a map, but navigating in three dimensions is as mysterious to me as echolocation. Which means that architects, like bats, make me slightly uncomfortable.

Except for Ben. Not that he wasn't a wizard of three dimensions; he was. It's that his professional mystery was offset by the fact that he reminded me of Scotia: compact and sturdy physiques, hair that flopped over their brows, large eyes (his blue, hers brown) that spoke of a frank and friendly nature, terrierlike persistence, and the enthusiasm—even in middle age—of youth. I wouldn't want to carry this too far, but still, from the first, there was something reassuringly familiar about Ben. So, when we met early one March morning in the living room and looked out over the deck that was to become a conservatory, I could cheerfully tell him that we required the impossible: a conservatory that didn't look like a conservatory but would gather enough light for tropical plants. In addition, it had to have good air circulation, 60 percent humidity year-round, cooling for the hottest summer days, and a heated floor because plants, sensibly, like to keep their feet warm. He would also need to find room for a dining table, a sink, and a bit of counter space for repotting.

And he needed to factor in the swimming pool.

About the pool: I am still a little embarrassed about it. I considered passing it off vaguely as a "water feature," leaving the details to the reader's imagination. But the pool exists, sunk into the floor of the conservatory, although at thirteen feet long, eight feet wide, and thirty-nine inches deep, it looks more like an outsize bathtub. It is a resistance pool, which means that it has a current that flows down the middle, making it, as the ad says, a treadmill for swimmers.

Until eight years ago, I was strictly a summertime swimmer. Every Memorial Day, I'd be at the community pool with children in tow, and when the whistle blew for adult swim, I'd dive in. All the pleasures of a summer swim—the weightless slide through cool water, the wavering patterns of refracted sunlight on the blue pool floor, the deep silence below the surface—would return. I reveled in the freedom of the aquatic realm.

That is, I did for a few laps. Then, my arms would start to ache, my breathing would turn to gasping, and soon I'd be clutching the edge, berating myself for being so out of shape.

Then one summer day it occurred to me that actually I wasn't in such bad shape. Maybe, instead, I wasn't swimming properly. Maybe the teenage camp counselors who had taught my six-year-old self had not been the ultimate authorities on swimming methods. Or maybe swimming methods had changed. Or maybe my counselors had been wonderful teachers using state-of-the-art methods, but I wasn't paying attention. When I thought back to my days of learning to swim, all I could remember was freezing cold lake water and the soft mud bottom in the shallow end that sucked nastily at my feet. There was little incentive to progress beyond guppy and minnow: in the even colder deep end, the older girls reported, there was gross seaweed.

In any case, I decided to start over and relearn how to swim. My goal wasn't to swim fast; I just wanted to go for a swim the same way I went for a walk: easily and without thinking about it.

This time I wasn't going to take group lessons. I was going to teach myself. I found a thirteen-lesson DVD course of instruction from a company called Total Immersion (an unfortunate name that seems to imply, inaccurately I can assure you, that there will be no breathing involved). I watched each lesson several times and practiced nearly every day. I can now affirm that, indeed, swimming methods have changed, and if you haven't learned recently, you might give the sport another shot. By the end of the summer I was swimming a half mile of freestyle in twenty minutes, up and down the pool with such regular strokes and every-third-stroke breathing that I nearly hypnotized myself. Swimming became blissful. By the summer's end, I was addicted.

For two years, when the community pool closed at the end of the summer, I swam at a neighbor's backyard pool. Charlie and Ann were polio survivors, and for decades they had had a small, bubble-enclosed pool in their backyard that they used for physical therapy. Famously generous people, they invited me to swim. But as I became a better swimmer, their pool seemed to shrink. Swimming began to feel like one long, wet somersault. I tried the full-length indoor pools at the local YMCA and a nearby sports club, but the water was so chlorinated that the air was thick and sharp with fumes, making me wheeze when I walked in the door.

I started looking into resistance pools. There were two problems, however. The first was we had no place to put one. The second was that the thought of owning a pool filled me with guilt. I know in many parts of the country owning a pool is quite unexceptional, but when I was growing up, a private pool was a luxury that only the very wealthy indulged in. Everyone else went to a swimming club. The thought of my own pool, even a single-serving-size one, made me feel like Leona Helmsley.

But now it dawned on me that a conservatory provided not only a place to put a pool but also a compelling, unimpeachable reason for having one: humidity. Tropical plants require high levels of moisture in the air. They have thin leaves, and when the air has less than about 50 percent humidity, they lose water as vapor through their leaf pores faster than they can replenish it through their roots. To keep tropicals healthy, conservatories and greenhouses employ overhead misting systems to infuse the atmosphere with moisture. But I could use water vapor from a pool instead. A one-hundred-square-foot pool, depending on the temperatures of water and air, vaporizes about twenty-five gallons a day. I could regulate the amount of moisture in the air by opening or closing the pool cover. A pool would save me the cost of a misting system. In addition, a heated pool, with its thick Styrofoam insulation, would do double duty as a heating system, acting as a giant radiator. And, think of the savings in YMCA or health club fees. How could I possibly have thought a pool was a luxury? It was actually an economy.

Besides, I now see that a fundamental part of the calculus of living had changed for me. My sister had died at forty-five. At forty-eight, breast cancer had tumbled me into cold and dark waters. I had a profound appreciation that there were no guarantees for me that the future stretched out long into the unseen distance. It wasn't a question of statistics, of what precisely my chances of surviving were. The message for me was that life could well be a lot briefer than an actuarial table would predict. What the hell, I would have a pool.

Exterior of Kassinger conservatory.   *From Ben van Dusen, 2009.*

Ben took in all our requirements, and others, with equanimity, and after a few revisions, he had a final design. The addition would be built as the rest of the house had been, that is, with wooden framing, wallboard on the interior, and cedar shakes on the exterior. A shed-style roof would slope down to the north from the second-story windows of the house. Two broad, flat-roofed dormers on the north side would intersect the roof along its midline. The dormer roofs would slope, unusually, upward. Viewed from the backyard, the conservatory roof would have a shallow-V profile, a neat reversal of the gable end of the house it adjoined.

Interior of Kassinger conservatory.
From Ben van Dusen, 2009.

The shorter back wall, which was west-facing, would be a large bay window. The longer side wall would have tall windows under each dormer plus a shorter one between them.

The highest points in the room—where the roof met the house and where the dormers met the outside wall—stood at thirteen feet. The old exterior walls of the house would be replaced by floor-to-ceiling, sliding glass doors that we could push aside, nearly erasing the barriers between the living room at the east end and the kitchen on the south side. Limestone tiles on the conservatory floor would extend into both of those rooms to further blur the boundaries between the new addition and the old house. The pool would be tucked into the bay. Twelve large skylights—three of which could be opened for ventilation—would march down the length of the room in two parallel rows. More than 50 percent of the roof would be glass, but from the exterior, no one would see how transparent the roof was. It was a conservatory that didn't look like a conservatory.

During the 1600s, the south windows of orangeries and greenhouses became more numerous and larger to admit more light. So you might imagine that one gloomy January day some seventeenth-century nobleman would have stepped into his orangerie or greenhouse, looked up, and thought of putting glass into the roof. But it didn't happen. When such a nobleman stepped in out of the cold to check on his valuable trees he would not have thought about light at all. He would have peered through the smoke that filled the space, coughed, wiped his tearing eyes, and wrung his pale and lace-cuffed hands. All his beloved and expensive trees would have been dingy with soot. Some would have been frost damaged, their leaves brown and curled and dangling from their twigs. Others would have been evidently fire-scorched. The most pressing problem to resolve in these structures was not light but heat.

England, France, Holland, northern Italy, and Germany were still in the midst of the Little Ice Age, and winters were colder than they are today. The Thames regularly froze over and was host to annual frost fairs. Greenhouses had to be heated most winter nights. But in the sixteenth and early seventeenth centuries, heating technology was remarkably primitive and ineffective, even for small rooms in houses, much less the large, high-ceilinged space in a greenhouse. Open hearth fireplaces—fired with wood or coal or, in Holland, peat—were the norm. They were not only smoky, but it was entirely possible to singe your skirts trying to keep warm at one side of the room and find a washbowl of water frozen solid at the other, while you endured a draft that blew at what felt like hurricane speed. "You will have a roaring fire that will melt gold, and a room in which no corner will be without its cutting current," grumbled one contemporary.

Fireplaces, therefore, were a poor solution for greenhouses. Braziers weren't much better. As one grower noted, "if the fire be large it will without doubt dry up the outward bark of the trees and twigs," but if it were small, the trees farthest away were frostbitten. At the Oxford Physic Garden, the director tried to solve the problem by having a man pull an iron wagon of burning charcoal back and forth in the greenhouse, but the technique didn't catch on. In addition, if charcoal heating went on long enough, the trees developed a "certain Languor or Taint discoverable by their Complexions." Even worse, at least from the gardeners' point of view, people were similarly affected and fell ill with what we now know was carbon monoxide poisoning.

The Dutch, inspired by the particular ineffectiveness and smokiness of their peat-burning fireplaces, invented freestanding "stooves," which were originally made of fired clay or tiles and later cast iron. They and the Germans used them to heat small, closed rooms in their homes. But for a stove (as it was called in English) to provide better heat than a fireplace, the room had to be nearly airtight. The result, as Fynes Morrison wrote in 1613, was that "it must needes bee that these ill smells [of peoples' wet clothes and sweat,] never purged by the admitting of any freshe aire, should dull the braine, and almost the spirits." In a greenhouse, which was a large, uninsulated room with lots of leaky windows, such a stove was ineffective.

In the mid-1600s, horticulturalists got the idea to connect a hearth or stove to masonry channels running under the greenhouse floor or in its back wall. The system was a great improvement and could do more than ward off frost. It could raise the greenhouse temperature to positively balmy levels. In 1684, the Chelsea Physic Garden had one "that conveys the warmth through the whole house, by tunnels; so that [the director] hopes . . . to bring or keep the air at what degree of warmth he pleases." Still, the greenhouse windows had to be kept open to avoid asphyxiating the plants and people. In 1691, John Evelyn, an accomplished horticulturalist and a founding member of the Royal Society, designed one of the first forced-air heating systems that drew in and circulated *fresh* air while pushing "imprisoned and effete" air out. Furnace-heated greenhouses became known as "stove-houses" or simply "stoves," and the technology was soon transferred to domestic buildings.

At the same time that horticulturalists were developing stove-houses, they were experimenting with another, more prosaic structure: the kitchen garden hotbed.[2] The hotbed had a venerable pedigree. Ancient Roman gardeners discovered that they could extend the growing season for vegetables by surrounding the plants with a low wooden frame covered with thin sheets of transparent mica. When Tiberius Caesar was told by his doctor that he needed to eat cucumbers for his health, his gardeners grew them year-round in wagons filled with well-manured soil and covered with a mica top that they could roll out in cool but sunny weather and roll inside during the cold spells. It is not clear whether the soil in the wagons was sufficiently manured that decomposition provided additional heat, but people understood that decomposing manure exuded heat: Aristotle noted that the Egyptians incubated eggs buried in manure, and Greek alchemists, whose experiments required long and slow heating, surrounded their retorts with dung. After the fall of the Roman Empire, ancient hotbed technology was kept alive in the Arab world. In the eleventh century, Arab gardeners were reposted to sprout squash and eggplant seeds in midwinter in deep beds of manure topped with soil and covered with cabbage and cauliflower leaves before transplanting them in

---

[2] The term "hotbed" wasn't coined until 1626. Thanks to its association with manure, the word developed unsavory connotations, as in "hotbed of disease" and "hotbed of intrigue."

the spring. Hotbeds only reappeared in Italy in the beginning of the fourteenth century and not until the late 1500s in England. The dung beds were most often covered with leaves or straw mats and surrounded by fences to break the wind. In the seventeenth century, the hotbed evolved into a more substantial structure. The dung was surrounded by a wooden frame and covered over with pieces of glass joined together in what looked like a picture frame or casement. The casements could not be larger than roughly four by six feet because they lacked hinges and had to be lifted up and off. A kitchen gardener could start all kinds of vegetables this way and get a jump on the short northern growing season. In 1675, John Evelyn wrote about a new hotbed method in which the manure was placed in a brick-lined pit, and wooden boxes of soil planted with seedlings were placed on top, so that the plants wouldn't be disturbed when fresh manure was added.

The prosaic hotbed grew up, both in size and status, when Europeans fell in love with the pineapple. The first European to taste a pineapple was Christopher Columbus when he encountered them in Guadeloupe in 1493. He called the plant a *piña de Indes,* or "Indes pine," because its fruit looked to him like a pinecone. When English traders began exporting them from the West Indies in the 1500s, first as a preserve and later whole, they added "apple" to the name so buyers would understand that this peculiar object, despite its rough surface and prickly leaves, was edible and sweet. (The Peruvian name for the plant, first recorded by the monk André Thevenet in 1555, was *ananas,* which became its name in many European languages, including Latin.) Europeans adored the taste—pineapples have a very high sugar content and, unlike oranges, no acid—and in the sixteenth and seventeenth centuries the pineapple became what the orange had been in the fifteenth century or what the truffle is today: rare, terribly expensive, and, when served at dinner, evidence of one's wealth and sophistication.

Fresh pineapples were difficult to ship. They couldn't be picked ripe because they would rot long before they reached Europe, but picked unripe, they might never mature. If picked somewhere between the two, though, they might last for weeks before suddenly ripening. Their finicky behavior inspired a unique business: pineapple rentals. If you weren't rich enough to buy a ripe pineapple, you could rent an unripe one, not to eat, but to display at a party, either as the pièce de résistance in a heap of other expensive fruits or on a special pedestal. The next day, you returned it. A pineapple could pass through several households before it ripened and finally was sold to someone who could afford to actually eat it.

A portrait of King Charles II painted about 1660 captures him in the act of receiving a pineapple, the "queen of fruits," from his kneeling gardener, John Rose. The pineapple that Rose presented was most certainly not one he had grown himself. Although the plant could survive in the window of a northern greenhouse, it couldn't be fruited with such limited light and warmth. Agnes Block, who had a famous botanical garden outside Utrecht, was the first person in Europe to fruit an *Ananas comosus* in 1687, no doubt in her stove-house. In October 1693, the Brompton Nursery in Kensington announced that there was "at this time a very fine Ananas near Ripe in the stove which is to be presented to ye Queen in a few days."

It appears that Pieter de la Court van der Voort, a Dutch merchant and one of the early theorists of indoor gardening, was the first, in the 1690s, to fruit the pineapple plant systematically and in quantity. The first step in de la Court's method was to root pineapple crowns in a hotbed. But because the plant grows to be four feet tall and then sends up an even taller fruit-bearing stalk from its center, it couldn't mature in a standard hotbed. So de la Court built a new kind, converting a hotbed by steeply angling a glass cover against a wall, thereby creating a tall, all-glass lean-to. The rooted crowns were moved to this "succession house" or "pinery," which was heated with a deep layer of horse manure and ground-up oak bark. Other Dutch and English growers quickly copied and refined de la Court's structure, adding benches banked like stadium seats and furnaces and flues adapted from stovehouses. In eighteenth-century Holland and England, pineapple growing became a serious—and profitable—hobby for the horticulturally inclined. Some noblemen had pineries several hundred feet long.

A pinery. *From* A Short Treatise on Several Improvements in Hot-Houses *by John Claudius Loudon, 1805.*

(The most exuberant expression of the nobility's affection for pineapples would later be found in Scotland. In 1761 at his estate in Stirlingshire, the fourth Earl of Dunmore constructed a forty-five-foot-tall stone pineapple as a summer house, a kind of folly, on top of a long storage building. The leaves of the plant and the crown, each individually sculpted, curved out in full and realistic relief from the building. Below, pineries ran the length of building, warmed by flues in the back wall. The earl left his estate in 1770 to become royal governor of Virginia where he committed follies of another kind, dismissing the Virginia Assembly twice and otherwise enraging the citizenry, until he sailed back home in 1776. The citizens of Dunmore County, Virginia, promptly renamed their county Shenandoah, but the Dunmore Pineapple still enlivens the Scottish landscape.)

In 1710, Herman Boerhaave, the newly appointed professor of medicine and botany at the University of Leyden, added steeply banked glass lean-tos to the university's botanic garden, and the structures became a tool of science. Today, a joint appointment in the departments of medicine and botany would be unusual, but in Boerhaave's day, it was common, inevitable really. Physicians had to be knowledgeable about plants because plant-derived medicines (known as *simples*) were about the only help they could offer their suffering patients. In fact, over the millennia, physicians and folk healers had found simples of real value—hawthorn extract for relieving cardiac symptoms, the bark and leaves of willow trees for headaches and fever, henbane as a sedative, and lemon balm for healing cold sores, to name just a few. But for every effective botanical treatment, there were hundreds of ineffective, and sometimes downright harmful, ones.

The problem was that physicians relied by and large on the works of the ancient pharmacopeias, especially the Greek-born physician Dioscorides's five-volume *De materia medica*. The information in Dioscorides's unillustrated work, generically known as an herbal, was a compendium of knowledge gleaned from his Greek predecessors, as well as from books and healers he encountered while traveling the Roman Empire with Nero's army. The book covered nearly six hundred plants and included discussions of their medicinal properties and their habitats, directions for transforming their roots, leaves, or flowers into drugs, and dosages and warnings of side effects. Much of the medical information, however, was simply wrong. Take, for example, the information on rhubarb, whose roots Dioscorides reported were good for "gaseousness, weakness of the stomach, all types of suffering, convulsions, spleen, liver ailments, inflammation in the kidneys, griping and disorders of the bladder and chest, matters related to hypochondria [indigestion with nervous disorder], afflictions around the womb, sciatica, spitting up blood, asthma, rickets, dysentery, abdominal cavity afflictions, flows of fevers, and bites from poisonous beasts," as well as bruises and skin disease. Nonetheless, for the next fifteen hundred years, *De materia medica* was the supreme authority on plants.

Putting questions of the drugs' effectiveness aside, the physician at the end of the Middle Ages faced a more immediate concern: identifying those plants recommended by Dioscorides, as well as those prescribed by the second-century Roman physician Galen and the eleventh-century Persian physician Avicenna, among his local fields and forests. One problem, of course, was that a plant native to Greece might not be native to, say, Holland. Another problem was that a lot of plants look alike. Even the best-written descriptions, much less those that had been translated from Greek or Latin into Syriac or Arabic and then back to Latin and subjected to fifteen hundred years of copyists' errors, were often little help to anyone trying to distinguish subtle details. To add to the confusion, Dioscorides often described a plant through an analogy to another plant. The rhubarb root, he wrote, was "outwardly black, similar to centaury the larger, yet smaller and redder within," which was not very helpful if you weren't familiar with centaury the larger.

Illustrations should have helped and occasionally did. But the early illustrators had a dull and limited palette, and their stylized representations often gave only a general idea of the plant's appearance, about the same way the John Deere trademark represents a stag. Dioscorides categorized plants and ordered his book by the diseases the plants treated. Over the centuries, writers revised his work by reordering the plants and managed, not infrequently, to link the wrong illustration to a description. By 1300, the whole thing was a muddle.

You could argue that since rhubarb root can't cure any of the illnesses Dioscorides claimed it could (although it does help with constipation), it didn't matter whether physicians could correctly identify the plant or not. But around 1300, according to Anna Pavord in her elegant and comprehensive *The Naming of Names: The Search for Order in the World of Plants,* a few educated men living in Naples and Salerno were troubled by the situation and set out to do something about it. They may well have been inspired by a new law that Frederick II, Holy Roman Emperor and founder of the University of Naples, had passed that required, in essence, that physicians vouch for the quality of pharmacists' products. In any case, a Salneritan scholar associated with the medical school produced a new herbal known as the *Tractus de herbis et plantis*. The text of the *Tractus* was a compilation of older works, but the illustrations were new, drawn from life, more detailed, and more accurate. The artist still used only a limited color palette, but leaves had veins and, if insects had nibbled the specimen, holes. Pine-cones had scales, and stalks were sometimes crosshatched or dabbed with paint to indicate texture. The representations were far from subtle, but as art historian Otto Pächt wrote, and he could have been speaking in general about the nascent Italian Renaissance, "A new critical spirit becomes manifest in their work and a new courage to explore the visual world and to find out things for themselves." Over the next two centuries, botanical illustrators—Albrecht Meyers, Hans Weiditz, and Jorge Ziegler—became botanical portraitists. Their best works were stunningly beautiful and nuanced, and because they depicted plants in their native habitats, at all seasons, and from worm's-eye to bird's-eye views, they were also visual encyclopedias.

Scholars at Italian universities from about 1350 to 1550 were in the forefront of advances in science, medicine, law, and philosophy. In the mid-sixteenth century, a professor at the University of Pisa, Luca Ghini, turned his attention to helping sort out the disorder in the world of plants. Ghini was born in the small town of Croara about 1490, studied medicine at the nearby University of Bologna, and then was named the first *professor simplicium,* professor of medicinal plants, before moving to the University of Pisa in 1544. In an oil portrait, he looks out from a pale face with kindly black eyes that dip down at the corners and a long nose overhanging a dapper moustache and a goatee. He is showing the viewer an open book, and on each page there is a plant with a paragraph of text above it. Possibly it is an herbal or maybe it is a *hortus siccus* or herbarium, the book of dried and pressed plants, each labeled and annotated and carefully mounted on special paper that Ghini invented.

The herbarium was a simple idea, but one that had an enormous impact on the course of botany. As exacting as botanical illustration had become, for a scientist, there was nothing like seeing the real object. Besides, illustrators couldn't possibly capture in a timely way all the plants, local and increasingly foreign, that were available and in need of chronicling. But a herbarium could be instantly and indefinitely supplemented, and without benefit of artistic skill. Moreover, as the spirit of scientific inquiry spread beyond Italy, physicians and scholars across Europe could send and share their herbarium plants and seeds with one another. In doing so, they might sort out whether indeed the Radix Marica, Gladiolus, Theklpida, Urania, Catharon, Opertritis, Consecratix, and Egyptian Nar were all synonyms for the same cough-curing, thick-humour-purging plant, *Iris illyrica.* They could sort the contents of their herbaria as Dioscorides did, according to the illnesses they cured, or in other ways that might be more meaningful, according to leaf or root shape or, as Ghini's successor, Cesalpino, did, by seed or fruit type.

But if a dried specimen was better than a painted image, Ghini realized, a living, three-dimensional plant was better than both, and in 1544 under his direction, the University of Pisa installed the first "physick," or medicinal, garden in Europe. Here, planted in neat geometric plots were the species deemed to have curative powers. The physic garden was a living reference book that physicians, pharmacists, and anyone else could read. The idea was quickly copied, and during the second half of the sixteenth century, universities and medical schools, as well as municipalities and some wealthy individuals, established similar gardens. Physic gardens opened at Padua, Florence, Ferrara, Sassari, and Bologna before 1559, Leipzig in 1580, and Leyden in 1587. The Oxford Physic Garden, founded 1621, was to be "a Nursery of Simples, and that a professor of Botanicey should read there and shew the use and virtue of them to his auditors." In 1626, the Jardin du Roi in Paris opened as a medicinal garden. The Chelsea Physic Garden, owned and run by the Worshipful Society of Apothecaries, opened in 1673 as a training ground for its apprentices.

Gradually, the purpose of the physic gardens expanded, and a broader scientific purpose came to rival and even supersede the medicinal purpose. The first scientific society in Europe, the Academia dei Lincei, was founded in Italy in 1603, but during the seventeenth century, the center of European intellectual inquiry moved from Italy to England, France, and Holland. The Royal Society (officially, the Royal Society of London for the Improvement of Natural Knowledge) was founded in 1660 and dedicated to the proposition that scientific truth and natural laws could be determined by building a body of facts verified by experiment. Nehemiah Grew, John Ray, and Marcello Malpighi, early Royal Society fellows, were looking at plants with fresh eyes, exploring their internal anatomy with newly invented microscopes and considering the significance of various species' anatomical similarities and differences. When Hans Sloane, a wealthy physician and member of the Royal Society, bought the Chelsea Manor and generously deeded the Physic Garden to the Society of Apothecaries in 1722, he took measures to ensure that the garden would have a broader scientific function. He required that each year the apothecaries would send samples of fifty new plants (no plant to be offered twice) to the Royal Society.

A competition developed among institutions across Europe for the most varied and extensive botanical collection. For both public institutions and private collectors, a first-rate botanic collection became a way of projecting national or personal prestige. In 1648, the Oxford Physic Garden could claim to have almost 1,600 plant species, only 600 of which were British. In 1665, the Jardin du Roi in Paris boasted of having more than 4,000 species, and Leyden listed 3,800 species in 1687.

Increasing numbers of these plants came from Asia and Africa. Bulbous plants, such as tulips, crocus, cyclamen, and hyacinths, arrived first, followed by imports from tropical America, including tobacco, morning glory, sunflowers, ranunculus, bananas, and tomatoes (as an aphrodisiac). Between 1678 and 1692, Henry Compton, Bishop of London, received 340 American species for his hothouses at Fulham

Palace from his protégé John Banister, an Anglican missionary in Virginia. In 1691, John Gibson, assistant gardener at Battersea Park, wrote an annotated list of twenty-eight private greenhouses near London, including the one at Hampton Court, which, he noted, had "no orange or lemon trees, or myrtles, or any greens, but such tender foreign ones that need continual warmth." Glass hotbeds were often used, too, to protect the smaller plants.

The glass lean-tos that Herman Boerhaave, thanks to de la Court, introduced about 1710 to the botanic garden at Leyden were perfect for nurturing the new tropical exotics. Not only did Boerhaave have one of the world's most comprehensive plant collections, due in part to the country's leading role in international trade, he was deeply interested in advancing glass lean-to technology. He determined the best angle to set the glass (perpendicular to the sun's rays on the shortest day of the year) and added sliding panels for ventilation, oiled paper in frames to act as double glazing, and canvas shades. Because he hosted a constant flow of European visitors, his innovations and ideas spread across the continent.

Books with designs for glass lean-tos appeared in English, Dutch, French, and German. By midcentury the glass lean-to had evolved, here and there, into what looks like today's commercial, all-glass structures. A drawing dated 1751 of the greenhouses at the Chelsea Physic Garden shows that two of the roofs were glass, the first glass-roofed hothouses in England. Philip Miller, head gardener at Chelsea and the author of the widely read *The Gardener's Dictionary*, explained the change: "The most tender exotic plants ought to have their glasses so situated as to receive the sun's rays in direct lines as great a part of the year as possible. For which reason the stoves, which have upright glasses in front and sloping glasses over them, are justly preferred to any at present contrived." Glasshouses—well-heated, glass-walled, and glass-roofed structures—had arrived.

Ben hurried to put the finishing touches on the plans for our glasshouse and get them first to the county and then the neighborhood zoning authorities for building permits. I wasn't worried about whether we would be granted permits, but I was worried about when. Many of the houses in our incorporated neighborhood were built after World War I as summer cottages for Washingtonians who would take the trolley a few miles out to the last stop on the line, Chevy Chase. By World War II, the area had been subsumed into suburban Washington, and as land values rose in the 1990s, developers began buying the original small houses, tearing them down, and replacing them with larger houses. The neighborhood government was gearing up to impose a year-long building moratorium while it considered new, more restrictive zoning regulations. It didn't appear that any new rules would affect our project, but I didn't want to wait a year to start construction.

From a previous building project, I was well acquainted with the two critical requirements of the county zoning code: a house could not cover more than 35 percent of its lot and, in the case of an extra-narrow lot like ours, a house could be no closer than five feet to the side lot lines. So I was shocked when Ben called me to say that the county had rejected our plans: the conservatory as designed would be two feet too close to the line. After a frenzy of conversations, it transpired that the zoning authority had been reviewing the history of its regulations. In the process, it had discovered a long-lost piece of paper that established seven feet as the setback for lots like ours.

There was nothing to do but redesign the conservatory. Ben narrowed it by two feet, and the county approved the new plans. Now all we needed was the neighborhood permit.

I walked the plans four blocks to the neighborhood office and handed them over to Mr. Sanderson, a man with a white moustache whose geniality contrasted with his rather forbidding title of zoning enforcement manager. Mr. Sanderson assured me that the approval would not be a problem since the neighborhood's regulations were based on the county's, and promised a review within ten days. I called the builder and we set a start date.

Ten days later, I got a call from Ben.

"You are not going to believe this," Ben said. "I don't believe it."

"Don't tell me," I said. "I'll believe it."

"I just got a call from Mr. Sanderson. He's rejecting the plans. He says the lot coverage is over the 35 percent limit. By nine square feet."

I spluttered, he spluttered, and when we ran out of splutter, we took ourselves off to the office.

Mr. Sanderson explained that the problem was the pair of single-step stoops at the back of the existing house. The county didn't count stoops when it calculated lot coverage. The neighborhood did, if the stoops were covered. Ours were covered by a three-foot roof, an overhang really, which ran above the stoops as well as the window well between them.

"Well," I said, "we'll just take those stoops out." It would be a pretty big step up into the house, but we would manage.

"No," said Mr. Sanderson, "that won't do it. You'll still have the overhang."

"So, it's not the stoops that are the problem?"

"Yes, they're the problem, because they're covered."

"But if they're not there, how can they be covered?

"The stoop area is still covered. It's still a stoop. It doesn't really matter whether a step is there or not." He said this, remarkably, with a straight face.

"Are you telling me I need to take down the roof?" I asked.

"That would solve the problem," he said thoughtfully.

"But then I'd have uncovered stoops. And there are lights in the roof above them. Someone might trip in the dark."

Mr. Sanderson nodded sympathetically. "Yes, I can see that could be a problem. But maybe you could put a fixture on the sides of the doors."

I asked if there was any other way around the problem. I could redesign the conservatory, he offered, reducing the area by nine square feet. But then we'd have to go back to the county for a new permit, which could take weeks. Again, he was all sympathy.

"How about if I took down the portion of the roof between the stoops, the section that covers the window well?" Maybe I could cover the well with a plastic cover.

Mr. Sanderson shook his head. "No, that wouldn't work.

That part of the roof is okay. Since it doesn't cover a stoop."

"So the answer is I have to knock two holes in the roof, right over each step?"

"Well," he answered agreeably, "that would do it."

"Could I put skylights in the holes?" I asked desperately. "That way at least it wouldn't rain on us."

Mr. Sanderson shook his head, "No, skylights are a covering," he said. "But," he added brightly, "you could take the shingles and plywood off the roof and get down to the framing. Yes," he said with the air of someone who had just deciphered the theme that unlocks the Sunday crossword puzzle, "that would work."

I looked at Ben; he looked at me. Was this guy channeling Joseph Heller? The back of the house would look like hell and be completely dysfunctional, not to mention this destruction would cost thousands of dollars.

"If I agree to put two holes in the roof above the steps, you'll issue the permit?" I asked. "Today?"

"Sure," he said. "Your architect here," he nodded at Ben, "just needs to draw in the changes and everyone initials it."

I wanted my conservatory. Mr. Sanderson handed Ben a pen. He drew two holes in the roof, and we all initialed.

The construction went smoothly and quickly. In the first part of December, the foundation was poured. After Christmas, the carpenters built temporary plywood walls and tore down the outside walls behind them. I watched from my office as the framing went up and the roof went on. Every afternoon after the workers left I would put on my coat, walk around the back of the house and climb in over a windowsill to note the day's progress, admire the craftsmanship, and try, futilely, to imagine how the space, currently filled with scaffolding, saws, compressors, stacks of lumber, and sheets of drywall, would look full of plants. In February, the plywood walls came down, the sliding glass doors went in, and the floor tiles went over the subflooring. In March, the plumbers and electricians finished their work, and in one day the pool, which is essentially a vinyl-lined metal box, was constructed in a concrete pit at the back of the room. At the end of March, the county inspectors approved the structure. All that was left was Mr. Sanderson.

I had done nothing about the promised destruction. I hadn't asked Ben to make drawings for it. I hadn't put it in the contract with the builders.

This was not like me. I am a follow-the-rules kind of person. "Good" was my maiden name and is now literally my middle name. My sister, however, had been a different sort of Good. And if Mr. Sanderson was channeling Heller, I seemed to be channeling Joanie.

The byword of Joanie's teenage years was a dismissive "tough!," as in "tough luck for you, I'm not cleaning up my room and I am going out, right now, with my friends." She wasn't really rebellious, not in any of the traditional teenage ways. It's just that if she didn't see a relationship between the state of her room on the one hand and going out with her friends on the other, she saw no reason that my mother's linkage of the two should inhibit her in any way. I could only watch these encounters with a mixture of amazement, admiration, and chagrin that, despite being the older sister by two years, I didn't have her self-possession. I have to admit, too, that I had a certain discomfort about her bold flouting of parental authority, an uneasiness about the subversion of traditional order.

Joanie always had a considerable confidence in herself. After college, she worked for a few years for a bicycle manufacturer, where she started as a gofer and quickly became the gatekeeper to the CEO. Barely twenty-two, five-foot-two, 105 pounds (two of which must have been her thick, waist-length hair), and with childhood's spill of freckles still faint across her cheekbones, she took no guff from anyone. No one traveled, made a purchase, took a vacation, or was hired or fired without Joanie's at least implicit approval.

At twenty-four, she decided the law might be for her, and she and her boyfriend, Ken, moved to Cambridge, Massachusetts, where she found a job as a paralegal in Boston and Ken worked in a physics lab at Harvard. The next year, she was accepted at the University of Pennsylvania law school, and she and Ken moved to Philadelphia. Joanie went to the first day of orientation . . . and quit. The law, she announced, was not for her. But how could she possibly know? I protested. She hadn't gone to a single class. Stay for a while, for a week or two at least, I urged, just to make sure; her tuition would be lost whether she left immediately or later in the semester. Joanie was having nothing of my cautious approach. She knew what was right for her.

She and Ken broke up, and Joanie moved to Maryland to take a job as a project manager for Siemens. She rented an apartment in a ten-story building that I could see from our backyard. I had three children under the age of six, Ted traveled, and I was grateful for her companionship and help in the evenings. We would watch the girls play in the backyard, take them to the park or out for ice cream, and, on a rainy day, she would invite Anna and Austen over to race up and down the long hallways on her floor and take a ride in those magical conveyances otherwise known as elevators. When Alice was two, Siemens offered her a promotion in San Francisco, and, although I argued against the move, she accepted.

Eight years later, I was telling the archetypal Joanie story, one from her days in Cambridge, at her memorial service.

Joanie and Ken lived on Trowbridge Street in an apartment on the top floor of a three-story house. It was early April, the season in Cambridge for the monthly street cleanings to start again. The schedule was difficult to obtain and changeable in any case, given the fickle spring weather in the Boston area. Given this, early on the morning of a street cleaning, a squad car with a loudspeaker would pass through the neighborhood, announcing that residents had thirty minutes to move their cars and warning that any remaining on the street would be ticketed and towed. Then, anywhere from thirty minutes to several hours later, a phalanx of squad cars would arrive, closely trailed by a fleet of commercial tow trucks to haul away the ticketed cars (no doubt at great profit), and soon followed by a couple of monster yellow street sweepers. The operation worked with military precision; they could ticket, tow, and clean an entire street in minutes.

At 8:00 A.M. that particular chilly morning in April, Joanie and Ken were eating breakfast when they heard the thirty-minute warning blared from the street below. Ken was still in his bathrobe; Joanie was dressed for work. They figured they had at least twenty-five minutes to get the car, time to finish a piece of toast. Almost immediately, though, they heard the growl of engines and the clanking of chains and realized the trucks were already hauling cars away. Joanie went whipping down the uncarpeted stairs of the house and into the street, only to find that a tow truck driver has already put a chain on her car.

Ken found a pair of shoes and hustled after her, arriving on the street in his bathrobe to witness Joanie standing between her car, ticketed and chained but not yet hoisted, and a tow truck, arguing with the tow truck driver. The driver was a mean-looking, beer-bellied fellow in a flannel shirt who had at least a foot in height and more than a hundred pounds on Joanie, and arms that made Ken think he wrestled alligators in his off hours. Joanie was protesting vehemently that she hadn't been given anything like thirty minutes, more like four minutes, and demanded that the driver unchain her car. The driver snarled that she had two choices: pay him forty bucks in cash that instant or she could bail her car out of the impoundment lot later for much more. Neither Ken nor Joanie had forty dollars on them, and when Ken started back toward their apartment to find or borrow the money, the driver turned away and immediately went to work on her car.

Joanie turned away, too, but with a look of righteous and steely determination, a look that Ken knew to be wary of. Before anyone knew what was happening, Joanie jumped into the open cab of the tow truck (the driver had left the door open and the engine running), slammed the door, slapped down the lock, and rolled up the window.

The driver immediately went berserk.

"Get the hell outta my truck, you crazy bitch!" he shouted at her, his face right up at the window. "Get outta there or I'm going to break the goddamn window and pull you out!"

"Give me back my car!" she shouted.

"Get outta my truck!" he shouted back, even more furious.

"Give me back my car!"

Meanwhile, Ken, who had only gone a few paces, was watching Joanie through the passenger-side window. She was sliding down in the seat, clearly trying to reach the clutch pedal—which given the size of the driver must have been a considerable distance away—and looking down, trying to figure out where the parking brake was, and which of all the levers and shifts in the truck was the one that put it in gear.

All of a sudden, Trowbridge Street became a scene. The cops in the next block writing tickets hurried back. The other tow trucks stopped and a couple more drivers, none who looked like they ate salad for lunch, lumbered over. The tow truck crew boss, who had been directing the trucks to the various targets, arrived. He started yelling, too, not at Joanie, but at his driver for being an idiot for leaving his door open and engine running. The driver went from macho to emasculated in ten seconds. Suddenly, he was pleading with Joanie to get out of the truck. Next, the yellow street-sweeping machines with their giant whirring brushes pulled up, their progress halted by the crowd and the commotion, and the sweepers got out of their machines, complaining. Ken was watching with a mix of horror and admiration; and the cops were trying to get everyone to back off.

Joanie meanwhile had reached over her shoulder and grabbed the seat belt, which probably had never been used before, and buckled up. She may not have found the clutch pedal, but she could definitely reach the accelerator. The truck revved and then revved again. No one dared stand in front of it. Joanie was staring out the windshield, and there was no doubt in anyone's mind that she had a destination in mind and was ready to go.

Finally, the cops pushed everyone back and one cop went up to the window.

"Ma'am," he said in a neutral tone, "you need to roll down the window."

Joanie rolled it down a nanometer.

"Ma'am, you need to get out of the truck now."

"I'm not getting out of here," Joanie declared. "We were getting the money, the forty dollars, but he wouldn't wait. He can't just take my car away with no warning."

The cop was not at all interested in joining a debate and simply told her that if she didn't get out, he was going to arrest her. He then turned to Ken and told him he needed to convince her to get out of the truck immediately or Joanie was going in the squad car.

Ken went up to the window. "Joan," he said with the calm rationality of a budding physicist, "they are not going to relent. You are right, it's completely unfair. But there's nothing we can do about it. And he's really going to arrest you."

Joanie unbuckled her seat belt, opened the door, climbed

down, and walked a few feet away. The truck driver huffily went about hoisting her car and drove it away. The other men began to return to their various vehicles. Joanie looked at Ken and the few remaining bystanders and said shakily and with tears in her eyes, "It wasn't fair. We only got four minutes' notice." Then she and Ken started home.

After they crossed the street and were headed down the sidewalk, a voice called "Ma'am, ma'am?" from behind them. They stopped. It was the beefy crew boss with his radio in hand.

"Ma'am, I just called the driver and he's going to bring your car back." Then he turned away without a word of explanation and went back to directing the tow trucks that were already rousting the other cars left on the street.

Did he see the justice of her position? Did he admire her spunk? Or was he afraid she would never give up and he'd find himself in court? Whatever it was, Joanie won.

I thought of that story in those months when I did nothing about putting holes in the roof. I couldn't go forward with such senseless destruction simply because it was commanded by an authority, and I put off calling to arrange for the final inspection. Unlike Joanie, I dreaded the confrontation—maybe if I waited long enough, Sanderson would forget the whole thing. But one day, he showed up of his own accord. He walked around inside the conservatory, admired the work, and chortled over the tiny pool. Then, he headed to the back door and stepped into the backyard, with me trailing behind. He looked back at the house, and then at me.

"You didn't do the work on the roof," he said in a puzzled tone.

"No," I answered.

I offered no explanation. I said nothing.

We stood there on the muddy ground in the bright but chilly spring day, looking at each other for what seemed to me a very long time.

And finally he said, "Well, I guess it doesn't matter."

It was time to think about plants.

Plant Hunting

four

Philodendron bipinnatifidum

It was late March, and one morning I found myself alone in a silent house for the first time since construction began. The day was already warm, and I opened the windows and slid back the glass doors to the conservatory. I stood in the center of the empty room. A breeze flowed from the east, through the front windows of the house, through the living room, through the conservatory, and out the west bay window, a ribbon of air lacing outdoors, house, and conservatory together.

It was to my eyes a beautiful space, but now I was worried: Would it work as a plant-growing space? In the planning stage, twelve skylights seemed more than adequate, and I fretted about the heat we would lose through them. Although the skylights and windows did let in a pleasant, diffuse light, no one would ever feel compelled to reach for the sunscreen. The north-tilting roof combined with the energy-efficient glass and insect screens on the operable skylights subdued the light much more than I had imagined.

Sunlight outdoors measures roughly 10,000 foot-candles. I got out my light meter and took readings at waist height at various points around the conservatory. At 9:00 A.M., when the sun had hours to go before clearing the ridge of the house, the dimmest corner measured 75 foot-candles and the brightest was twice that. At noon, the measurements doubled; at 3:00 P.M., the range was 250 to 400. Only in front of the west-facing bay window, and where the skylights dropped slow-moving rectangles of direct sun in the afternoon, did the readings reach four figures. What plants could survive with less than 5 percent of sunlight? The answer, I was afraid, was plastic ones—although maybe no one would notice the difference in the gloom.

I called up Edie, who was beginning to seem like a therapist. She dismissed my worries out of hand. A tropical forest, she pointed out, is not in fact a sunny place, at least for those plants that live on the forest floor. The tree canopy is extremely dense and only about 2 percent of the sun's light filters down to the bottom. Low-light tropical plants can survive with as little as 100 foot-candles, although they would probably need twice that to grow. Even many medium-light plants can survive with only 150 foot-candles.

How do they manage with so little light? The leaves of low-light plants are thin and large and have a single layer of cells on the upper surface. Their chloroplasts are arranged horizontally to trap every photon that manages to slip through the gauntlet of limbs and leaves above. Some plants have leaves with deep red or purple undersides that reflect light passing through the leaves back to the chloroplasts above, as well as capturing greenish light reflected from the forest floor. I would have to recognize, Edie said, that low-light plants are not the gay blades of the plant world; it takes a lot of energy, provided by sunlight, to produce copious flowers. On the other hand, my recompense would be leaves with an infinite variety of patterns and some rich but subtle colors.

I made several trips to Johnson's, just scoping out their stock and getting Edie's advice on various species. The plants I wanted had to be novice-proof. I wanted nothing that would expire instantly if I forgot to water it or watered it twice. When I was finally ready to make decisions, Edie helped me collect a variety of ultrareliable, low-to-medium-light foliage plants of varying heights. I chose two five-foot "dragon trees" (*Dracaena marginata* grown to a tree form) with braided trunks and leaves as long and sharp as letter openers; a pot with four tall *Dracaena fragrans* 'Massangeana', whose trunks looked like fence posts and whose leaves looked as if they had been filched from a cornfield; four species of striped, streaked, and mottled *Dieffenbachia;* two Chinese evergreens (*Aglaonema modestum*); a *Xanthosoma* 'Lime Zinger' with sagittate leaves the color of green Kool-Aid; two *Colocasia esculenta*—one a 'Black Magic' variety with velvety, dark purple leaves and one a 'Fontanasii' with shiny green ones; and some white-veined *Syngonium* appropriately nicknamed "Arrowheads." I saw an *Aspidistra* and selected it out of affection for George Orwell and because Edie told me it could survive in a closet with a night-light. I also bought two *Aucuba,* woody plants whose jagged-edged leaves are flecked with bright yellow as if sunshine filtered through trees were falling on them. I snagged a variegated variety of my friend the *Spathiphyllum;* a large *Philodendron bipinnatifidum,* whose leaves looked as though a deer had eaten the soft parts and left the tougher veins; four baskets of lacy *Nephrolepis exaltata* 'Bostoniensis', or Boston fern; and the surefire *Pothos,* that vining plant with heart-shaped, marbled leaves that tumbled from the tops of filing cabinets in every office I'd ever worked in. I pondered the three species of palms that Edie said could take low light, but large specimens were expensive, and I decided they would cause me too much heartache if I killed them. Then, a tree form of variegated *Schefflera actinophylla,* aptly known as an umbrella plant, caught my eye. This would need brighter conditions, especially since it was variegated—the white parts of the leaves lack chlorophyll and are unable to photosynthesize— but I had a place in mind for it, near the west-facing bay. For color, Edie suggested *Caladium* with piebald green, pink, maroon, and white leaves and *Anthurium* with spathes that looked like red plastic plates that had been left too close to the stove and warped.

As I checked out, Edie had one final piece of advice for me.

"Do not feel bad," she said sternly, "if you kill a few, or more than a few, of your plants. Believe me, even the best growers, even those born with a green thumb, have failures. Everyone has a kind of plant they simply cannot grow. For the life of me, I can't keep a *Nephitis* alive, I don't know why.

"I know it's easy to get attached to a plant," and she fixed me with a penetrating, knowing look, "but remember this: a

Peperomia is not a puppy. If it's not working, throw it out, and get something that will."

I drove the two miles home from my plant-hunting expedition as if I had a newborn in the car, slowing gently at red lights and going carefully over the neighborhood speed bumps. The trip was uneventful. I certainly arrived in good shape, and not a single plant expired on the journey.

It was an entirely different story for the plant hunters of the eighteenth century, especially those collecting in tropical regions. They faced challenges that are hard to fully conceive today. They suffered—and sometimes died—from malaria, dysentery, sepsis, and scurvy; food poisoning, sunstroke, dehydration, and volcanic eruptions; a fall off a cliff or into a hippopotamus wallow or through the covering of a pitfall trap; snake, scorpion, and bat bites; robberies, kidnappings, and imprisonments; pirate attacks, run-of-the-mill shipwrecks, and spectacular mutinies. More plant hunters by far died or were seriously injured in their earth adventures than astronauts have been on their voyages into space, both in absolute and in percentage terms. As for bringing back live plants, John Livingstone, an amateur plant collector and surgeon who worked in China in the early 1800s, estimated that only one in a thousand plants sent to England from Asia arrived safely.

Tropical plants, the ones that at northern latitudes can only survive in the shelter of heated glasshouses, were particularly difficult to transport. Botanist Hans Sloane was one of the earliest collectors of tropicals, hunting in 1687.

His appreciation of medicinal plants, he wrote, dated to his childhood in Ireland where he saw people eat seaweed to counteract scurvy. He studied botany with John Ray, a former Cambridge don who had published an influential book on plant classification, and at the Jardin du Roi in Paris under the famous botanist and collector Joseph Pitton de Tournefort. When he was twenty-seven, Sloane applied for a position as family physician to the Duke of Albemarle, a job that was primarily attractive because the duke was about to sail for Jamaica where he would be governor. Sloane thought the island would prove good hunting grounds for more of the New World plants that had medicinal value, like the Peruvian cinchona tree whose bark treated malaria.

Sloane had only about fifteen months abroad; the duke died in the autumn of 1688, and Sloane accompanied his widow and children home early the next year. In that short time, however, he collected some eight hundred botanical specimens, plus lizards, birds, fish, and small animals, either dried or pickled in jars. He also brought a collection of live creatures, including an iguana, a seven-foot yellow snake that followed him around like a dog, and an alligator in a tub. Most of his plants were dried specimens, but he may have brought a few onboard alive. It's not clear if any arrived in that condition. If Sloane's record with his animals is an indicator, probably none did: his iguana leaped overboard, the duchess's footman shot the snake, and the alligator, fed on "Guts and Garbage of Fowl," simply expired.

It was hard enough for western European collectors who hunted in temperate zones, regions like North America, eastern Europe, Russia, and most of China and Japan where temperatures swing from warm in the summer to cold in the winter, to sustain plants on long voyages home. At least many of the temperate-zone plants they chose to send home were woody species whose bark made them less vulnerable to desiccation. Many also had a natural period of dormancy that collectors could take advantage of, either by timing shipment or by putting the plant into a dormant state by withholding light and water. Temperate-zone bulbs were also excellent candidates for long-distance travel, so it was no coincidence that many of the early imports from Turkey and Russia were crocuses, hyacinths, lilies, and, of course, tulips.

Tropical-zone plants were far more challenging to ship. Tropical trees have bark, but it is thin since the underlying tissues need no protection from water loss or freezing temperatures. Understory plants were even harder to ship: their thin leaves dry out quickly and their stems are made of soft tissue easily damaged. And, of course, because tropical plants have evolved in climates where temperatures and humidity are high year-round, they are devastated by cold temperatures and dry conditions. At least plants sent from the Caribbean needed only three or four months to arrive in England, and if a collector sailed in spring, as Sloane did, then he and his finds arrived in summer (if, of course, they arrived at all), which minimized the stress on the plants.

The fifteen months in Jamaica made Sloane's career. His herbarium immediately became famous, establishing his reputation in the scientific world. His medical practice took off, too, despite his patient's death. (Everyone knew that the Caribbean climate was dangerous. The average age at death of Europeans in the region was thirty-five, exactly the duke's age.) Sloane would eventually become physician to Queen Anne, King George III, and King George IV. He had a knack for making money, and he developed "Sir Hans Sloane's Milk Chocolate," based on a drink of milk, cocoa, and sugar that he had seen Jamaican mothers feed to their sick children. Advertised for "its Lightness on the Stomach and its great use in all Consumptive Cases," it was available in apothecaries' shops everywhere. (Decades later, Cadbury Brothers would buy the recipe.) And, in 1695, he married the wealthy widow of a Jamaican plantation owner. He sold her Jamaican property in order to purchase the manor that included the Chelsea Physic Garden, which he then leased to the Society of Apothecaries for £5 annually in perpetuity.

Sloane's collection—and his financial backing—inspired other collectors to return to the Caribbean in search of seeds and living plants. In 1690, James Harlow collected in Jamaica for Sir Arthur Rawdon's hothouse; James Reed was sent to Barbados by a syndicate, to which Sloane subscribed, the same year. Around 1730, William Houstoun, a ship's surgeon, sent home numerous specimens from Jamaica and the coast of Mexico, and Robert Millar collected seeds and dried specimens in Mexico, Panama, Jamaica, and Colombia. Many of these West Indian plants were woody types rather than soft-tissued ones more difficult to transport.

Plant hunting in Jamaica, which Britain had controlled since 1655, was a walk in a botanical garden compared with botanizing in the humid tropics of Africa. In 1749, Michel Adanson, a twenty-one-year-old protégé of Bernard de Jussieu, director of the Jardin du Roi, was the first botanist to go on a collecting venture in the continent's equatorial region.

Adanson had come to botany not through the usual channel of medicine, but through a love of the natural world and a deep interest in taxonomy. As a young teenager in Paris he had been reluctantly heading toward a clerical career when he began visiting the Jardin du Roi to escape the boredom of the classroom. At fourteen, he started attending lectures there and at the science-oriented Collège Royale. At nineteen, he compiled a catalog of the Jardin's recent acquisitions, and then resigned the ecclesiastical position that had been waiting for him. Botany, he decided, was his real calling.

Adanson was fortunate in his timing. His father understood his ambition, and the fact that he did was a sign of a new era, the Enlightenment. At the end of the seventeenth century and in the eighteenth century, pursuing an interest in natural history and owning a "natural history cabinet," a herbarium, or an exotic plant collection had become fashionable, the mark of a modern gentleman. "As we no longer live in rude and barbarous times, thanks to the reestablishment of letters, . . . there is no longer any excuse for the nobility to take pride in crass ignorance," wrote one gentleman physician living in Aix-en-Provence, the town where Adanson was born. Botanical research was a sign of intellectual sophistication, or at least, as the doctor pointed out, a "pleasant occupation, hardly less diverting than hunting." And while the wealthy were unlikely to risk their own lives hunting plants, they were willing to pay others, educated in botany, to do so. A career in natural history was a respectable alternative for a young man of good family and education.

Adanson's father tried introducing his son to the duc d'Ayen who kept a large and renowned botanical garden.

The duc considered Adanson too inexperienced, but nobles were not the only ones who were sponsoring collectors. French trading companies had gotten into the business, too, although their interest was in "economic" plants that had a marketplace value. Fortunately, Adanson père had another contact, a director of the Compagnie des Indes, who did extend an offer. Adanson would go to the company outpost in Senegal as a clerk. The Compagnie administrators did not expect the young man, expert in Greek and Latin and trained in the sciences, to do any bookkeeping. They were hoping instead that he would find animals, plants, or minerals that would bring the company some financial return, as tea from China and spices from East Asia had for the Dutch.

Adanson was delighted with the assignment. "Senegal," he wrote before he left, "is of all the white settlements, the most difficult to penetrate, the hottest and most unhealthy to live in, the most dangerous in all respects, and so the least known to naturalists." It was, in other words, perfect for a young man besotted with botany and eager for fame and an invitation to join the Académie des sciences. He studied all that had been written on equatorial Africa; boarded a ship at L'Orient on the Britanny coast armed with a few books, a microscope, and other scientific instruments; and set sail on March 3, 1749. His enthusiasm was hardly dampened by his instant discovery that he had no stomach at all for water travel. He was constantly and violently seasick until the day he disembarked at Fort Saint-Louis six weeks later.

Although no one at the time left the fort without armed guards, Adanson was soon venturing out alone, dressed in his knickers, white stockings, a voluminous shirt, and shoes with metal buckles and with his waist-length, reddish hair wound up under a round hat. The soldiers were probably glad to see him off: Adanson would have been a strange duck in their eyes, uninterested in gambling or drinking, a young man whose first activity after arrival was to lay out a garden in the fort. Over the next five years, he traveled into the country repeatedly, going by canoe to the thorn-covered island of Sor where he discovered the enormous baobab tree, overland to the mosquito-infested Senegal River delta, and by boat up the Gambia River for days on end, despite unrelenting mal-de-mer and heat so extreme it melted the boat's caulking. He nearly lost his right hand to an infection, came close to drowning (once in a sudden tornado and once in a capsized canoe), and endured a debilitating fever that lasted for months. He faced lions, tigers, wild boars, huge "serpents," mosquitoes that descended in black masses, and red ants that blistered him all over. He was smitten with the country, nonetheless: "I cannot repeat enough that [this] is the most fruitful country in the world and the least known," he wrote in 1750, "and that no other place shows such a variety of plants and merits more of our observations." The country was, he pronounced, "delicious" in all ways, and he approved of almost everything he saw and ate, from the fat fishes that jumped into his canoe to the tender hedgehogs, tastiest, he wrote, just before they turned in for their annual hibernation.

He made an intensive study of the Wolof language, came to speak it fluently, and would later compile the first Wolof dictionary. He lived and dined with local families, admired the beautiful women, listened to the elders' stories, and watched the festival dances. He let children play with his hair—at least those who didn't run away at the first, ghosty sight of him. There was nothing he didn't want to see, whether it was salt-pans or lime-kilns, crocodile hunting, dyeing methods, or a Moorish wedding. He gave thought to how the plants and animals he found fit into the larger environment and into human lives, and his journal was a kind of anthropological study. He was deeply committed to his work (he extended his stay from two years to five), occasionally rash (he fought a duel with a local king), certainly brave, and obsessively thorough. He asked questions about every aspect of life in Senegal, took censuses, made measurements, and collected everything, including, of course, chests and chests of plants.

Getting his hard-won treasures back to France was as great a challenge as gathering them from the wild. His first shipment of preserved fish and birds he packed in a barrel, only to have them eaten by insects before he could even get them to the dock. Ultimately, he discovered that the best way to keep dried plant specimens safe and at a proper temperature and humidity was to put them under his mattress and sleep on them.

Shipping live plants successfully was impossible. Seeds were a better bet, but keeping them from drying out, going moldy, germinating prematurely, or getting eaten by dockside or shipboard vermin—after all, seeds are little packages of food for the developing embryo—was extraordinarily difficult. Collectors and botanists had been giving much thought to how to pack seeds. They experimented in coating nuts in gum arabic, gum seneca, pitch, rosin, brewer's loam, mutton fat, charcoal, beeswax, or a combination of those materials. They wrapped seed pods in linen or writing paper and put them in canisters, jars, or snuffboxes, which they then filled with rice, mullet, bran, or Indian corn, depending on the port of embarkation, and sealed. Linnaeus had his own method, which involved putting seeds in a glass bottle, filling the bottle with sand and sealing it, then putting the glass bottle in another one, and filling the gap between the bottles with a mixture of nitre, salt, and ammonium chloride. Once seeds were packed, they were stored in linen bags, bottles, pots, wicker baskets, or hung in string bags below deck. But no matter how they were prepared, after seeds and nuts had waited weeks on a dock for a ship and traveled from hot and humid climates to cool ones, they were often no longer viable by the time they arrived. We know that Adanson shipped seeds of a thousand species, most of which were new to Europe, but there are no data on how many survived to produce plants.

What we do know is that by the time he returned to France in 1754, Adanson had sent or brought back 500 samples of minerals, ores, and stones; specimens of 250 birds and 40 quadrupeds; 600 insects; 100 crustaceans; 30 snakes and amphibians; and 900 shells, corals, sponges, and other small marine life species, all of which he stuffed, dried, or preserved in glass vials. His herbarium contained 600 species of dried plants. He waited to ship live specimens until he could accompany them on his homeward voyage, when he took 200 plants with him. But after a four-month journey that started with weeks of being becalmed, continued with "a boisterous south-east wind [that] spread itself over the Deep and assailed us with a storm that lasted two months," and ended in Brest on a snowy day in February, most were dead.

Adanson was admitted to the Académie in July 1759, and, in addition to reports on his voyage, he wrote a groundbreaking, two-volume work, *La Famille des Plantes*, that proposed classifying plants according to an examination of a plant's total morphology—leaves, stems, flowers, and roots. Not surprisingly, Adanson's approach provoked rabid criticism from Linnaeus, whose artificial "sexual system" grouped plants according to the number and position of their pistils and stamens. (Granted, Adanson's insistence on returning to plants' ancient Greek names or using the names in the local dialects didn't help his cause.) Feuds with Linnaeus and other botanists, as well as his insistence on spending years writing a twenty-seven-volume encyclopedia of the philosophy of knowledge (never published), meant that his contributions to botany went largely unrecognized for many years.

The most famous of all the plant hunters, Joseph Banks, made no attempt to bring back live plants (and few seeds) from his trip to the South Seas in 1768. This was hardly surprising given that he was en route for three years. Banks was an extremely wealthy and well-connected twenty-five-year-old who had studied botany at Oxford and was already a member of the Royal Society when he learned of the society's plans for its first major scientific mission. With financing from the king and a ship from the Admiralty, the society was preparing to send Captain James Cook to Tahiti to take measurements of the transit of Venus across the sun, measurements that would help determine the distance between the sun and the earth. A second and secret goal of the mission was to find and claim for England a rumored southern continent. Banks had gained some experience in scientific exploration on a trip to Newfoundland but was nonetheless a very young man. He proposed, however, to pay for himself and two other naturalists, two painters, four servants, and a large quantity of scientific equipment and supplies. The Royal Society was pleased to accept his offer.

Banks and his companions were nine of the ninety-four adventurers who left London on the hundred-foot-long *Endeavour* that August. The group traveled in great harmony, despite the impossibly crowded conditions onboard, and successfully circumnavigated the globe from west to east, explored Tahiti and other South Seas islands, charted the New Zealand coast, discovered Australia, and survived shipwreck on the Great Barrier Reef. Banks arrived home in July 1771 with more than 3,000 dried plants representing 1,300 new species, 1,000 preserved fish and birds, and a great trove of cultural artifacts. The voyage was hailed as a colossal scientific achievement. (The loss of a third of the shipmates— including all but one of Banks's entourage—to disease was not unusual and did not undermine the perception of the venture's success. In fact, because Cook took barrels of sauerkraut with him and made sure to take on additional greens in New Zealand, no one died or even suffered from scurvy.) "The celebrated Mr. Banks" became the darling of the press and an increasingly intimate friend of the royal family, and he was soon elected to the Council of the Royal Society.

Banks's trip with Cook was the last major exploring voyage he made. His career moved in a different direction when King George III turned to him as his adviser on the royal gardens at Kew. The gardens were already a repository for exotic plants donated by travelers, colonists, and sea captains. One of Banks's first acts in his new capacity was to send out the first royal botanical collector. The king was a man of considerable and intelligent curiosity about the natural world—he had had an observatory built at Kew in time for the transit of Venus—and supported Banks fully.

Banks set about to turn Kew into a serious botanical garden and British plant hunting into a profession. He chose Kew gardener Francis Masson, a thirty-one-year-old Scottish undergardener, for a mission to the southern tip of South Africa. Banks had briefly reconnoitered the Cape of Good Hope on his way home from the South Seas and had visited the Dutch East India Company's botanical garden there. The plants reminded him of many of the hardy types that he had seen in Australia, and it struck him that they might withstand the rigors of transportation.

Masson journeyed out from Cape Town in 1773 in a wagon propelled by oxen and large sails. He, fellow horticulturalist Charles Peter Thunberg, and their native guides covered more than nineteen hundred miles, collecting plants in the mountains, the temperate veldt, and the dry, stony, red desert of the high plateaus. He sent back to England at least four hundred species no one had described before, including varieties of hardy bulb species of *Gladiolus*, *Iris*, and *Amaryllis* (among others, one that the natives used to make poison arrows), as well as cacti and succulents like *Aloe*, tiny *Lithops* that camouflage themselves as pebbles, *Euphorbia* that survive the dry heat by storing water in their leaves, and *Protea* with leathery or hairy leaves that restrict evaporation or underground stems that store water. He successfully sent home new species of dainty, multicolored *Portulaca* (which have somewhat succulent leaves); daisylike, red and mauve *Mesembryanthemum*; *Aspalathus* with brilliant yellow flowers; fifty species of the drought-tolerant geranium; and, most famously, the bird-of-paradise (*Strelitzia reginae,* named in honor of Queen Charlotte's birthplace). Masson's specimen of *Encephalartos longifolius,* a primitive cycad whose cones can weigh up to eighty pounds, still grows in the southern wing of Kew's Palm House. Banks had guessed correctly, both about the hardiness of South African plants and about Masson. No single plant hunter would ever successfully send so many living, new species to Europe.

Masson hunted for plants for the sake of botany and the glory of the king's garden. But Banks was equally interested in plants for commercial purposes. In 1770, French adventurers Pierre Poivre and his clerk, Provost, had stolen nutmeg and clove trees from the Dutch Spice Islands and carried them off to the Isle de France (modern Mauritius), ending the valuable Dutch monopoly. Banks saw opportunities for similar plantations of "useful" species— he had *Opuntia* cactus (the host plant for cochineal insects, which were made into a costly red dye), tea, and indigo in mind—in India. He strongly supported the founding of the Calcutta Botanic Garden by the British East India Company in 1786, not only as a botanical research station but also as a nursery for such valuable export crops. Robert Kyd, the director of the Calcutta Garden, urged experimenting with the cultivation of sago palms from Malaysia, date palms from Persia, and cotton plants. The palms were to feed starving Indians; raw cotton would supply the thread manufacturers of England.

Banks was interested in developing British raw cotton resources overseas. Like many others, he advocated the economic model in which colonial outposts provided cheap raw materials that British manufacturers processed. But independent Indian farmers cultivated cotton, which meant that the quality was impossible to control. Bales were routinely contaminated with seeds, leaves, unpicked bolls, and dirt. Besides, the journey to England could easily take half a year, and raw cotton was prone to rot. (India, therefore, exported the cloth and thread to Britain instead.) The government's Board of Trade saw more potential for raw cotton in the West Indian colonies where English plantation owners controlled the quality of the crop and had lower shipping costs. The plantation owners were eager to grow more cotton, but their varieties were not as fine or productive as East Indian varieties, and they pressed the board, which pressed Banks, to get them better plants to try.[3]

So it was that Anton Pantaleone Hove, a young Polish-born doctor and Kew gardener, became the second plant hunter Banks sent out. In January 1787, Hove received two communications from Banks. The first was a letter confirm-

---

[3] Cotton plantations in the southern colonies of North America were in their infancy at the time. According to Henry Hobhouse in *Seeds of Change*, the first bale of cotton from the North American colonies arrived in London in 1785. A Liverpool customs officer, believing it could only be a West Indian product illegally shipped in an American ship, refused it entry. The first American cotton to reach England rotted on the dock.

ing his assignment to Gujarat Province in India as a plant collector. The second was a secret attachment, stating that the primary object of his mission was to covertly collect seeds of Indian cotton plants, learn all aspects of their cultivation, and discover how the Indians manufactured their cloth. Hove was to be an industrial spy for the British government, stealing cotton plants and technology from under the nose of the British East India Company. In addition to his regular reports, he was to send secret reports, written in Polish, on cotton. As an inducement to take on the job, Banks promised him the superintendency of any West Indian cotton plantation that developed from his findings.

Hove left for India in April 1787 and promptly set out on his mission, traveling slowly in the region around Surat, north of Bombay, and collecting cotton species as well as novel plants of all kinds. He got no help from the East India Company, which was rightly suspicious of his intentions. Although he traveled with as many as two dozen armed guards, he was robbed three times in ten weeks: once by a local official, once by a band of dissident tribesmen, and once by a criminal gang that burned his tent and everything inside. The last time he lost almost everything he owned, including his clothes and medicines, managing to rescue only his papers, seeds, and plant specimens that he had hidden elsewhere. Soldiering on, dressed in local clothing purchased with borrowed funds, he continued to collect, sleeping wherever he could. One night, he was badly stung by giant ants; another night, he and a companion slept in a storehouse so overrun by rats that his companion's pomaded hair was devoured during the night.

When it was time to head back to Bombay in November, all the European ships were filled, so Hove had to send his plants, seeds, and dried specimens in one local cotton boat and his personal belongings in another. One of the two boats failed to arrive, having either sunk or been hijacked, but he counted himself lucky that it was the boat with his belongings that disappeared. He then transplanted the live plants into a friend's garden in Bombay until he could find passage home. Only one East India Company ship had yet to set sail for Europe that season, and he tried to book passage. The captain insisted that his plants had to travel in the hold: he didn't want the boxes to clutter up the deck. Hove knew his plants would never survive. The company refused to intervene.

The captain's attitude toward hauling plants was not unusual. Life onboard an oceangoing vessel was rough in the extreme, and taking care of delicate plants was a burden. In addition to watering, they needed circulating air to prevent mildew and disease, the right mix of sun and shade, and protection from sea spray. Collectors of the era used a variety of packing devices, but one of the best was an open case with metal hoops arched over the top. The crew would cover the hoops with netting on fine days and replace the netting with canvas "whenever the waves have frothy curls upon them." And if spray did land on the plants, the crew would sprinkle them with freshwater to wash the salt off. That, at least, was the theory.

The problem was that the caretaker—the captain or more likely some tarry-handed sailor—often paid little attention to such instructions. The deck of a ship, even the more isolated poop deck, the captain's domain, was a crowded place, busy with the comings and goings of the crew. Sailors had more pressing duties than playing nursemaid to plants, even if, as Banks advised, they had been "sweetened" before the ship set sail. From the crew's point of view, the boxes were not only a bother but a potential danger. Thomas Manning, an English academic and explorer who was in charge of a consignment of plants sent to Banks in 1806, complained that "the first mate does not approve of having a garden on the poop at all. He says it wracks the ship to pieces. The captain agrees in the same story and when the beams creak in the [cabin] they all turn to me sometimes and damn the flower pots." When Sir George Yonge went to Kew to inspect a shipment of plants from India in 1790, he found "nothing, but four stumps of plants! . . . The fate of all these has been like all others, and the cause the same viz. total neglect & inattention almost wilful of what was committed to the [crew's] care." Sometimes, the plants didn't make it to shore at all. In an emergency, when the deck needed to be quickly cleared or the ship lightened, plant cases were the first items to be tossed overboard.

It was February 1789 before Hove found the *Narge,* a Danish ship that would transport him and his five cases of plants, which included cotton plants; breadfruit, mango, and nutmeg saplings; and a full-grown *Garcinia* (whose fruits are mangosteens), home. They got as far as the Cape in South Africa where ships usually stopped to resupply. The *Narge* was to make only a brief stop, but when the captain learned that war had broken out between Denmark and Sweden, he insisted on waiting for a convoy.

Hove passed the time with Francis Masson who had returned to the Cape. Masson asked him to take back some of his finds, too, but Hove had to decline, "as I had lost a great many of my own for lack of water, and the Captain was very particular respecting it, I could not well venture taking them." Using freshwater for plants was another contentious issue for the crew. Freshwater was always in limited supply and often rationed. When it rained, everyone onboard turned out to collect rainwater in whatever baskets, blankets, and leather buckets they could lay their hands on. Plants had last call on the scarce resource.

The *Narge* arrived at the Isles of Scilly just off Cornwall, tantalizingly close to home, in late June, but then contrary winds kept the ship from landing week after week. "Losing almost daily some of my collections, and none of us free from the scurvy which began to make great progress on the ship on account of the badness of the weather and deficiency of water and fresh produce," Hove wrote. He finally hired, at his expense, a pilot boat to take him and his plants to shore. He arrived at last at Plymouth on August 8, 1789. By now, his tropical plants had been en route for ten months. The official report on his collections was, not surprisingly, "unfavourable."

Hove went on to a medical career, which was just as well since British production of cotton in the West Indies would be overtaken by cotton grown in the American South. In any case, Banks had a far grander adventure in economic botany under way at the same time. In the winter of 1787, he sent off Captain Bligh in the *Bounty* to the Society Islands to pick up a large cargo of breadfruit trees and take them to the Caribbean where, transplanted, they were to provide cheap food for slaves in the British colonies. Bligh was accompanied by Kew botanist David Nelson, a quiet and unassuming man who had accompanied Captain Cook on his last and fatal voyage.

Bligh set sail in a ninety-foot ship that had been completely reconfigured for the botanical adventure. Never had a ship been outfitted less for the comfort of captain and crew. As Banks wrote in an early memorandum for the ship's captain, "the difficulty of carrying plants by sea is very great; a small sprinkling of salt water, or of the dew which fills the air even in a moderate gaile, will inevitably destroy them if not immediately washed off with fresh water." The captain's cabin was therefore turned into a greenhouse. Extra skylights and air scuttles were made for the plants' convenience. There would be none of the traditional shipboard animals like parrots and monkeys that might harm the trees.

The sailors were to be nursemaids. Trees in half casks would be stored belowdecks, and the crew would have to frequently lift these very heavy pots up to the deck "for the benefit of the sun." Other tubs, as tall as the trees planted in them, would be lashed to the quarterdeck and would be covered with canvas whenever Nelson so ordered. All efforts would be made to destroy pests with poison, "and the crew," Banks wrote, "must not complain if some of [the rats and cockroaches] who may die in the ceiling make an unpleasant smell." Sir Joseph Yonge, the minister of war, on seeing the physical changes made to the *Bounty* harrumphed that "the Captain of a ship cannot be expected to take his orders from a gardener." But, in fact, he did.

The journey started on December 23, 1787. The *Bounty* lost months trying to take a shortcut to Tahiti, on orders of the Admiralty, by sailing west around Cape Horn. Bligh finally turned east and nine months later, landed in Tahiti. Normally, port stops were as brief as possible and sailors were confined as much as practicable to their ship to maintain discipline and avoid desertions. But the breadfruit trees could not simply be dug up, plopped in pots, and taken away. To survive the rolling of the ship and other stresses, Nelson had to get them properly rooted first, and that took time. Bligh, whose character—according to Caroline Alexander's *The Bounty*—has been unfairly maligned, decided to allow some of his crew to live on the island, this "Paradise of the World," and others had plenty of opportunity to experience the hospitality of the islanders. By April 4, the *Bounty* set sail for the West Indies with over a thousand small but rooted and healthy trees, as well as seven hundred other plants, including hibiscus, tree ferns, bananas, and other native fruits that Nelson planned to take back to Kew.

Twenty-four days later, eighteen crewmen on the *Bounty* mutinied and set Bligh, his loyal crew, and Nelson adrift in a twenty-three-foot-long boat with little food and only twenty-eight gallons of water. The last Nelson saw of the *Bounty* was the mutineers throwing the breadfruit trees over the side. The reasons for the mutiny are many and complex, but it certainly had something to do with the trees. The undertaking was a civilian takeover of a navy ship, with naval traditions and rules broken willy-nilly. In the eyes of some of the crew, the mission was a demeaning one: it was one thing to suffer great privations for king and Crown, another to die for a bunch of breadfruit. In such a rigidly hierarchical and tradition-bound world, the sight of the captain ousted from his cabin and relegated to a closet undermined Bligh's authority. And if the trees hadn't required potting, Bligh would never have allowed his men the freedom and enticements of Tahiti.

Bligh, in an astounding demonstration of seamanship, sailed more than thirty-six hundred miles west to Timor. From there, he and his remaining crew caught a ship back to London. Neither Banks nor Bligh gave up. In 1791, Bligh and two other Kew gardeners (Nelson died on Timor) sailed again for Tahiti in the *Providence,* this time successfully transporting trees to Jamaica and returning with Caribbean plants for Kew.

One of the *Providence* gardeners, Christopher Smith, went on to hunt plants in the Moluccas, and in 1804 became the superintendent of one of Kew's new overseas botanic gardens, this one on Prince of Wales Island in the Torres Strait between Papua New Guinea and Australia. The establishment of botanic gardens in the Southern Hemisphere by European powers in the late eighteenth century did much to help stock the gardens and glasshouses of the Northern Hemisphere. They also functioned as way stations for plants headed to Europe, and they allowed gardeners to understand plants' habits and requirements before they were relocated.

The numbers of species available to European horticulturalists exploded after the turn of the century. The overseas botanic gardens, plant hunters, travelers, and overseas residents kept sending seeds, and botanists regularly traded plants across national boundaries. In the 1800s, commercial nurseries began sending plant hunters to collect abroad, too. Although most of the tropical specimens continued to die en route, it took only one successfully imported plant or seed to create hundreds of new specimens in a few seasons. "In truth," Sir Joseph Banks grumbled in 1812, "our hothouses overflow at present so much with intertropical plants, that I scarce wish for additions of that kind."

My conservatory was far from overflowing with plants, but what I had was certainly growing. The summer sun heated the air inside, and I closed off the rest of the (air-conditioned) house and ran the overhead fans on high. I watered with a coiled hose attached to the sink spigot roughly every other day and fertilized according to package instructions. Nearly every day, I would discover that one of my charges had extended a new leaf or a new frond.

Then, one morning I noticed with shock that one of the *Dieffenbachia,* a lovely plant that put out pale green leaves with darker green veins and that had looked perfectly fine the night before, had collapsed entirely. Its three stems were leaning far out of the pot, nearly parallel with the floor, its leaves as limp as much-laundered handkerchiefs. When I touched the soil, it was dry, so I immediately flooded the pot with water. Then I left the conservatory: I couldn't bear to stand vigil on the patient.

Four hours later, my *Dieffenbachia* was standing upright, oblivious to its near-death experience. But later that week, the same thing happened again and then to the other *Dieffenbachia.* The *Syngonium, Xanthosoma,* and *Alocasia* swooned, too: it was like a contagious hysteria. By August, all of my plants were so thirsty I was watering every day, and if I forgot one day, several were sure to get the vapors. Finally, it dawned on me that the plants, which were in the original pots from Johnson's, might need repotting. All those new leaves were transpiring so much water vapor that the soil was going dry almost instantly.

Clearly, bigger pots with more soil were required. But I hesitated. The plants were doing so well otherwise and I was afraid that I would damage or maybe even kill them in the repotting process.

I consulted Edie. She rolled her eyes, told me to buck up, and sent me home with a bag of potting mixture, a trowel, gardening gloves, a bunch of plastic pots (each two inches larger than the current ones), instructions, and encouragement. I dragged a table outside, took a deep breath, and gave the pot of *Dieffenbachia* some sharp raps against the table. Nothing happened. I tried again, with more force but with equally unsatisfying results. I realized, on closer examination, that this was not surprising because the plant's roots had grown through the holes on the bottom of the pot and were clutching its underside. Like a toddler with her arms wrapped around her mother's leg at the nursery school door, the plant was hanging on for dear life.

I held the plant upside down and tried to poke the roots back through the holes. No dice. I could see only two other options: either cut off the roots or try to cut up the hard-plastic pot. I called Edie. Cut the roots, she said: the plant wouldn't miss them. I winced and did it. The root ball, with a delicate but dense veil of rootlets enveloping it, fell neatly into my hand.

There were no other moral dilemmas. I put an inch or two of soil in the bottom of the new pot, plunked the root ball in, and filled in around it, tamping it down firmly. After repotting the second plant, I got over my squeamishness, abandoned my gardening gloves and trowel, and dug into the potting soil with both hands. Soil went into the pot, onto the table, into my hair, and sifted down to dust the tops of my running shoes. In not much time, all my plants were in their new digs and watered, and they were looking much more comfortable. I noticed, with satisfaction, the dirt under my nails and began to feel that I might become a gardener.

Beyond Foliage

five

Platycerium

It was September when I moved the four Boston ferns from the conservatory to the backyard. I had enjoyed watching each new frond emerge, as tightly wrapped as a watch spring, and slowly unwind over the course of a few days, until finally, fully extended and fluffed out with frilled leaves, it relaxed over the edge of the pot and toward the floor. But the plants had become enormous, puffed up with layer upon layer of fronds until it looked as if I'd hung ballerinas' full tulle skirts, in bright green, at the north windows. They were blocking too much light.

So I exiled them. Outside, hanging beneath the infamous overhang at the back of the house—Boston ferns would be burned by too many hours of direct western sun—they were in proper scale. Even better, they complemented my citrus trees, with their rounded heads of leaves spangled with fruit, that I'd clustered in full sun on the stone patio nearby. My citrus collection had been bolstered by friends bearing gifts: I now had a variegated pink lemon whose purple buds gave way to green-and-yellow-striped fruit, a lime tree, and a Ponderosa lemon tree. With Ted's *Impatiens* blooming in purple, pink, and red mounds at the edge of the patio, the backyard was looking vibrant.

In contrast, the conservatory, especially with the citrus trees and the ferns outside, struck me as sparse and a little dull. I turned my attention to the bay window, eight feet long and two feet deep, at the back of the conservatory. The bay got long hours of western light and even some southern light through the two skylights in its roof. Flowering plants in hanging baskets would work there.

The space was difficult to get to. The far end of the pool bordered the width of the bay, which meant that in order to get to any potted plants there, I would have to take a large step across a corner of the pool and onto the bench that hid the pool cover, and with watering can or hose in hand, edge my way along, stepping between the pots without falling backward into the water. I could see it would be even trickier to water plants hanging above my head while engaged in this balancing act, but I was feeling a little cocky with my successes so far.

But for all that effort, I wanted some spectacular hanging baskets. I decided I needed to branch out beyond Johnson's. It was time for a road trip.

I pulled up to Logee's Greenhouses, one of the oldest tropical plant retailers in America, improbably located in the northeast corner of Connecticut in the small town of Danielson. It was an unseasonably warm October morning, all coppered leaves and cottony clouds and cobalt sky. From the outside, Logee's looked like another of the many white clapboard New England houses I had passed on the road. I half expected, as I pushed open the front door, to find myself in a living room with wingback chairs by a fireplace, polished oak floors, a sampler on the wall above a gateleg table, and a golden retriever wagging its tail in the doorway. Maybe someone would be sitting in one of those chairs, needlepointing.

Instead, the room I entered had never been fully constructed. Its floor and walls were dark, unfinished lumber. The only light was attenuated daylight that managed to penetrate some remarkably dusty windows. Along one wall was a potting bench heaped with black dirt and a clutter of clay pots. In the middle of the room stood a few shelves with a meager supply of gardening paraphernalia. By the front door a few large plants were available for purchase. Behind a wooden counter, a run of narrow, worn, and rickety-looking wood steps disappeared into the ceiling. But the ceiling! The ceiling, wood rafters and planks, was completely and deeply carpeted in small, dark green leaves. Here and there, lengths of leafy vine hung down as if strands of the carpet had been snagged and pulled free.

No one appeared to be home. I walked to the back of the room, drawn by a low doorway of radiant daylight. The door frame, deeply furred in the same vines, led down to a steep and narrow wooden stairway. I took a few steps down.

I felt like Dorothy at that moment she steps out of her

house, just blown in from black-and-white Kansas, and finds herself in the Technicolor world of Oz. Before me was a sun-lit paradise of flowers. Fuzzy blossoms that looked like fat, magenta caterpillars hung from a basket at the base of the steps. Just above the basket was a tree with orange crepe-paper blooms like poppy flowers. A hip-high begonia with leaves polka-dotted in white and sprinkled with creamy flowers stood next to a bush heavy with clusters of impos-sibly turquoise flowers. From my left came a *plinkity-plink-plink* of trickling water. I looked to see if I could spot the source of the sound. It came from somewhere behind a deep bank of foliage and spiky, pink bromeliads.

A few yards away a young woman, dressed in jeans and a T-shirt, was busy turning what looked like an old-fashioned ship's wheel mounted on a tall metal pole. The wheel was turning a vertical gear chain that turned a smaller, silvery wheel at the top of the pole. Above, a creaking sounded.

"Be right with you!" she called. "Just opening the vents a bit." I looked up and could see glass panels in the ridge of the greenhouse roof opening slowly.

She came up the stairs and I explained that I had an appointment with Byron, and she said she'd go look for him and invited me to come down.

"I haven't seen him today, and it may take me a while to track him down. Just wander around," she suggested, wav-ing her hand toward the back of the greenhouse, where I saw passages to other greenhouses.

Logee's was founded in 1892, and I suspected this long greenhouse, with its earthen floor, was original. The peaked roof, made of long panes of glass, felt oddly low, as if over the decades either the walls had been slowly sinking into the ground or the ground had gradually risen. The eaves were about waist high, and a continuous bench snugged into them and circled the greenhouse. A metal grid covered the bench; the grid neatly accommodated the small, square, black plastic pots of young plants that Logee's sells. Almost all the spaces in the grid were filled with plants, which were segregated by species. At the rim of each pot a white tag had been stuck into the soil. In the midst of each cluster of species, a sign on a stick announced its name, its attributes, and care instructions.

A narrow alley, wide enough for only one person, ran along the inner edge of the bench all the way around the greenhouse. On the other side of the alley, the center of the greenhouse was filled with rows of broad benches running crosswise, with passageways between. These benches held more little, tagged plants in grids, but they also displayed many large and luxuriantly blooming specimens. Other well-grown ones hung from an iron scaffolding above. These, I would learn, were the grandes dames of the place, the mother plants from which cuttings were taken to create offspring. At the end of each bench, venerable vines, their lower trunks gnarled and mossy, grew up the poles of the scaffolding and then traveled horizontally, creating a flowery arbor overhead.

I had started my second, goggle-eyed circuit of the greenhouse when Byron Martin, owner of Logee's and grandson of its founder, walked down a path toward me. The man who approached was in his early fifties, wearing an orange T-shirt neatly tucked into jeans. He was fit-looking, with an open and nearly unlined face and just a little gray in his closely trimmed brown hair. He looked, well, Byronic.

There were four greenhouses connected to the first one and open to the public, and we moseyed from one to the next. As we went, I questioned Byron about Logee's. He stopped frequently as we walked, interrupting himself to praise a plant we passed or give me its history at Logee's, to pluck a fruit for me to taste, or to pull off a blossom so I could smell it.

Logee's, he said, specializes in flowering container plants and is primarily a catalog and Internet business. Each year, the company mails about 600,000 catalogs, offers about 1,100 different species for sale, and has about 40,000 plantlets in stock at any one time. The vast majority are sold in two-and-a-half- or four-inch pots.

I had learned of Logee's through its catalog, which I had signed up online to receive. I love the catalogs and often keep an issue in the car. The Logee's catalog is perfect red-light reading. Each page features three or four tropicals, each with a photograph of a mature Logee's specimen. Beside each photo is a wonderfully literate paragraph describing the plant and giving tips about its culture. *Begonia* 'Richardsiana', for example, is "always growing and freely flowering, its pearly white blooms hang like jewels among sprawling branches and small maple-shaped leaves." And "remember," the catalog advises vis-à-vis the *Bougainvillea* 'California Gold', "to stress it a little with dryness and grow it in full sun." Sidebars are interspersed on such subjects as how to coerce scented geraniums into flowering or how to overwinter banana trees in Zone 7 gardens.

Logee's did not start as a catalog business or even as a

tropical plant business. Byron's grandfather, William Logee, developed an interest in horticulture as a young man. After a few years as an apprentice at a rose nursery in Boston, he looked for a place to establish himself, and he settled on Danielson, a small town about twenty-five miles from Providence, where a cobbler was looking to sell the private greenhouse on his property. William bought it, empty, in 1892, and in a few years he was successfully producing flowers for the cut-flower market—snapdragons, mums, and roses, among others—in beds in the greenhouse. He married the girl across the street and they started producing children—there would be thirteen—with equal success.

An older son, Ernest, got interested in the business and stepped up as a partner in the 1920s. He became fascinated with begonias and collected, hybridized, and sold them locally, but the bread and butter of the business remained cut flowers. So it was hard times for Logee's when the Depression hit. Cut flowers were one of the first luxuries people gave up. But if people were not coming in to buy flowers, they might still be tempted if the flowers went to them. The Logee children, including Byron's mother, Joy, born in 1912, peddled violets on the streets of Danielson and offered bouquets door-to-door in the wealthier sections of Providence and Hartford to keep the business solvent.

Most of the Logee children left the family cut-flower business behind when they grew up, but Joy, Ernest, and another brother, Richard, loved it and stayed.

"My mother was always a real plant collector and not just those that they grew to sell as stems." Byron smiled with the memory. "Everything appealed to her, although her particular love was scented geraniums and herbs, and she kept her potted plants on benches that ran along the sides of the greenhouse. In 1939, they were running short on space and needed to get rid of some of her potted plants. My mother thought she'd mail out a list, just a simple, typewritten list, of the plants she wanted to get rid of. People responded, and before she knew it, Logee's had a mail-order business. Which was good, because after the war, cut flowers really went to the dogs."

Byron's father, Ernest Martin, grew up in Providence but always had a strong interest in the natural world and spent his twenties working on a large farm in Ohio. After his return from World War II, he became the head gardener on an estate in South County, Rhode Island, and a devoted member of the National Begonia Society. At the society meetings he became friendly with Joy's brother, Ernest Logee, and through him, met and fell in love with his sister, Joy. If ever a man was destined to have a green thumb, it was Byron Martin.

Byron and I were standing under a tree-form *Allamanda* whose yellow double flowers seemed an expression of purest joy. "My father was the one responsible for planting all these vines in the greenhouse. He wanted these production spaces to feel like conservatories, places where customers could enjoy the flowers and see what the small plants would look like grown up. But he was also a real grower, which my mother was not. There are people who really, really love plants and are very good at growing them on a windowsill. But it's something else to grow them beautifully and profitably in large quantities, like a crop. Seldom do you find both those people in the same body. My father was one of them."

Byron's father's death at sixty-three in 1972 was therefore not only a personal tragedy for his family but also a potential disaster for the business. Byron was a senior in high school at the time, and his mother came close to pulling him out of school to work in the greenhouses. Fortunately, the principal was accommodating and gave the boy a pass so he could walk home—the school was a block away—to water the plants, prune, help out in shipping, or whatever else was needed.

"As a kid I ran around the greenhouses, but I never really worked there. I had botanical names in my ears all the time, but I never paid any attention to them. My father had always said, 'Don't make the kids work in the greenhouses; when it's their time, they'll do it.' My mother was from the old Yankee school of child rearing and wanted to put us to work right away. Fortunately, my father prevailed on that one. I'm not sure how I would have felt about the business if I'd been forced into it.

"It was really only when my father became ill that he began to teach me. But he died before I could get it all, and I had to do a lot of studying on my own." He told me he still has the college textbook on propagation that his father gave him just before his death.

"It's been an evolutionary process for me. I started out just wanting to grow beautiful plants, and only gradually did I get interested in Logee's as a business. When I was about twenty-nine, I looked around and realized this place was my future. It had never been more than a family business—meaning family members were the only employees—but it had been going backward since the death of my father. We were using maybe a third of the available space, plants had rooted into the benches, and it was just an overgrown mess.

"So, one day I went in there with a chainsaw and cut it all out. I just leveled it from one end to the other." Twenty-five years later, I could still hear in his voice how satisfying that moment had been. "My mother and my uncle went through the ceiling, but it just had to be done. Then, I took out all the benches and rebuilt them and reorganized everything." Under Byron's direction, the business grew; it now employs forty people in the peak season—spring and summer—and sells a quarter of a million plants each year.

After a couple of hours in the Logee's manicured paradise, I was feeling a bit overwhelmed. One plant was more flower covered or more fragrant or both than the next, and I asked Byron if there was anything he couldn't grow.

"The cacao plant," he said promptly. "Have you ever seen a cacao tree?"

I admitted I hadn't.

"I've always been very into economic plants, like coffee and matte and vanilla. But the cacao is really challenging, not like a coffee plant, which is really simple to grow. It's a very strange tree. It's got a straight trunk, and tiny flowers bloom right off it, up and down the trunk. When the fruits develop, they're shaped like big footballs and they stick straight out from the trunk, too. I've been growing the plants for years now, hand-pollinating them, but," he said with frustration, "I always get this dark, burnt edge around the leaves. I've never been able to figure it out."

I said it didn't sound to me like he couldn't grow it, just that he had a minor cosmetic issue.

"But for me, Logee's is not just about keeping plants

alive, but about growing beautiful plants. And not just beautiful anywhere, but beautiful in a pot. So, as long as I've been growing the cacao tree, I still don't sell it.

"You go back a generation, and this wasn't the case. My elders would collect everything. They had to have every plant there ever was, somewhere, and they kept anything that came in and never threw anything out. But I'm not interested in that. I'm interested in plants that are going to perform." He paused. "I hear there's a grower in Georgia who doesn't get that leaf burn. So I'm going to get in my car and drive like a thousand miles, so I can see this guy and figure out how the heck he's getting around this problem."

"He'll tell you?" I asked.

"I don't know." He paused. "He may not even know. There may be some micronutrient in his soil that he doesn't even know about."

We were walking down a dirt path in a cool greenhouse, past a banana tree whose reddish leaves were brushing the roof peak, past *Brugmansia* trees dangling pale yellow flowers the size and shape of coronets, when our path was suddenly blocked by the most extraordinary tree I'd ever seen. Its limbs, much furcated, reached in a tangle to the roof. On the branch in front of my face were several clusters of tangerines. To the left, on a different branch of the same tree, I recognized kumquats. Lemons, oranges, and pink-skinned and yellow-skinned grapefruits hung on other branches nearby. If this were Oz and this tree had thrown its fruit at me, I would have had a tropical fruit salad.

The root stock of the tree, Byron said, was actually a sour orange, a sturdy and vigorous species onto which he had grafted ten to fifteen other citrus species and varieties, including blood oranges, Valencia oranges, Washington and Robertson navels, and two kinds of tangerines. Many of the cuttings for Logee's citrus offerings came from this tree. Another tree behind this one was similarly bedecked with clusters of dissimilar fruits. The root stock of this one was a kumquat onto which he had grafted four varieties of kumquat, Calamondin orange, and a number of hybrids, including a sunquat, a 'Meyer' lemon–'Meiwa' kumquat mix that, he enthused, had the sweetness of the kumquat and the freely flowering habits of the lemon.

Our talk turned to raising citrus trees and the bane of potted citrus growers, the dreaded root rot. Byron led me over to a section of a smaller greenhouse, past an area where a gardener was nipping one little vining plant after another with a small clippers. Hanging high on a rod were a half-dozen hanging baskets with some rather scrawny-looking plants in them.

"These are our 'Meyer' lemon mother plants," he said. "We take all our cuttings from these plants. In fact, as you can see, they were recently sheared." I noticed small, new leaves sprouting from the ends of branches.

He lifted a pot down, pulling out the plastic drip lines in the process. He turned the pot over and the plant fell out into his hand.

"Look," he said, inviting me to peer closely at the dense web of roots on the outside of the plant's pot-shaped root ball. "See these soft brown ones?" He rubbed with his finger on the surface and little pieces of root fell off. "Those are dead. But look: here's a live one—you can see the little feeder roots coming off it." The root in question was a light yellow, with even more delicate, whiter branching. It didn't detach itself when Byron picked at it. "You can see it's a mix in here, and this is definitely a healthy plant.

"There are always roots dying and there are always roots growing in a healthy plant. It's a question of balance, a question of whether you get to some tipping point where there are no longer enough healthy roots to support the plant. Certainly, excessive moisture fosters disease. Roots need to take up oxygen, and if they're always surrounded by water, they're not going to get enough oxygen. That stresses the plant and gives root disease good conditions for multiplying. But root rot is definitely not an all-or-nothing proposition."

The thing to do, he said, is to frequently tap the plant out of its pot and look at its roots. If there are a lot of brown ones that rub off, cut back on the water. As long as there are a decent number of healthy ones, all is not lost.

I wanted to take everything at Logee's home with me, but in my bay window I had room only for five hanging baskets. I had to have the bright yellow *Allamanda*. I suppose, for the aesthetics of the room, I should have planned to make five baskets of a single species, but I was too entranced by the colors to limit myself. Instead, I selected an *Acalypha pendula* with those fuzzy red caterpillar flowers, *Bougainvillea* 'Orange Ice', *Passiflora* 'Purple Haze', and *Plumbago auriculata* 'Imperial Blue'. I bought four two-and-a-half-inch pots of each and had them packed up so I could take them on the plane with me. I was going home, but taking a bit of Oz with me.

Two weeks later, I was on Route 50 heading west through the Ohio foothills of the Appalachian Mountains. It was a mark of my provincialism that despite having lived my entire life on the East Coast and having driven all of I-95 from Maine to Florida, I had never driven west, never crested the eastern Continental Divide and headed down what was to me the back side of the mountains. My destination was Glasshouse Works in Stewart, Ohio, twenty-five miles west of Parkersburg, West Virginia, and about six hours from home.

I turned off Route 50 onto State Route 144, a winding two-lane road that flirted with the placid Hocking River to the right. Where the road parted from the river, fields of dried cornstalks filled the flat bottomland. Trailer homes and houses, a few windowless and abandoned, appeared from time to time among gentle hills covered in trees that wore the tatters of the season's hues. After twelve miles, the voice on the car GPS announced that I had arrived at my destination, but I saw nothing except fields and the river. I poked along—not a single car had passed me in either direction—wondering whether to turn around, when the road took a sharp turn and a dozen clapboard houses appeared in a cluster. On the right, I spotted a rusty, Victorian wirework trellis, partly obscured by tall grasses, from which hung a sign that read:

GLASSHOUSE WORKS
Open All Year, Fri—Sat, 10—6

The trellis was in a rough-hewn rock garden that hosted, even at the end of October, a spill of pink flowers and an array of plants, none of which looked familiar. There was a large house nearby, its clapboard painted pale gray, its trim an orangey-red that glowed like neon in the midday sun. There didn't seem to be any other building that could be Glasshouse Works, so I walked up the steps to the porch. It was crowded with a collection of white wicker furniture, a few hanging baskets of plants that had been partially nipped by frost, a stack of folding chairs, a half-dozen wooden birdhouses (one at least five feet tall), and a collection of empty cardboard boxes. A strip of beadboard was missing from the porch ceiling. In the yard directly below was a haphazard assemblage of ceramic pots and statues, including one of St. Francis of Assisi, a large pig, two Mayan-looking creatures with open mouths, Pan, and a stylized ox covered in hieroglyphics and sporting two stunted wings but missing a head. A full set of child-size, Victorian cast-iron garden furniture stood nearby.

There was a glass door at the top of the porch steps, and I could see an office inside, so I opened it.

"You must be Ruth!" exclaimed a balding, bespectacled man seated at a desk. He was partly shielded from view by a stack of computer components and a network of cables, but I saw he was wearing a loose shirt printed with pineapples. Pinned to the walls, which were lime green, were photos, calendars, notes, and cartoons. Two sets of shelves flanked the door: one had plastic bins filled with stacks of papers; on the other were rows of plastic folders, unlabeled, in which papers stood like sheaves of wheat.

"So you found us! Not everyone does! Welcome!"

Tom Winn, co-owner and cofounder of Glasshouse Works, got up to shake my hand. Tom was a tall and somewhat portly man who radiated good cheer. I told him that in fact I hadn't been sure if this was Glasshouse Works or whether I was barging onto someone's private porch.

My uncertainty was understandable, he said. The building had started off as a private house, then it became a hotel, then an old-age home. By the time he and his partner, Ken Frieling, bought it in 2000, it was a home again, owned by a recluse who lived in three rooms at the back with her seventeen cats and three dogs. On the hottest days, he added ruefully, evidence of the cats could still be detected in his office.

Tom and Ken had started their horticultural adventures when they were graduate students in English at nearby Ohio University in the early 1970s and decided to rent a greenhouse in Stewart just for fun. They had a knack for growing plants and began to sell their plants to a few grocery stores in the area. Then a grower/retailer in the nearby town of Corning who sold by catalog contracted with them to provide about half her stock. They completed their master's degrees, but the plant business occupied more and more of their time, and their work on their doctorates fell by the wayside. In 1978, they found themselves with a full-time business and several contiguous properties in Stewart, including the former town post office that now serves as their shipping department, seven greenhouses, a barn, and four run-down houses. Although they were often advised to focus on a couple of highly marketable plants like poinsettias, and although that advice was in fact very good advice, they saw no fun in it. Instead, they decided to grow the most exotic, rare, and unusual of tropical plants, plants with improbably colored and peculiarly shaped leaves, varieties that few people owned or even knew existed. They now have about five thousand different species or varieties, including more than 150 *Coleus,* one hundred plus *Begonia,* and more than fifty *Philodendron.*

Tom took me on a quick tour of "the hotel" (which I suppose is a more appealing nickname than "the old-age home") first. We went through the back of his office, through a lavender foyer, past a staircase guarded by a stone Chinese lion on every step, and into a room painted the color of French's mustard. Tom told me he and Ken purchased the hotel for two reasons. One was to have a "really nice place for customers to check out, instead of just a table in the barn." They also thought their customers, fans of the exotic in plants, might buy similarly exotic garden and home goods. "We looked for objects you wouldn't find at Wal-Mart or even a normal specialty store. They're rare objects to complement our rare plants."

We zipped through four rooms on the first floor, which were painted, in order of appearance, mustard, navy blue, maroon, and teal. They were crammed with a marvelously eclectic assortment of objects, including picture frames (punched metal, ceramic, and tiger-striped); mirrors of all shapes and sizes; glass and brass chandeliers of all eras; a lamp whose blue shade was gripped by a smiling Buddha; assorted sconces and statues (Venus, Diana, and David were among those present); vases in multicolored glass; wind chimes as tall as I; boxes of marble eggs; a bin of glass apples; bowls of Indonesian carved wooden balls; two dozen or so etched granite plaques hanging on or leaning against the walls; candles in glass jars; three elegant

Victorian terrariums; two terra-cotta, child-size cupids in midflight; artificial banana trees; stuffed animals (to occupy customers' children); mobiles spiraling from the ceilings; plant cabinets with fluorescent lighting; shelves with mugs and ceramic cows; stands hung with purses; Tiffany lamps; marble cats; brass garden ornaments; Chinese gargoyles; a surrealistic oil painting of the Abduction of Europa; three-foot-tall wooden candlesticks; a collection of colorful ceramic chickens; stone carvings of horses' heads, stylized sheep, and lifelike rabbits; rotating displays of note cards; shelves of gardening books; dozens of African masks; sepia-colored, imitation baroque wall hangings; rattan baskets; leather elephants; stained-glass windows; a seven-foot-tall wooden giraffe; an enormous, antique church organ with three banks of keys, an impressive set of copper pipes, and two turquoise Foo dogs on its lid; and a full-size Egyptian mummy case elaborately carved and painted in red, black, and gold.

"A little something for everyone," said Tom cheerfully.

We ended up in the small kitchen (bright yellow) where Andrew, an Ohio University graduate in anthropology, part-time band member, part-time barista, and part-time employee of Glasshouse Works, was washing up yesterday's dishes. A computer sat on the kitchen table next to an enormous pot of *Euphorbia tirucalli,* or pencil cactus, that Tom said he was going to auction on eBay. It looked like there would be just enough room to open the refrigerator on one side of the table, but only if no one was working on the computer. As we walked in, we startled the cat, Licorice, who knocked a frying pan off the stove and onto the floor.

The kitchen, it turned out, was a really nice place for people to check out.

I was totally, completely, utterly charmed. It brought back memories of my sixteenth summer, which I spent as an unpaid intern in Washington, D.C., working for a tiny environmental group. It was 1970 and I lived in a house that had been rented, room by room, to summer interns. The door to my bedroom had a curtain of purple beads, all the radiators were painted gold, all the floorboards were swaled, and flower decals decorated the bathroom walls. If Logee's had felt like Oz, then Glasshouse Works felt like a happy, hippy Brigadoon.

As Tom continued his tour outdoors, we ran into Ken walking toward us. He, too, was tall, but he had a rugged look compared with Tom's more academic mien, and his thinning gray hair was pulled back into a ponytail at his neck. After a brief introduction, Ken urged us to look into a particular greenhouse before he watered in there. Anyone who went in afterward was sure to come out drenched.

Tom teased, "You're sure you're going to let us go in there?" and explained to me that Ken was very protective of his greenhouses. Not even he, much less strangers, often got a chance to go inside.

"Oh, it's okay." Ken chuckled. "I've just dumped a couple dozen trays in the alley that I've got to get in before tonight's frost. You're not going to get in very far, anyhow."

The three of us walked toward the greenhouse, past a dense stand of variegated bamboo and a mulberry tree with zigzag stems. Tom explained that most of their plants are sold in two-and-a-half-inch pots, although they often had four-inch or even six-inch sizes in the summer. About 85 percent of their stock is tropical, and the rest is for outdoors in Zone 7.

Ken said, "I like to think of us as a Noah's Ark for plants. I can never bring myself to throw away the last plant of its kind. Invariably, if I do, someone will turn up asking for it. You see, many of our customers are just as hopeless about plants as we are. They're going to get intrigued with *Pilea*, for example, and then want to collect as many different varieties as they can. A surprising number of our customers have home conservatories or a dedicated plant room with lots of grow lights. You wouldn't imagine it, but we ship a lot of plants to New York City apartments." He paused and then said thoughtfully, "Really, our most basic group of customers are more like stamp or coin or model train or antique doll collectors."

"I just got a call this morning," Tom chimed in, "by way of example, from this guy in upstate New York who fills, absolutely fills, his yard in the summer with tropicals. He once called me to ask how he could winter over his canna lilies. Normally, I would suggest putting them in the basement, but this guy lives in a trailer, so I told him to put them under the bed. Years later, I heard from him that he put his *Alocasia* and *Colocasia* and *Caladium* in there, and I guess others, too, because when there was no more room under the bed, he pulled the curtains closed and gave his bedroom over to the plants. He had so many plants inside, he spent the winter sleeping on the couch in the living room."

"That's a little extreme," said Ken, shaking his head, "but it gives you an idea."

Ken left us at the greenhouse door, and Tom and I stepped in. It must have been nearly 100 percent humidity inside; my glasses instantly fogged over. I put them in my pocket and looked around in awe. I could have been in the depths of a rain forest. Inside, every inch, every millimeter of space—high, low, middle, floor to roof—was filled with plants. As at Logee's, benches circled the greenhouses under the eaves. Actually, I had to assume benches were there because I couldn't see any surface beneath the trays and pots of plants jumbled together. I stumbled over potted plants peeking out from below the benches and a few stray vines that crossed the dirt alley. Other, larger vines, some close to trees in form and height, had grown up and across the roof. "We don't use shade cloth in the summer," Tom explained, "we just let the vines provide the shade. It gets so hot in here, Ken just dashes in, soaks everything with a hose, and escapes. But he and Andrew will start cutting it back next week."

The broad center of the greenhouse was a solid mass of plants. All of the stems and vines and leaves and hanging pots of flowers were so intertwined and tangled, plants appeared to be growing in midair. As we sidled sideways down the narrow alley, leaves tickled my face at every step. When our way was blocked by the trays heaped in our path, we cut across the central jungle and down the alley on the opposite side until we made it to the far end where a fan roared. At every step, I spotted something that interested me. I would poke in the pot among the leaves, looking for a tag but only rarely found one.

"What's this one? What's that lovely one?" I asked again and again, touching or pointing to some striking specimen.

"What's the one with those thorny, striped leaves? What's the one with the little purple flowers? Is that a kind of philodendron, the one with the pink and green leaves?"

Tom knew them all, and when he wasn't naming the ones I was interested in, he was pointing out, naming, and elaborating on others. He has a deep, resonant voice with a born lecturer's precise articulation. His native Maine accent broadened short "a"s into "ah"s, so he sounded almost English. "*Equisetum diffusum!*" he proclaimed, "*Billbergia pyramidalis striata!*" and "*Pereskia aculeata godseffiana variegata*, very unusual!" The Latin names—binomials, trinomials, quadranomials—rolled off his tongue like marbles down a chute.

He stopped by a maroon pot hanging at his chest height and parted the foliage.

"Ah," he asked with affection and relish, "see the little squill?"

A squill. I thought I'd heard of a squill before, some kind of little animal, something with quills, a sort of hedgehog maybe, something cute. But how had it gotten up there into the pot?

I peered in eagerly, but there was nothing I could see. How small was a squill? Uh-oh, I thought, maybe a squill wasn't an animal, maybe it was some sort of insect. Then I noticed that Tom was fondly stroking a delicate, narrow leaf about three inches long.

"A squill is actually a *Ledebouria*. It's a little plant in the lily family, but the leaves are spotted, and this one also has yellow margins. Judah Livesay at the Cox Arboretum in Dayton selected it out, so we call it *Ledebouria judah*."

At least it wasn't a bug.

Many of the hanging pots had several, very diverse species growing together, and this mixing contributed to the junglelike feeling in the greenhouse. Tom stopped in front of one such pot and commented on its occupants: the pink-tinted, deeply corrugated leaves belonged to a *Peperomia caparata*; the furry, rippled sea green leaves edged in lime green of *Plectranthus fosterii* 'green-on-green'—they'd gotten it from a collector in Houston; a horsetail fern—"it's suddenly back in fashion"; and a *Plumbago capensis* with powder blue flowers—"this might work in your setting"—twined up the pot's wire hanger.

Not only did the mother plants grow mixed together, the plantlets growing in trays on the benches were also intermingled. A tray might have three or four individuals each of a half-dozen species; even those three or four were not grouped together. The Glasshouse Works theory is that in the tropics plants grow haphazardly mixed, not in homogenous patches. Tom and Ken believe that they reduce insect problems by arranging their plants in a similar, natural way. An infestation of one plant that would quickly jump to its neighboring siblings would be less likely to spread to neighboring plants of different species, which could well be less attractive hosts. And when an order comes in for a plant, they are sure to have insect-free specimens somewhere in one of the greenhouses.

Somewhere, but where? Their theory sounded reasonable to me, but how, in what seemed to be a random collection of as many as ten thousand plants and plantlets, did they ever find anything when it came time to fill an order?

"Oh," said Tom blithely. "Ken just knows where everything is. It's amazing. But that's why he doesn't like people in his greenhouses. They might move something and he'd never find it again."

We walked through, or stepped into, the other six greenhouses, all equally verdant. Then we toured the shipping department and finally arrived at a small pond. Connie, an effusive employee who lives with her family on a nearby farm, was using a long stick to fish a water plant out of the middle of the pond. A call had just come in, she sang out to Tom, from the Dayton Conservatory: they were in need of *Myriophyllum aquaticum.*

This was not an isolated call. Glasshouse Works maintains relationships with a number of public conservatories, including Winterthur in Delaware and the Atlanta Botanical Gardens. Over the years, Ken and Tom have bought, traded, and sold plants with these and many other institutions. In the early days of their business, they acquired plant stock from overseas, from hobbyists and collectors in Borneo, India, Japan, and throughout South America, but now the movement of plants across borders is highly restricted, both in the United States and abroad. Instead, they rely on a network of contacts at conservatories, public and private, and they sometimes trade with customers who purchased a plant that has since disappeared from their own stock. When he gets something really rare, Ken told me, he always divides it or gives cuttings to at least one other grower, out of fear he'll fail with it and it will be lost forever.

My last stop of the day was the sales greenhouse. Here, there was order: plants had tags and were grouped by species. Andrew walked with me down the aisles with a large box in his hands, pointing out those species he thought would work in a north-facing conservatory.

Between my trip to Logee's and the trip to Glasshouse Works, the weather in Maryland had turned cold. Nighttime lows had dropped into the thirties, and with Ted's help, I had wrestled all my citrus shrubs and trees from the patio back into the conservatory. After much reading and consultation with vendors of grow lights, I had purchased two high-intensity discharge (HID) lights. These are the brightest lights for growing indoors and are about twice as efficient as fluorescents. They also concentrate more light in a smaller space. There are two types of bulbs that fit in HID fixtures: metal halide and high-pressure sodium. I chose the metal halide ones because the light they give off is strongest at the blue end of the spectrum and looks most like natural sunlight. High-pressure sodium bulbs emit light at the red end of the spectrum, which is excellent for producing flowers and fruit, but the light has a distinctly yellow-orange cast that makes people look as if they'd contracted a liver disease.

I had hung the HID lights on the side of the conservatory where it joined the kitchen; the fluorescent fixtures I already owned went on the opposite side of the room. To my surprise, I found that the HID lights were so strong that they not only cast about 1,000 foot-candles of light on the tops of my citrus trees, their glow also provided about 250 foot-candles to the plants I had arranged on the floor in the middle of the room. My conservatory would be more brightly lit, for more hours, in the winter than in the summer. I still wasn't going to be able to grow *Abutilon, Hibiscus, Passiflora*, or *Bougainvillea*, but my foliage plants should get fat and happy on this rich diet of photons. Better yet, with 250 foot-candles I might have a chance with some flowering plants that were not quite so light hungry as those.

With Andrew's help I picked out plants. Most were foliage plants like *Philodendron* 'Pink Princess' that has washes of pink on its leaves; a staghorn fern (*Platycerium veitchii leoinei*) with unusually fuzzy, almost white leaves; an *Alocasia cuprea* 'Blackie' whose leaves looked like turtle shells; three varieties of tiny bird's nest *Sansevieras*; and a stunning *Begonia* 'Cathedral' whose maroon leaves were marked with patches of green shaped like cathedral windows that glowed when the light shone through them. But I also picked out four varieties of *Anthurium*—two with peach-colored spathes that smeared into green at the edges and two with spathes in shades of reddish orange—and I couldn't resist a half-dozen blooming bromeliads, including a *Billbergia pyramidalis* 'Kyoto' with a flower bract like a fireworks explosion, an *Oxalis variabilis purpurea* 'Grand' whose soft, cloverlike leaves held clusters of silky, lavender flowers, and a *Hoya* 'Indian Rope' whose thick leaves, folded in half and twisted, were blushing pink.

We carried the plants to the kitchen where I could pay, but I was reluctant to leave. Would I ever get back here? Maybe after I drove away, the whole thing—the pastel houses, the overstuffed greenhouses, the old post office, the funky hotel—would just disappear?

I went back for another look. At that moment, the over-the-top, jungly, steamy spirit of the place grabbed me. I picked out more plants, lots more plants: *Pilea, Colacasia,* more *Alocasia, Stromanthe, Pelagornium,* more *Begonia, Chlorophy-*

tum, Dracaena of all varieties, ferns of all textures, anything that Andrew said didn't need absolutely bright light, and a couple that did. Winter was coming, and I wanted, wanted, wanted all this living, breathing green stuff.

I had planned to stay in a hotel overnight in nearby Athens, Ohio, and drive home the next day. But I didn't want to transfer all these plants in and out of a hotel room (and wasn't sure if they'd be admitted, in any case), and with the forecast for frost, I couldn't leave them in the car. So I drove six hours, pulling up to a silent, dark house at midnight, and unloaded everything into the conservatory. What wouldn't fit on the wirework table went on the floor.

Austen had gone off to college in September, leaving only Ted, Alice, and me at home. I met them at breakfast, which they were eating standing up in the kitchen for lack of a place to rest their cereal bowls.

"Oh my God, Mom, there are so many!" Alice said. "They're beautiful! I love those ones that look like they've got yellow paintbrushes growing out of them."

"Aphelandra," I said, beaming. "Aren't they great?"

Ted said nothing, but looked grumpy. Early morning is not his shining hour, and breakfast without a chance to spread out and read the *Wall Street Journal* in no way improves his mood.

"They'll be off the table by tonight," I promised.

He harrumphed, and the two of them left their bowls in the sink and, Alice bent under her gigantic backpack and Ted with his briefcase in one hand and his *Journal* in the other, vanished for the day. Ted would drop off Alice at school on his way downtown.

I faced the task of arranging a zoo of tropical plants. I had decided to go for the jungle look of Glasshouse Works. Since most of my acquisitions were young plants in small pots that could only be appreciated at eye level, I needed some benchlike structures. I scrounged in the basement and came up with some old plastic-coated wire shelves that had once done duty in a closet, and that, resting across plant stands and some stools, would do. I unearthed a set of old side tables whose wood tops were irrevocably marred with the circular traces of glasses long ago drained, but which I had saved with the improbable intention of refinishing. I arranged the shelves and tables around the wirework table, interspersing my larger plants that stood on the floor, as well as four seven-foot-tall bird-of-paradise I'd recently acquired with their many and magnificently arcing leaves. There was just enough room to pull back the chairs from the table. With the citrus trees, full of fruit, at the sides of the conservatory, the rest of the house disappeared from view. When I sat at the table, I felt ensconced in a verdant cocoon. This was more like it—I could have been Dr. Livingstone in Ujiji beside the shores of Lake Tanganyika.

Ted was less than enthralled. Alice, who had yet to fully make up her mind about the conservatory generally—was it cool or was it weird? (and was her mom cool or was she weird?)—also had reservations. My arrangement felt a little creepy to her. Claustrophobic, was Ted's conclusion. I liked the way the bird-of-paradise dipped their leaves over us at dinner, but Ted had the feeling he was in a restaurant with people hovering behind his chair, anxious to claim the table. He wanted to ask them to go wait at the bar.

There were a few practical problems to living in the great warm heart of green-ness. Ken was able to water the Glasshouse Works greenhouses with a hose, soaking everything indiscriminately from glass ceiling to dirt floor and leaving all the plants dripping wet and puddles on the ground. This was not an option for me; I had to water all my plants individually. I couldn't use the hose very well—the coils got caught around the table and chair legs and tipped over the lighter pots on the floor. It was safer to use a watering can, but it took numerous trips back and forth to the sink, which was hard on my middle-aged back. Still, I was willing to put up with the inconvenience in exchange for the junglelike feeling.

After a couple of weeks of stoic silence on the subject, though, Ted had had enough: would I please make a clearing in the jungle? I knew that this was not really a question.

Now that I look back on it, his declaration was a turning point, a positive sign. While I was living through Joanie's illness and then my own, friends would ask with concern, "How are you coping with all this, all at the same time?" My answer was perplexity: I was simply dealing with life as best I could day to day. It is only in retrospect that I can see how greatly the two events upended our lives. I was most concerned about our children's perceptions, and Ted and I carefully planned when and how to tell them about Joanie's death and then my diagnosis. (Of course, how they perceived it all turned out to be far different from what we thought we were conveying.) I had little time for thinking about how Ted was coping.

Both of us strove to maintain an atmosphere of normality, for our own benefit and the girls'. I channeled my anxiety into researching treatments and comparing outcomes and managing the side effects of medications. Ted, naturally reserved as well as naturally generous, expressed his anxiety by offering me an extra portion of largeheartedness. The conservatory was, no doubt about it, a product of his concern. It was an extravagance, especially given that we had three children heading to college and that new rounds of medical expenses were possible. Others would have sensibly retrenched. Ted could have made that case, and I would certainly have agreed, but he didn't.

But now, as we headed into the fourth postcancer year, the man who had been standing all that time on that metaphorical beach, eyes fixed on me and holding his breath while I struggled in rough seas, was breathing normally again. He had concluded that I was going to remain in the here and now and not disappear over the horizon, at least not for the foreseeable future. I wasn't so sure yet, and wouldn't be until the five-year anniversary, but he knew it was time to get back to where we left off, to recalibrate the balance in our marriage.

So I deconstructed Ujiji. Frankly, I was beginning to feel a little uncomfortable in there, too.

Entertaining

six

Passiflora

Long before there was Glasshouse Works and more than a hundred years before there was Logee's, there was Loddiges. Loddiges (rhymes with cottages) Nursery was one of England's first and largest commercial nurseries, and it specialized in tropicals. Founded in 1774 by a German immigrant, Joachim Conrad Loddiges, the nursery offered plants from around the world, gathered by a network of overseas correspondents. Over the course of several decades, the Loddiges family constructed more than eleven hundred feet of connected glasshouses. The early structures, arranged in a giant, squared-off U shape, were mostly lean-tos, but about 1820, George Loddiges, the founder's son, ordered the construction of two extraordinary buildings, both designed by the glasshouse innovator, John Claudius Loudon.

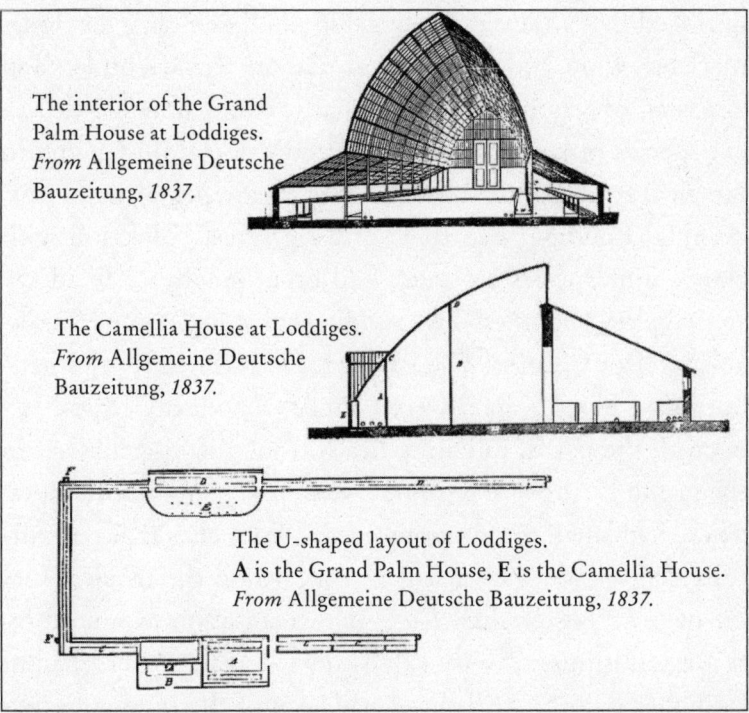

The interior of the Grand Palm House at Loddiges. *From* Allgemeine Deutsche Bauzeitung, *1837.*

The Camellia House at Loddiges. *From* Allgemeine Deutsche Bauzeitung, *1837.*

The U-shaped layout of Loddiges. **A** is the Grand Palm House, **E** is the Camellia House. *From* Allgemeine Deutsche Bauzeitung, *1837.*

Imagine a 140-foot-long football made of glass panes held in an iron webbing. Cut the football into quarters along its long axis. Take one of the quarters and nestle it into the angle made by the ground and a long wall. That was Loudon's design for the Loddiges Camellia House. When construction was complete, Loddiges so filled it with camellias that it seemed to one visitor, "a complete wood of that shrub, so much so that blackbirds have repeatedly built their nests and reared their young in it."

Across the U from the Camellia House was the Grand Palm House, in 1820 the largest and most unusual hothouse in the world. It, too, was built entirely of iron and glass, and it looked like an upside-down ship's hull at eighty feet long, forty feet wide, and about four stories tall. Inside, buyers and gawkers, of whom there were many, could find 170 different species of palms from thirty countries, from Ceylon to Jamaica, from South Africa to Egypt. Pitcher plants, ferns, orchids (Loddiges had the world's greatest collection with eighty-four species for sale), and other epiphytes filled the space below the trees. The buildings also had some remarkable interior features. The Palm House was heated by small-bore iron pipes, which were connected to a boiler and ran beneath the paths, radiating heat through iron grilles set in the ground. Above the canopy were more small-bore pipes. These had small perforations every two inches that periodically sent gentle showers of warm rain on the tropical forest below. "Never shall I forget the sensation produced by this establishment," wrote a visiting German nurseryman of Loddiges in 1829. "All that I had seen of the kind appeared nothing to me compared with this. I fancied myself in the Brazils."

Both the architecture of the glasshouses at Loddiges and the technology that enabled their construction were new and fundamentally different from anything that had gone before. By the first decade of the 1800s, Europeans had become familiar with two kinds of structures that housed plants: the glass-fronted lean-tos that had developed from hotbeds and pineries, and the older, "architectural" greenhouses descended from orangeries. The former were strictly utilitarian, with no room for people inside them. The latter mimicked the architecture of other buildings on an estate and employed the same materials—brick, masonry, or wood—for pilasters, cornices, and friezes while substituting floor-to-ceiling windows for walls. While the architectural glasshouses did duty as winter shelters for subtropical plants and trees (and might house a few for decorative purposes during the summer), they were often just as important to their owners as entertainment spaces where their houseguests could take a winter promenade or dine on a summer evening.

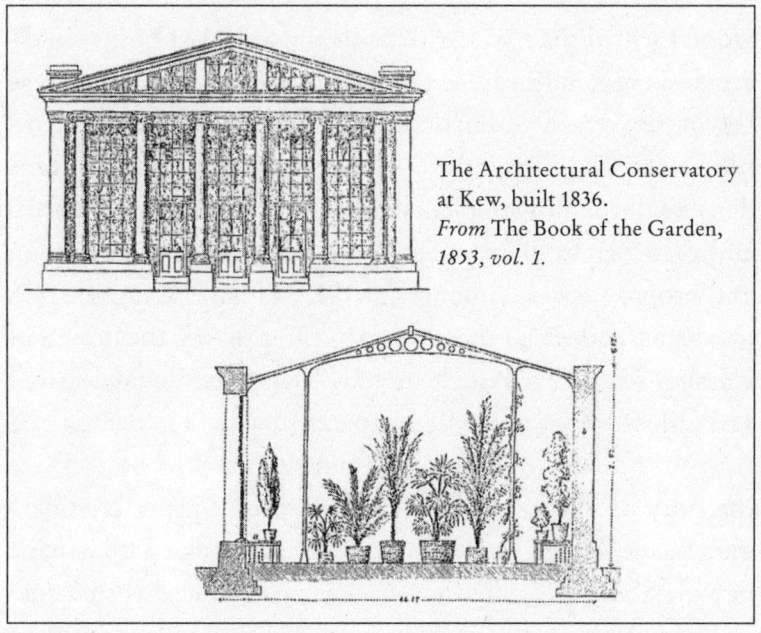

The Architectural Conservatory at Kew, built 1836.
From The Book of the Garden, *1853, vol. 1.*

But however much these buildings pleased the partygoers, as habitats for flora, especially the sun-loving tropicals flooding into Europe, they were mediocre at best. The load-bearing columns and the wooden frames that held the glass in the walls and roof had to be substantial, thereby blocking the transmission of light. The most sun-demanding tropicals, like the beautiful palms that whispered so seductively to northern Europeans of balmier climes, would not thrive. And even if the light had been sufficient, because the buildings could be no more than about two stories high, many palms and other tropical trees would have outgrown their homes.

In the first years of the nineteenth century, horticulturalists had begun to consider how to better sustain tropicals in northern climates. In 1804, Joseph Banks and John Wedgwood formed the Royal Horticultural Society (RHS) whose aim it was to collect information about plants and encourage the improvement of horticultural practice. The RHS members met twice a month to report on their efforts to standardize the naming of plants, consider the potential of useful and ornamental plant varieties, and discuss acclimatization and propagation techniques. In 1811, Thomas Knight, RHS president, addressed the question of improving the design of glasshouses. They were, he noted, "generally very defective" and failed to maximize light, space, or heat. He recognized that even the glass lean-to was not designed to best utilize the sun's rays, and he had already written a paper considering the ideal angle at which light should strike a glass pane in a glasshouse. Sir George Mackenzie advanced the discussion in 1815 with a paper that proposed that a glass building shaped as a perfect half sphere or as a quarter sphere backed onto a wall would be the ideal home for tropical plants. It would, he wrote, make "the surface of your green house parallel to the vaulted surface of the heavens, or to the plane of the sun's orbit."

In 1817 and 1818, John Claudius Loudon, a landscape architect and author of books on hothouses, farming, and estate architecture weighed in with two articles on the subject. He admired Mackenzie's general idea, but, as was his wont, criticized almost all the details. A perfect half sphere, or dome, was too deep for its height, he wrote. Where the ribs came together at the dome's apex, they would block too much light. Furthermore, the top of a half sphere was too flat. Condensation that would inevitably collect there would drip directly down on the plants, damaging tender leaves and flowers. Instead, he presented a more elliptical structure, the sort of blunted quarter football he would soon design for Loddiges. With an upper part that was more steeply angled, condensate would slide down the inside of the glass panes to the ground rather than fall like rain.

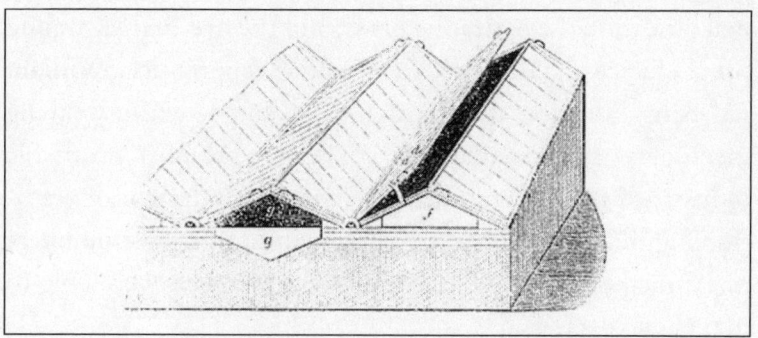

Design for a ridge-and-furrow roof.
From The Book of the Garden *by Charles McIntosh, 1853.*

He also suggested a revolutionary "ridge-and-furrow" roof, a roof that looked like it was made of deeply pleated glass. Knight, Mackenzie, and others were correct in recognizing that when sunlight hits glass obliquely, some rays, instead of passing through, are reflected back into the sky. In a pleated roof where the ridges and furrows are oriented along a north-south axis, Loudon argued, the panes would present a more perpendicular surface to the sun in both the morning and afternoon hours, and would capture more light than a horizontal surface. As a secondary benefit, the furrows could be used to channel and collect rainwater running off the roof.

Loudon belongs in that group of Englishmen born at the beginning of the Industrial Revolution who, without benefit of upper-class expectations and education, managed to make remarkable contributions in science, technology, and business. In the same period, Michael Faraday, son of a blacksmith, invented electromagnetic motors; John Dalton, son of a sheep farmer, made fundamental discoveries about atomic structure; and Joseph Bramah, who invented the machine tool, the hydraulic press, and the fire engine, among other devices, started as a carpenter's apprentice. William Fairbairn, the son of a gardener, invented textile-weaving machinery that created one of England's most profitable industries. By entering fields outside the purview of traditional guilds (which had an interest in limiting the numbers of its members), these able and energetic men were able to make unexpected advances.

Loudon was born near Edinburgh in 1783 to a yeoman farmer. He was luckier than many of his cohorts; he received a good primary education at an Edinburgh school where he studied botany, chemistry, drawing, and modern languages. At fifteen, he worked as a draftsman and assistant to a landscape gardener who had an extensive range of hothouses. Thanks to the Scots' enlightened belief that access to higher education should be broadly available to the citizenry, he was able to take courses in agriculture at the University of Edinburgh. In 1803, at twenty, he felt ready to make a name for himself and left for England. With glowing recommendations from his professor and employers, he immediately won commissions. Before the end of his first year, he had published a blistering article criticizing the plantings in London's public parks and started his first book.

Loudon was an appealing-looking young man with large eyes and curly hair, but he had little interest in being charming. A workaholic nonpareil, he stayed up all night twice a week to work on plans or write, drinking tea as a stimulant. Over the next forty years, two million words would flow from his pen into articles, pamphlets, books, and four encyclopedias on subjects including ornamental plants, hothouses, agriculture, estate management, and architecture. In addition, he founded and edited several botanical and architectural magazines and maintained a busy landscape design and architecture practice. He could be pleasant, especially to his clients, but was more frequently tactless and sometimes plain offensive. At a time, for example, when hothouse fruit cultivation was the first concern of the RHS and a hobby of many of his clients and potential clients, he wrote that growing fruit indoors could be recommended only to those who "from indolence or bilious complaint are apt to sink into a sort of torpid unenjoyed existence."

If Loudon was fortunate to live at a time when genius could trump birth, he was astute in transplanting himself to London. In the early 1800s, England was the center of the world, horticulturally speaking. From Paris to St. Petersburg, the "English" or "natural" style in gardening was supplanting all other designs, and estate owners were tearing up their formal gardens, and in their stead building up hillocks, rerouting streams, creating waterfalls, and naturalizing trees and shrubs. When it came to both outdoor and indoor gardens, the English nurseries had the most diverse selection available, the result of imports from their colonies in Asia, Africa, North America, and Australia. And when it came to constructing buildings best suited to growing tropical plants, Britain's superiority in iron manufacturing technology would give it a leading role.

The British had a long history of iron making, but the manufacture of iron required huge amounts of wood. Fifteen to twenty pounds of wood (in the form of charcoal) went into the furnace for every pound of iron that came out. Great tracts of English forest had fallen to the axe to fuel the furnaces, and in the late 1600s, the government moved to limit iron production to save the remaining forests. Coal, abundantly available in the Midlands, could substitute for wood in fireplaces, but it was useless in the iron furnaces: the phosphorous and sulfur in coal contaminated the iron, making it brittle. Abraham Darby, son of a yeoman farmer and locksmith and another of the era's self-made men, rescued the industry in 1709 when he discovered that coke, a fuel made from coal burned in an environment with limited oxygen, could fire the furnaces without spoiling the iron. By 1800, English coke-burning blast furnaces were smelting three tons of high-quality iron for every ton that Germany and France produced. That iron, poured into molds and cooled to create cast iron, became factory machinery, bridge trusses, steam engines, railroad tracks, and locomotives, the muscle and bones of industrial England.

Some of the first buildings to use cast iron for support were, appropriately enough, the new factories that housed the iron machines. Load-bearing columns were the first structural elements to be made of cast iron; the material is at its best under compression. Cast-iron beams were more problematic, though, because the material does not hold up well under tension, that is, under a bending force, such as the weight of a roof. A cast-iron beam needed to be enhanced on its underside by other elements, such as a perpendicular flange (e.g., an I-beam) or struts that spread that force to a column or wall.

It would have been difficult to build the large, glassy, and precisely curved glasshouses that Loudon imagined with a masonry or wood superstructure. But molten iron could be cast into long, curved molds that would produce the slender and perfectly identical parts needed. Iron wouldn't warp or rot, and coating its surface in paint or coal tar greatly retarded the development of rust. There was only one problem with using cast iron in a dome-shaped glasshouse: it couldn't be used for the structure's major vertical arcing elements, what were known as "sash bars," because the force exerted on an arc is, in part, a bending force. The sash bars would have to be braced on their undersides, which meant that they would look more like bridge trusses than simple arcs. Trusses would come between the sun and the plants below, casting shadows on the plants below.

Wrought iron—iron that has been reheated and mechanically formed rather than poured into a mold—performs much better under tension than cast iron. However, at the time there was no way to produce large, identical, curved wrought-iron pieces. When such a piece was required for a building, several short wrought-iron pieces were sometimes bolted together, but each joint created a weakness. Loudon solved this problem in 1816 by inventing a machine that produced long, curvilinear, wrought-iron sash bars that were exceedingly strong. Loudon's sash bar opened new frontiers in architecture. With them, the traditional divisions between roofs and walls could be made to disappear. Building design limited to the horizontal and vertical axes was suddenly liberated. When traceries of iron were filled with glass, buildings suddenly escaped the confines of the rectilinear and their forms became almost infinitely variable. To demonstrate those possibilities, Loudon built an assemblage of glasshouses at his Bayswater home, each in a different shape and made of thirteen types of sash bar and seven types of glass. The drawings published in 1818 in his *Sketches of Curvilinear Hothouses* show a curved pyramidical structure, curved lean-tos of various sorts, arcades, and a half dome (all juxtaposed against the backdrop of a medieval crenellated wall). Bayswater was Loudon's advertisement that his wrought-iron buildings could, as he said, have "every conceivable variety of glass surface."

Bayswater was effective. Almost immediately George Loddiges contracted with Loudon for the Camellia and Grand Palm House designs to be built by W. & D. Bailey and Sons. Then Bailey, having obtained the rights to the wrought-iron sash bar from Loudon (for free—Loudon was no businessman), built Loudon-designed glasshouses for pineapples, grapevines, and tropical ornamentals across England and in Holland. Other firms quickly got into the business, and curvilinear glasshouses were soon as popular as architectural ones.

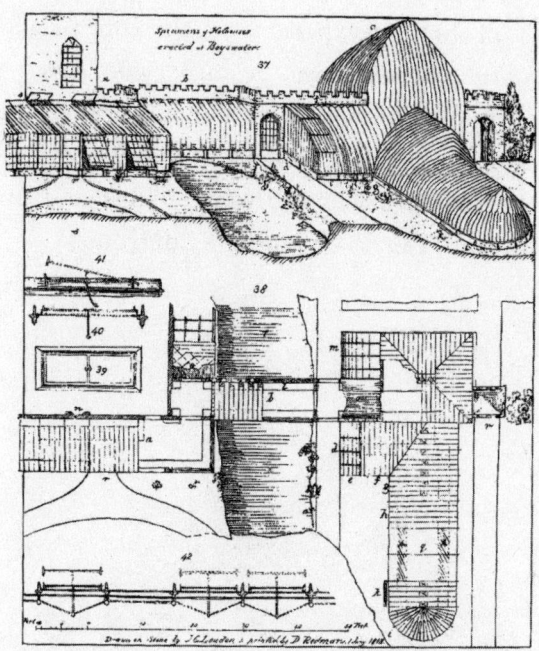

John Loudon's Bayswater home with demonstration glasshouses. *From* Sketches of Curvilinear Hothouses *by John Claudius Loudon, 1818.*

The beautiful, fanciful new structures seemed to require a special word, and "conservatory" came into vogue at this time.[4] A conservatory described an aesthetically pleasing

---

[4] The word had been used before for buildings designed to conserve plants over the winter, but now it took on a more specific meaning. Also at this time, the terms "hothouse" and "stove" generally came to mean a building used for scientific purposes, the propagation of

structure where people enjoyed the company of plants while also enjoying the company of one another. A conservatory could be freestanding or attached to a manor home or an in-town mansion, and the plants inside could be arranged in beds in the ground, on trellises, or in pots. The point was to present an artful, exotic experience to the upper-class owners and guests who came to visit. A conservatory was "a place for frequent resort and agreeable assemblage at all seasons," a place for meandering down well-tended paths alongside tropical flowers and other "curious" plants and under the boughs of fruit trees and drooping palm fronds.

The conservatory at Bretton Hall, Yorkshire, completed 1827. *From* An Encyclopaedia of Cottage, Farm and Villa Architecture and Furniture *by John Claudius Loudon, 1832.*

tropicals, or kitchen gardening, while "greenhouse" continued to indicate a building for storing plants over the winter, but the words were used with maddening inconsistency.

In the first decades of the nineteenth century, the editor of *Famous Parks and Gardens* wrote that a "mania for conservatories spread contagiously among all the richer classes of the cold and temperate countries of Europe." The fifteenth Earl of Shrewsbury began renovations to the grounds at Alveton Lodge, later renamed Alton Towers, in Staffordshire, an estate that had been in his family for four hundred years. He commissioned two architectural glasshouses, one a classic Greek temple, the other a rambling confection built of masonry with window-filled walls and seven gilded, glass-and-cast-iron domes topped by pineapples. (Elsewhere on the property, he constructed a pagoda, "a cottage for a blind harper," a reduced-scale Stonehenge, Indian temples, caves and waterfalls, and a small Matterhorn.) Sir Charles Cockerell, who had made a fortune in India, built a home at Sezincote in Gloucestershire with an attached Indian-style conservatory with deeply scalloped window frames, a remarkable sight in the English countryside. Lady Diana Beaumont, owner of Bretton Hall estate in Yorkshire, commissioned a palm house from Loudon. He designed her a freestanding, glass-and-iron structure shaped like a bell, a hundred feet in diameter and six stories high, with a circular ventilation opening at the top with a shock of cast-iron feathers sprouting from its apex. (It was supposed to bring to mind a wigwam, but Loudon had obviously never been to the American West.) At Syon House, the Duke of Northumberland built a semicircular, classical Greek building that was topped by a huge glass bubble of a dome. The Earl of Stamford and Warrington had a fanciful structure that mixed Gothic windows with domes and towers reminiscent of Arab tents. At the Dalkeith Estate in Edinburgh, parts of which dated to the twelfth century, the family added a twelve-sided conservatory with slender Roman Doric columns at the angles and elaborate cast-iron roof girders. The Palm House at Lord Rolle's Bicton estate in Devon, one of the few estate glasshouses of the period still standing, has a delicate curvilinear structure, perhaps designed by Loudon, covered in hand-size, overlapping panes that shimmer like fish scales.

The conservatory at Dalkeith Estate, completed 1832.
From The Book of the Garden *by Charles McIntosh, 1853.*

The Earl of Stamford and Warrington's conservatory at Enville Hall,
Stourbridge, completed 1853. *From IPC Media Limited.*

A conservatory was a highly visible sign of status because only the very wealthiest could afford one. The cost stemmed, in large part, from the materials. Wrought iron was two or three times the price of cast iron, and cast iron was many times the price of wood. It was the glass, though, that levered conservatories out of the category of very costly into the category of astronomically expensive. In England in the early 1800s, window glass was still made in either of two old and labor-intensive ways. In the first method, which created "crown glass," a glassblower twirled a blob of molten glass on the end of an iron rod until it spun into a flat disk. Then he cut it into pieces that measured roughly six inches by eight inches. The alternative method produced "cylinder glass." To make a piece of cylinder glass, the glassblower used a hollow iron rod, dipped a blob of molten glass onto one end, and blew through the other, creating a sphere of glass. He rolled the sphere against a piece of stone or metal, shaping it into a cylinder. While the cylinder was still soft, he cut down its length and finally flattened it into a pane. The length of a piece of English cylinder glass depended on how forcefully the glassblower could expel air from his lungs, but although the panes were somewhat longer than crown glass pieces, they were still only about ten inches wide. It was not until 1832 when Chance Brothers and Company enlisted the help of French glass inventor Georges Bontemps that longer pieces blown with compressed air—up to three feet long—became available in England. Glass by either method would have been a luxury item, but a tax increased its price six- or sevenfold. A garden laborer would have had to work a half day to pay for one small pane.

There was more expense to a conservatory, of course, after

it was built. First, it had to be stocked. In 1833, Loddiges sold its palms for about £5 each (a sum roughly equivalent to £400 today). Once stocked, a conservatory required intensive labor. Gardeners had to satisfy the requirements of both the plants, which needed constant hand watering, weeding, insect treatment, and fertilizing, and of the visitors who expected the space to look both natural and perfectly manicured, without a single yellowing leaf or spent flower. To keep his gardens, indoors and outside, in prime viewing state, the estate owner employed large numbers of "bothy men." These were single men who lived and ate together in a cottage (a "bothy") on the grounds and worked twelve-hour days, six days a week. A good-size country estate might have twenty glasshouses of various kinds—mostly for supplying the great quantities of fruit and vegetables and various flowers out of season needed by the family and their constant flow of guests—tended by a garden staff of twenty-five. Another twenty-five gardeners would care for the outside grounds. Although ordinary garden laborers were paid less than £1 a week, the aggregate labor expense was formidable.

My conservatory, I had imagined, would be a quiet sanctuary, *my* quiet sanctuary. Sometimes it was, but it also became the social hub of the house. We ate every meal there; the "real" dining room was nearly abandoned. General hanging out— chatting, reading the newspaper—that had taken place in the living room now happened in the conservatory.

Alice decided the conservatory was the best place to do her homework, better than the desk in her bedroom, not only because her desktop was obscured beneath a dense bracken of papers, books, lotions, and other teenage paraphernalia, but because she could thereby avoid the multifarious distractions of her computer. She and I had been debating for years whether it is possible to truly absorb geometry while listening to iTunes, checking out the sales at American Eagle, and responding to messages on Facebook, so I could hardly ask her to go back to her room. So the conservatory became her study in the evenings and on weekends.

Come May, Alice was not the only one in my refuge. My parents, back from Florida until fall, were frequent visitors. Together with my aunt and Anna, who was home for a summer internship, they played bridge at the wirework table. The snap of cards, a round of bidding, postplay analysis, and a certain amount of kvetching—yes, the cards do tend to slip between the wires and, yes, the skylights do create a glare—filled the air. Then, around five o'clock, it was the cocktail hour for the older generation, and out came the crackers and cheese, a bucket of ice, and the liquor bottles. There was always general astonishment and mild disapproval that I was passing on a cocktail, but my eccentricity was deemed offset by my cleverness in growing a lime tree that provided the garnish for their gin and tonics.

Austen was also home for the summer, combining a part-time job at the county public defender's office with a part-time job at the county skeet-and-trap shooting range. She and her friends tended to occupy the conservatory for the late-night shift. I would find empty soda cans, jars of salsa, and chip bags on the table in the morning, so I knew they'd been around. From time to time, I would also discover damp towels on the floor, although never any damp bathing suits. Ah, youth.

The pool was a draw during the day, too. My aunt was a regular swimmer, as were several neighborhood friends, and two young cousins. A pack of Alice's buddies would sit around the edge, chitchatting and dangling their legs. One athletic girl figured out that she could tie her Boogie Board to the grab bar that overhangs the motor at the front of the pool, crank up the current, and surf. Ted thinks swimming is an activity to be engaged in only should the boat from which he is fishing be sinking faster than he can bail. But he mulled the possibility of getting a large inner tube and a cold beer and drifting around the pool in slow circles.

My book group met in the conservatory, too. We discussed *A Few Short Notes on Tropical Butterflies,* a collection of short stories by John Murray, ate spiced shrimp, and drank piña coladas. My daughters have always loved this book group, "the gossip group," whose members live in the neighborhood, as opposed to my other, more serious group. This one, with its wine-fueled laughter, shouts of approval or dissent, and overlapping conversations, seemed like fun. As little girls, Anna recently told me, they sneaked down the steps to listen in to what sounded like a really good party. I told her how Joanie and I once did the same thing, sneaking down the hall to listen when it was my father's night to host the monthly poker night. (How disconcerting and strange it was to hear those deep-voiced men, usually so serious, playing a card game, ragging one another like boys our age.) Now, I think my book group gives my children confidence that full-fledged adulthood will not bring an end to the friendships that are so important in their lives.

The conservatory has hosted many other gatherings: Thanksgiving and Christmas dinners, seders, school potlucks, and celebrations of all kinds. When the crowd exceeds ten, I push back the plants and add two round plastic tables. When we pass twenty, I also set the table in the "real" dining room, but those are always the last seats taken. Even at night, without the benefit of a flood of sunshine, the conservatory draws visitors. Maybe people are attracted by the implication of sunshine inherent in large and lush green plants. Maybe we've all been conditioned by those advertisements of happy couples and families frolicking in tropical locations, and unconsciously presume that good times are going to happen in a tropical conservatory. Or maybe, lingering deep in our primate psyche is the sense that there is safety in a place that feels like the high treetops. Whatever the reason, the fact is that guests walk in the front door and immediately head to the plants, without passing Go or collecting anything but a rush of serotonin.

Those of us who live here gravitate to the conservatory. Even the dog prefers the wicker chair where she can keep the maximum number of her pack members in view, as well as get a jump on anything interesting that drops on the floor. I have noticed that we spend less time in separate rooms and more time in the wide-open conservatory. Having a rendezvous, I have concluded, is better than having a refuge.

Extravagance in entertaining, as well as in drinking, philandering, and gambling, was a hallmark of the upper classes during the extended Regency period, defined as the last decade of the eighteenth and the first three decades of the nineteenth centuries. The period is named for the Prince of Wales, son of the periodically insane George III, who was either unofficial regent or actual regent from 1788 to 1820 and then wielded power as King George IV until his death in 1830. It was the prince who set the social tone of the period.

The prince had a few redeeming character traits: he was amiable and gracious, and he had a fine appreciation of and commitment to the arts. He helped found the National Gallery and King's College London. But he was also a voluptuary of the highest order, an alcoholic, a spendthrift, an opium addict, a glutton whose middle-aged body was said to resemble a feather bed, and "an egregious coxcomb" (before he ate himself out of the running). He was a man of whom it was written on the occasion of his fiftieth birthday in 1812 that he had "just closed half a century without a single claim on the gratitude of his country or the respect." When the prince was only twenty-five, Parliament had to pay off the £210,000 (more than $10 million) in debts he had accumulated by that tender age. Three years later, he had amassed new debts amounting to £300,000. Nonetheless, his expenditures increased dramatically when he became regent and then king. There is no question that his profligacy contributed to the political unrest in the 1820s that could have led, as similar royal extravagance had in France, to revolution.

The prince spent a good portion of his money, inherited and borrowed, on entertaining, which included the construction, outfitting, and constant redecoration of his various residences, the settings for his elaborate entertainments. (Other large sums went to his tailors; George was obsessed with clothes and designed his own military uniforms.) The parties were legendary, not for their witty conversation, but for their flamboyance. The prince stage-managed his productions down to the smallest detail, choosing lighting, crystal, silver, and the food, and, of course, his attire. His first party as regent, given on June 11, 1811, was typical. He spent weeks happily preparing for it and invited two thousand of the European nobility and gentry to a sit-down dinner in the conservatory at Carlton House. The main table was two hundred feet long and extended into the house. A stream, bubbling from a silver fountain at the head of the table, ran down the center of the table between banks of moss and flowers and under fanciful bridges. Goldfish swam in the water. Thousands of lights and flowers and vases of burning perfume made the evening "magically impressive," according to the *Times* report of the event.

Although no one could truly keep pace with the prince in dissipation, many tried. Scions of some of the great families spent fortunes in building and maintaining houses and gardens and in constantly hosting one another. Visiting country houses and entertaining at one's own country house were the major occupations of many in the upper crust of society who, by definition, had no other employment. ("He is not a gentleman; he works," scoffed the fifth Duke of Devonshire in speaking of his cousin, Henry Cavendish, a scientist who, among other achievements, was the first to measure gravitational force in a laboratory and determine Earth's density.) Those country houses were in essence five-star resorts complete with elaborate amusements, spectacular meals, expansive libraries, excellent shooting (with dogs, guns, horses, and beaters provided) and fishing, and an attentive house-hold staff. Hosts had to accommodate, often on short notice, entire families and their many retainers—servants, maids, valets, nannies, governesses, and even family doctors—for days and sometimes weeks. A visit to the host's conservatory, with a tour given by the head gardener—or the host if he happened to be one of those Enlightenment men—was a welcome diversion for jaded houseguests.

When the sixth Duke of Devonshire opened the doors to the Great Stove at Chatsworth in 1840, the premier county seat of the Cavendishes, he brought the private conservatory to new heights of grandeur, technological development, and horticultural display. The sixth duke, known by his family as Hart because he was also the Marquis of Hartington, was born in 1790 into a Regency family that seemed to exemplify the excesses of the period. His father, William Cavendish, that sniffy fifth duke, was wealthy on a royal scale, with an annual income derived from eight country estates and London properties. His mother, the Duchess Georgiana, was one of the era's great beauties, equally famous for her warm heart and heavy gambling debts. The Cavendishes philandered in Regency style: a year after Hart's birth, Georgiana delivered again, although this time the child's father was a handsome young nobleman who would later become Prime Minister Lord Grey. This was just one more bastard in the family. Hart had four older siblings: two were the offspring of his parents and two were the result of a continuing liaison between his father and Elizabeth Foster, Georgiana's best friend.

The fifth duke entertained on a grand scale. When Hart

turned twenty-one, in 1811, the duke gave a birthday ball at Devonshire House in London for a thousand guests while simultaneously throwing parties, with unlimited food and drink, for the tenants at all the other Cavendish seats. It turned out to be his last hurrah; the duke died two months later. Hart's inheritance included two hundred thousand acres of land and debts, contracted by his mother at the gaming tables, that would have done the prince regent proud.

The sixth duke was an attractive young man, six feet tall with pale skin, light brown hair, and blue eyes. There would be some of the Regency excess about him as well. He drank too much, had affairs with many women, and married none. Invitations to his parties were almost as sought after as invitations to the king's, and he entertained constantly and lavishly. At one party at Chiswick House just outside London, an immense elephant appeared, which gave "an air of Asiatic pageantry to the entertainment . . . ," according to one guest, Sir Walter Scott. The duke was an avid and intelligent collector of things—coins, medals, books, antique furnishings, English and Italian paintings and sculpture, and exotic plants—and money ran through his fingers. The expansion of his Chatsworth country home, which he doubled in size in order to house his collections and entertain even more grandly, cost tens of thousands of pounds. As wealthy as he was, he would have to sell his estate at Londesborough in 1845 to pay off pressing obligations.

Yet a moral conscience and a strong sense of civic duty equally defined the man. He was an early advocate of the abolition of slavery and the equal treatment of Irish Catholics, and he worked as an influential member of Parliament and as

Lord Chamberlain to effect those changes. When William IV ascended to the throne in 1830, the duke spoke passionately and repeatedly, publicly in Parliament and privately to the king, for support and passage of the Reform Bill. That bill, which enfranchised portions of the middle class and abolished "rotten boroughs" (boroughs with tiny populations represented by a Member of Parliament in the pocket of a noble) was naturally, albeit shortsightedly, opposed by a majority of the members of his class. The bill, which became the Reform Act of 1832, probably saved the country from revolution.

Horticulture became one of the duke's intelligent passions. In 1813, two years after he inherited his title, he began renovations at Chiswick House near London, improving the interior and creating an Italian garden on the thirty-three-acre grounds (to which, with a Regency flourish, he added kangaroos, elks, emus, goats, and a pair of Indian cattle). He also constructed a three-hundred-foot-long glass lean-to with a central glass-and-wood dome. In 1821, he leased much of the Chiswick grounds to the Royal Horticultural Society. All the duke required was a private door to the gardens.

In November 1823, twenty-year-old Joseph Paxton, a garden laborer with little education, began work for the RHS. He soon was assigned to work under the gardener in charge of ornamentals, and he cared for, among other species, the newly introduced *Aspidistra* from China and *Fuchsia* from Mexico. Friendly, smart, and hardworking, he was promoted to undergardener within the year, a year when the society was building a number of new glasshouses. Sometime in that period, the duke visited the gardens, and he must have met the new undergardener. In April 1826, the thirty-six-year-old duke hired him to become the head gardener at Chatsworth.

It was as if the CEO of Exxon had met a twenty-two-year-old technician on a facility tour and asked him to head the corporation's refining operations. It reveals a lot about Paxton that he had such extraordinary self-possession and enthusiasm about horticulture that he was able to impress the duke. It says something about the duke that unlike most men of the era so well-born, he related to people as individuals no matter what their station. It may also say something of the times, of how evident it had become that self-interest demanded one pay attention to clever, energetic young men. In any event, Paxton immediately took a coach to Chesterfield, the nearest town to Chatsworth, and then walked through the night the final twelve miles. No one was awake when he arrived at 4:30 in the morning to let him in, so he climbed over the wall, explored the grounds, and at six o'clock set his new employees to work.

Paxton devoted most of his early efforts to restoring the gardens—the fifth duke and the duchess had preferred London life and neglected Chatsworth—maintaining and adding walks, fixing drains and pipes and fountains, refurbishing the planting beds, as well as transplanting acquisitions. Then, in 1827, with significant input from the duke whose interest in horticulture grew as Paxton transformed the grounds, he turned to repairing the pineapple and peach houses, designing an orangerie, and experimenting with new greenhouses and hothouses for other fruit trees and vegetables.

The duke's confidence in his gardener grew and by Paxton's third year, he had tripled Paxton's original salary and given him authority over the woods of the estate as well.

One of the first jobs Paxton faced as head forester was planning the transplantation of a forty-year-old, eight-ton ash tree from a nursery twenty-eight miles away. He designed a machine to transport it and then oversaw the forty laborers who moved it over the course of four days and replanted it in the Chatsworth courtyard. The duke was thrilled with the feat and Paxton's star rose higher.

In the 1830s, the duke's love of collecting rare and beautiful things merged with his horticultural interests. In the five years between 1830 and 1835, the duke began a serious study of horticulture and spent £2,500 on plants, many of which were exotics for the new glasshouses. Paxton, meanwhile, converted a stone greenhouse into a hothouse by putting glass in the roof and modernizing the heating system. He also took the ridge-and-furrow roof design that Loudon had published in 1818 and turned it into a reality, with excellent results. In the same period, he designed a variety of new or refurbished glasshouses for which the duke paid about £3,500. One large glasshouse went to sheltering his valuable collection of orchids; others housed mushrooms, strawberries, pineapples, melons, cucumbers, grapevines, and peaches.

The duke, enchanted with tropical plants and delighting in what was becoming, despite the social chasm between himself and his gardener, a great and productive friendship, took Paxton with him on visits to horticultural shows, private gardens, nurseries, and public conservatories across England. He walked the grounds with Paxton nearly every day when he was at Chatsworth, and when they weren't both at Chatsworth, they wrote back and forth at length about gardens and glasshouses and their latest ideas for acquisitions and construction. They were like a couple of boys, full of the fun of a shared enthusiasm and the excitement of a grand and somewhat conspiratorial endeavor. They were out to make the Chatsworth grounds the most impressive in the country, with the most creative and exuberant landscape design and an unsurpassed horticultural collection.

In 1835, in the duke's continuing efforts to achieve the unsurpassable, he funded a plant-hunting expedition to India. Paxton picked William Gibson, a Chatsworth gardener, as the collector and sent him to study orchids at a nearby estate and other exotics at nurseries and conservatories. Well aware that finding exotic plants had always been only half the challenge, he also sent him to Loddiges for an education on how to pack and care for plants on shipboard.

The duke was sending out Gibson at a propitious moment in the history of plant hunting. In 1830, Dr. Nathaniel Ward, a physician with a practice in the dirty, sooty heart of London, had also been an amateur botanist and entomologist for a number of years. He hated living in London and would have much preferred a country life, but he had inherited his medical practice from his father and was bound to city life. Instead, he went "herborising" on the weekends, collecting ferns and other plants that he tried to transplant in his backyard garden. To his disappointment, the city air was so polluted that little grew.

One day, he noticed that in a covered glass bottle in which he had put a hawk-moth chrysalis and a bit of moist dirt, some tiny seedlings were sprouting. Curious, he put the bottle on a ledge and found that the plants—some grass and a fern— continued to grow without any addition of food, water, or fresh air. He was astonished: he, like everyone else of the time, assumed plants needed a regular new supply of all three. He turned to George Loddiges and together they began experiments on a larger scale, growing thirty species of plants in airtight glass containers. Ward realized that water was recycling inside the containers, condensing on the glass and dripping down to remoisten the soil. The plants' ability to survive without additional nutrients and fresh air, however, he could not explain. (Joseph Priestley had discovered that air was made of several gases, including oxygen, and that plants improved the life-giving quality of air, but no one yet understood that plants exhale oxygen.) In any case, the plants thrived.

The Great Stove at Chatsworth before it was dynamited in 1920.
From Gardeners Chronicle, *1904, vol. 35.*

Loddiges understood the commercial implications of Ward's discovery. For one, he might be able to sell more plants to city dwellers who otherwise couldn't get plants to survive in London's poisonous atmosphere. Second, plants shipped from overseas, 95 percent of which still died en route, might survive the voyage in Ward's cases. In 1834, Loddiges proposed an experiment. He and Ward constructed two glass cases, planted them with grasses and ferns rooted in moist earth, sealed them, and sent them by ship to Australia. Four months later, the cases arrived with flourishing plants. Then the cases were replanted with plants native to Australia and sent, via Cape Horn, back to London. Eight months later, Loddiges and Ward rushed down to the dock to meet the ship: the plants, including one species never successfully transported before, were in perfect shape. Gibson would be one of the first, if not the first, plant hunter to take advantage of what became known as Wardian cases. George Loddiges would report in 1842 that his plant hunters had reversed the odds on shipping plants, with 95 percent of their finds arriving in healthy condition.

Gibson departed in September 1835 and his ship arrived in India six and a half months later. Meanwhile, the duke and Paxton, inspired by what they had good reason to expect would be a fantastic haul of new plants, planned a new conservatory to house them, along with the tropicals they had already collected. Paxton had a radical new design in mind. Chatsworth would have the largest conservatory ever built, containing about eighteen times the volume of space of the Loddiges Palm House. At 227 feet long, 123 feet wide, it would cover an acre of land; at 67 feet in height, it would shelter the tallest palms. It would look from the outside like a long, two-layered wedding cake, only each layer would be curved. The arcing sashes would be made of the beveled wood that Paxton preferred, although the roof would be supported inside by hollow iron columns that also collected rainwater. The rainwater would be warmed and used to water the plants.

Eight subterranean boilers and seven miles of iron pipe buried in the building's foundation would heat the conservatory. The boilers would be supplied with coal by wagons drawn along a train track through an underground tunnel. Buried flues would channel the boilers' smoke to a distant chimney. No unsightly mechanisms would mar the view of the glittering building in its bucolic setting.

The most remarkable aspect of the building, however, would be the shape of the glass skin that covered its curvilinear frame. Paxton had used the ridge-and-furrow concept on the flat roofs. Now, he would adapt the concept to a structure where walls and roof were one, extending the ridges and furrows from the apex of the structure down the sides to the ground. The entire exterior of the Great Stove would be composed of glass pleats, which would not only capture the maximum light but would provide, Paxton believed, greater strength to the structure. Nothing like this had ever been dreamed of, much less built.

When construction started in the fall of 1836, Gibson was exploring the rainy plateau near Cherrapunji, an Indian town on the high plateau overlooking what is today, Bangladesh. "I never saw nor could I believe," he wrote, "that there was such a fertile place under the Heavens." He collected hundreds of species of orchids and other plants, including a hundred orchids new to the West, and began sending them, sealed up in Wardian cases, on various ships heading to England. In March 1837, he headed home himself, nursing thousands of plants on shipboard, including orchids still attached to their branches that he hung from his cabin's ceiling. The duke and Paxton were overjoyed with Gibson's collection.

The success of the venture, which also brought the most vivid proof of the efficacy of Wardian cases, inspired a new wave of privately and publicly funded expeditions.

By early 1838, construction on the Great Stove was under way and Paxton was supervising five hundred workers. Two years later, the wood and iron superstructure was complete, and the glazing began. Paxton worked with Chance Brothers, pushing them to figure out how to make longer panes than they had ever made. Not only did they succeed, but they sold them to the duke at cost, figuring their use in such an extraordinary building would draw other buyers. Fitting the four-foot-long, six-inch-wide panes into a skeleton of curving sash bars nearly seven stories high posed another challenge. But Paxton invented a wooden wagon designed so that its wheels fit exactly on a pair of parallel sash bars. A man and a boy in the wagon could push themselves along, laying panes on the diagonal, which gave the glass skin of the house a unique herringbone pattern, as they went.

When the conservatory opened, visitors found the world inside. The space was divided by geographical regions, a piece of South America here and a patch of Japan there. The duke had gone on a buying spree and purchased plants by the thousands, including the best palm collection in Britain, a collection from the king's Wimbledon House that had outgrown its space, and much of Baron von Hugel's South African garden. He ecstatically described part of the collection in a letter:

> *The Walton date-palm, growing every day more like that of Posilippo;* Hibiscus splendens; erythina arobrea; . . . *the various creepers and* passiflorae;

> Bougainvillea spectabilis; *and* Stephanotis
> floribunda, *ascending even to the roof;* ... Sabal
> Blacburniana, *the very first stove plant I acquired,*
> *from Mrs. Beaumont of the North: then* Cocos
> plumosa, *easily surpassing all others, a present*
> *from the Sheffield Horticultural Society; the Rose*
> *Hibiscus, and more lofty* Musa *[bananas];* ... *Lord*
> *Fitzwilliam's present,* Dracaena Draco, *that promises*
> *to rival the Dragon tree of Java* ...

And on and on he went. A delicate wrought-iron gallery that circled the interior gave guests a view up into the tops of palms and down on orange trees, papyrus, and sugarcanes. A broad carriageway stretched the building's length. Colorful birds flitted in and out of the greenery of palms, cacti, ferns, and vines, and among the brilliant flowers of *Hibiscus, Bougainvillea,* lilies, *Impatiens, Hoya, Bignonia, Melastoma, Strelitzia,* and orchids. Goldfish swam in small pools.

The duke opened the estate to the public at least five days a week. In the coming years, thousands of visitors would visit. The most prominent visitor to Chatsworth was Queen Victoria, who came for a stay with a royal entourage in 1843. (Chatsworth could accommodate visitors in forty-five bedrooms, but the duke also reserved all the rooms at the inns in the nearby towns.) The queen and Prince Albert were driven through the conservatory, which was lit for the royal visit with twelve thousand oil lamps. The Great Stove was awe-inspiring: the greatest glasshouse, with the greatest collection of tropical plants, in the world.

At least for a while.

Wintergardens

seven

Asclepias incarnata

The duke was driven by an authentic interest in horticulture (assiduously nurtured by Paxton), and the Great Stove at Chatsworth was organized according to botanical principles. Other European aristocrats were also bitten by the exotic plant bug and competed with one another for the most comprehensive or rarest collections. But some had little scientific interest in plants, and they took conservatories—or wintergardens as they were known on the Continent—in a different direction. The naturalistic landscapes of the era, those purposefully contoured hills and redirected streams, moved indoors. With them went the exotic architectural follies, the miniature Greek temples, Chinese pavilions, rustic bridges, and hermits' cottages that the wealthy liked to strew about their estates. If dallying in a garden's Gothic ruin or Temple of Hymen was romantic on a summer evening, it was even more alluring to do so when the outdoors was snowy and cold.

Russian prince Potemkin, the powerful favorite of Catherine II, finished building a notable wintergarden at Tauride Palace near St. Petersburg in 1789. The indoor grounds were sculpted with little hills, flowering hedges, and meandering paths that produced, according to one enchanted visitor, "at every step, fresh occasions of surprise." Those who tired of the scenery could look instead at fish in crystal vases or gaze at themselves in a mirror-lined grotto. John Kibble, a wealthy Scottish industrialist, provided another kind of visual refreshment for his visitors. In the 1860s, he adorned the round conservatory at his home on Loch Long with fifty full-size copies of Greek, Roman, and Renaissance sculptures. In 1867, the handsome and highly cultured Bavarian king Ludwig II was at a low point. He and his Austrian allies had lost the Seven Weeks' War, a defeat that would lead to the loss of his country's independence to Prussia. On the personal front, he had just agreed to an engagement to his cousin, despite the fact that he was homosexual. In the face of such extreme unpleasantness, he commissioned an exotic wintergarden on the roof of his palace. Under an acre of glass, he re-created the high hills of India. Not for him a few small pools as at Chatsworth, but a pond large enough to row boats on (the boats were made to look like swans), a brook, a fountain, a reed hut, birds, a nomad's pavilion made of bamboo and silk, and a grotto with stalactites and a waterfall. A panoramic painting of the Himalayas completed the fantasy setting.

King Ludwig II's roof garden on the Königsbau, Munich, 1867–71.
From Bayerische Verwaltung der staatlichen Schlösser, Gärten und Seen, 1981.

King Leopold II of Belgium took the private winter-garden to its most extravagant expression, but then, he had a most extravagant need for an alternative world. Leopold was a scrawny, notably ugly man with a limp, a bushy beard, and a nose that, according to Benjamin Disraeli, could only have been arranged by a malign fairy. He had a personality to match his appearance. His wife, a beautiful and lively sixteen-year-old Hapsburg princess, wrote to a friend after a month of marriage that "If God hears my prayers, I shall not go on living much longer." Leopold was no more charming to his daughters. He so rarely interacted with his oldest daughter, Louise, that when she was thirteen she was "simply stupefied" when he offered her a gardenia.

A small portion of Leopold II's Laeken Wintergarden, Brussels, construction started in 1865 and completed in 1899. *From* The Gardeners Chronicle, *vol. 6.*

The distress he visited on his family was, however, nothing compared with the misery he inflicted on millions of Africans. Under the guise of philanthropy and scientific exploration and aided by the explorer Henry Stanley, he established a vast and lucrative private colony—some sixty times the size of Belgium—in the Congo River basin and turned himself into the all-powerful dictator of the Congo Free State. He essentially enslaved the Congolese, who tapped the wild rubber trees for Leopold's profit, paying them a pittance and holding their families hostage until they produced outrageously high quotas of rubber. When the workers rebelled around 1900 and set the forests on fire, Leopold's private army of sixteen thousand hunted down the rebels and murdered the wives and children of men who refused to return to work. Those tribal chiefs who failed to enforce Leopold's commands had their hands cut off, introducing a ghastly practice that continues to haunt parts of Africa today.

In the midst of his international cruelties, Leopold built a monumental wintergarden at his Laeken Palace outside Brussels. The complex, started in 1874 and under construction for the next three decades, would ultimately include sixteen graceful, interconnected iron-and-glass structures covering nearly four acres. Several miles of paths crisscrossed the grounds. There were separate houses for palms, camellias, ferns, azaleas, and citrus, as well as houses that doubled as a dining room, theater, reception room, and a church. (The only glasshouse, it is said, that was not a success was the Congo house. The plants would never flourish there.) The king, who was intimately involved in the construction and stocking of the Laeken glasshouses, created a spectacular dream of flowers and foliage. "Tropical and sub-tropical plants . . . rose to form a green dome, their branches rustling down in flowery cascades," his younger daughter wrote of her father's wintergarden. "Orange-tinted sand covered the paths, which led through this forest of blooms, amid fountains and mysterious grottoes." The walls of the Great Gallery, a glass tunnel six hundred feet long, were lined with six-foot-high red geraniums trained up wires, and the ceiling was a mass of fuchsia in pink, white, magenta, and purple. In the last years of his life, after his atrocities came to public attention, Leopold became an international pariah and moved into an apartment in his Palm Tree Pavilion. He lived alone in his wintergarden, ever more hypochondriacal and churlish, until he died—in the Pavilion of the Palms—in 1909.

It was early January and I was in the depths of the seasonal blues I suffer through every winter. The excitement of the holidays had evaporated. Anna and Austen were back at college, and Alice had entered a teenage funk, living behind her closed bedroom door from which only occasional minor chords of her guitar emerged. The days were abominably short and the sun at midday barely hoisted itself over the top of my neighbor's hickory tree. I read the weather page of the *Washington Post* the way Etruscan seers studied the organs of slaughtered sheep. Some seers believed in the prognosticative powers of the liver, others the spleen or intestines. I looked to the graph of the normal average temperatures in the D.C. area for the next ten days. Every morning, I scrutinized the graph, hoping to discern a hint of an upward slope to the line. But the line was utterly flat, as were my spirits and productivity.

I decided to move my office from the attic to the conservatory for the winter, and each morning I lugged my books and laptop downstairs and set myself up at the wirework table. The table was too high, the chairs were too hard, and if I put my pen down carelessly, it slipped between the wires and fell to the floor. Still, I felt better. The air in the conservatory was moist and warm, and if there was no direct sunlight, the skylights at that season provided enough daylight to work. The citrus trees were still bearing the fruit they'd set in late summer. Much of it was overripe, but I refused to pick any. It pleased me far more to look at the kumquats, lemons, and Calamondins than to eat them.

I had rearranged the plants, distributing them around the conservatory. In the center of the room, several varieties of *Anthurium* with waxy peach and red spathes, neon-orange *Gloxinia,* and goldfish *Nematanthus* brightened the busy, green backdrop of my foliage plant collection. I was moderately successful with varieties of begonias like 'Cracklin' Rosie','Curly Fireflush', and 'Christmas Candy', which cheered me with their swirls of pink and chocolate and pinwheels of silver and purple. I had discovered *Streptocarpus,* small members of the African violet family, that produce their velvety flowers quite prolifically even in low light. The tall bird-of-paradise and *Ravenala madagascariensis* (traveler's palms) at the northern windows obscured my view of the brown grass and bare branches in the backyard.

The purpose of the wintergarden, M. Neumann, foreman of the hothouses at the French Jardins des Plantes, wrote in 1852, was "to imitate the rich disorder of a virgin forest by artistically concealing all obvious traces of artifice, and if possible hiding all material evidence that one is walking under a glass roof." Neumann would have approved of my work to date: the few vertical surfaces in my conservatory that weren't either glass doors or windows were greening over. In the fall, I had ordered six *Ficus pumilla,* the vine that so thickly covered the rafters at Logee's, and planted them in a long, narrow planter at the base of the four-foot-wide wall that separated the conservatory from the living room. Already, tendrils had climbed up six feet and were poised to transit the wall clock. (I'd had to redirect a few errant vines that headed into the living room.) There were two slices of wall between the three windows on the north side of the room: *Hedera helix* 'Buttercup', a sprightly yellow-and-green English ivy, was headed up one, and I'd hung a plaque of staghorn fern mounted on moss on the other. Even the counter I used for potting was disappearing. The vines of two *Pothos,* a species whose heart-shaped leaves looked etched in aluminum paint, spilled down over the cabinet doors below. I couldn't, as M. Neumann suggested, create a brook cascading through rocks, but I did figure out how to adjust the pool's filtration system so that it made an occasional quiet chuckle.

Still, something was missing. The space needed movement, activity. Birds maybe, like those that nested in the Loddiges camellias or that still sweep in flocks through Laeken. Maybe some zebra finches, tiny black-and-white birds with red beaks and clownish circles of orange on their cheeks, would be fun. But they'd have to be caged, and that would be a depressing sight. I wondered how a school of goldfish would do in the pool. (The pool water, filtered by a copper/silver cartridge, is no more chlorinated than tap water.) But although swimming with fish had some attraction, swimming with fish poop had none.

M. Neumann also believed that a wintergarden without some faunal life would fall short of the ideal. He proposed a solution: "One may well exclaim in sceptical admiration," he wrote, "but we are not afraid of expressing the opinion that the introduction of these brilliant lepidoptera, though difficult, is not impossible." At the time, although aquariums were the rage in English middle-class homes, no one had thought to create an indoor habitat for butterflies. But was there any reason not to?

Introducing butterflies into a conservatory was not only not impossible, Connie Hodsdon assured me over the phone, it wasn't even difficult. I figured Connie would know: she'd been in the business of breeding butterflies at her Bradenton, Florida, farm, Flutterby Gardens, since 2000. She urged me to visit right away. January was a slow month, but she would have monarchs and maybe some Gulf fritillaries ready to go. I could take them back on the plane with me, which would be better than risking UPS in the middle of winter. She brushed off my worries: she shipped thousands of butterflies a year, one each to a small envelope, and yes, they could go through airport x-ray machines, no problem.

Two weeks later I was in suburban Bradenton, standing in Connie's sunny backyard. Connie turned out to be a small, quick-moving person, with a cap of auburn hair and large brown eyes. In her black pants and a lime green shirt, she looked like a garden pixie, albeit one who sounded like Joan Rivers. She and her three dogs, including two of the fattest border collies I'd ever seen, took me on a tour.

We stood for a while on the concrete back patio in the shade of a towering avocado tree, getting acquainted. A couple dozen avocados had fallen to the ground. I picked one up: it was almost perfectly round and as large and heavy as a cannonball. Connie smacked one on the ground, breaking it open and offering it to the dogs.

"They're crazy about avocados," she said, "but the tree is something of a hazard. One of these bruisers fell the other day, hit me on my right shoulder, and about took my arm off. But I could never take it down, it's such a gorgeous tree." I looked up and was glad to see I was not in the direct line of fire.

Connie's livestock consists of fourteen species of butterfly, including monarchs, julias, Gulf fritillaries, white peacocks, zebra longwings, painted ladies, and eight varieties of swallowtail. Her customers, and the customers of the other hundred-plus breeders in the Butterfly Breeders Association, are mostly brides. There is a new tradition (a quintessentially American oxymoron) at weddings: instead of tossing rice at the newly married couple after the ceremony, the guests release butterflies. I hadn't heard of butterfly releases, but the idea struck me as a lovely one, and certainly a more inspiring gesture than wasting food. Flutterby Gardens ships about five hundred butterflies a week in the peak of the summer wedding season.

Connie led me through the backyard. The garden beds were nearly bare, with just a few patches of grass and a smattering of what looked like weeds. In fact, they *were* weeds, varieties of milkweed, which are the only plants monarch caterpillars will eat. Connie also pointed out a few short twists of vine hugging the ground. These were corky-stem passion vine (*Passiflora*), or rather the remnants remaining after a December frost. The passion vine was a twofer: Gulf fritillary caterpillars dined on its leaves and after they pupated, the butterflies drank its nectar. In the spring, the passion vine would start growing back; by summer, its vines and spiky sunbursts of purple flowers would carpet the backyard. Near the driveway, a pipevine (*Aristolochia*) had nearly taken over a thirty-foot mango tree. Its blanket of oval leaves was studded with pipe-shaped flowers that looked as though they'd been crafted out of calico-patterned cloth. The flowers were the size of my hand. The leaves and nectar of the pipevine are favored by pipevine and polydamus swallowtails. Here and there in the garden were *Penta,* shrubby plants with brilliant blossom heads composed of dozens of tiny orange and red flowers. *Penta* are the dark chocolate of the butterfly world: it's hard to find a butterfly that doesn't like *Penta* nectar.

In the middle of the backyard were four butterfly vivariums, each consisting of a wooden frame covered on the four sides and top in closely woven netting. We headed for the largest one. After pushing through the first and then a second flap of netting, I took one step inside—and then stood very still. All around me butterflies wobbled through the air: some small tangerine-colored ones and large black swallowtails, but mostly magnificent monarchs with their dramatic black-veined, orange wings. They flittered past my nose, blundered into and rebounded from the netting, lighted for a moment on potted plants, and generally set the air all aquiver. I wasn't sure where to look, there was so much motion, but decided the ground was a good place to start: I didn't want to step on a butterfly. In fact, there was a tangerine one—a Gulf fritillary, according to Connie—resting on the crushed-shell floor just in front of my feet, opening and closing its wings lazily, completely oblivious to impending disaster.

Then I noticed that there were bright red, upside-down toilet plungers planted all around. The business ends of the plungers were at eye level. I wondered if this was the latest in garden sculpture, an avant-garde version of silvery gazing balls or those brass sculptures that doubled as sprinklers, and, tentatively, I asked.

Connie gave a throaty chuckle and explained that these were her homemade butterfly feeders.

"There just isn't enough nectar in the flowers to feed all the butterflies I've got in here, so I have to give them an artificial nectar. I make it myself. It's a sugar solution mixed with a bit of soy sauce. I know that sounds weird," she added, "but it's for the minerals."

A feeder, she explained, was made of a plastic soda bottle spray-painted bright red that she then cut off just below its shoulder to form a dish. She stuck the neck of the dish onto a length of polyethylene pipe (from the plumbing department of Home Depot), glued the plastic lid of a coffee can into the dish, and put a round sponge, saturated with her artificial nectar mix, on top of the lid.

"Of course, butterflies aren't born knowing that my contraptions have nectar in them, so I have to train them." She turned to a monarch resting on the netting, gently pinched its wings closed, and picked it up. Then, she dipped a pink lacquered fingernail from her other hand into the sponge and held it up to the butterfly's head.

"There aren't too many gardeners that bother having long fingernails, but this is why I do." The monarch uncoiled a threadlike black tongue and dipped it into the proffered underside of her nail. "Then," she whispered (we both instinctively whispered, although I later learned that butterflies can't hear), "I take it over here." She carried the butterfly, still pinched between the fingers of one hand and drinking from her nail, over to a feeder and lowered it to the sponge. "Then I put its little feet on the sponge, like this— they taste through their feet, too—and lead its tongue down to the nectar," she said, and opened her fingers. The monarch continued to drink, opening and closing its wings slowly and peacefully, reminding me of a baby at the breast, sucking rhythmically, eyes closed in contentment.

We hung out in the vivarium for a time while I oohed and aahed over the butterflies. I learned that although their lives are sweet, they're short: usually two to four weeks, depending on the species, the season, and the climate. Monarchs— and monarchs were certainly the species that most appealed to me—that emerge in the spring or summer might survive as long as five weeks. Only those born in the autumn migrate; autumn monarchs live eight or nine months, long enough to journey to their southern habitats and lay eggs.

In the wild, only about two monarch eggs out of a clutch of dozens laid on the underside of a milkweed leaf will survive to adulthood. Because the caterpillars eat only milkweed, which is poisonous, the caterpillars and butterflies also become poisonous, and birds generally avoid them. Disease, however, takes a toll, especially a parasite known as OE (*Ophryocystis elektroscirrha*). Connie battles constantly to keep OE out of her flocks. She tests any butterfly she acquires by pressing a piece of Scotch tape against its abdomen and examining the tape under the microscope for spores. Butterflies with spores are destroyed. She and her part-time assistant frequently clean all the butterfly cages with a mild bleach solution. She rinses the milkweed leaves with bleach and dips the eggs, as well as newly formed chrysalises. A high concentration of OE will kill a young caterpillar. If the concentration is lower, the caterpillar may go on to pupate, but the butterfly that emerges will be weak or deformed. If it lives, it will pass along OE through its eggs and by spreading spores on leaves. In a population like the one at Flutterby, the pathogen can exterminate all the livestock within a couple of generations. Since monarchs go from egg to butterfly in one month, OE could put Connie out of business very quickly.

The spread of disease, or the potential for spread of disease, is just one reason some wildlife organizations oppose butterfly releases. Farm-raised butterflies, the National Wildlife Federation fears, might introduce nonnative species into new areas, with unknown impacts, or introduce a local disease to a wider population. Even if the species is native to the release area, the farmed population might introduce slightly different genes into the existing population. Could captive monarchs raised in Florida, for example, lack the instinct for migrating to Mexico and, interbreeding, pass on their ignorance?

The Washington (State) Department of Fish and Wildlife also frets about the growing numbers of released butterflies. Not only is it concerned about the thousands of butterflies that newlyweds introduce every year but also about the thousands released by schoolchildren doing science projects. "Releasing non-native animals of any kind teaches a poor lesson," according to Ann Potter, a WDFW wildlife biologist, "because their effect on the local environment is unpredictable and potentially devastating." Nonlocal butterflies have the potential to swamp the natives.

The situation sounded worrisome, and I was prepared to think that wedding butterfly releases were less than charming, until I read the literature from the other side. OE, it turns out, is pandemic in the wild, and captive monarchs are significantly less likely to carry it since breeders have a huge interest in eliminating it from their livestock. In fact, wild monarchs carry a host of non-OE infestations, including parasitic fly and wasp larvae not found in captive flocks. There is no evidence that released monarchs get lost, according to Monarch Watch at the University of Kansas and other organizations that track tagged butterflies to their overwintering site in central Mexico. Moreover, the monarch's range has been expanding naturally over the last few hundred years. Monarchs, originally native to North America, have established themselves as far away as the Azores and Canary Islands to the east and Indonesia, Australia, and New Zealand to the west. Even if as many as 50,000 farm-raised monarchs were to be released each year, the number is insignificant in relation to the 355 million wild monarchs already fluttering about the world.

Besides, Connie pointed out, the butterfly-breeding business is well regulated by the U.S. Department of Agriculture. Only nine butterfly species can be bred and sold across state lines, and sales are limited to states where the population and its traditional plant foods are native. So she could ship monarchs, Gulf fritillaries, and painted ladies to me in Maryland, but not her swallowtails or zebra long-wings. The fines for shipping unauthorized butterflies are substantial, and the USDA can revoke a breeder's license for a violation. The sale of a few illegal butterflies, Connie said emphatically, would never be worth the risk of the penalties.

Our next stop was the "lab." This was where Connie takes the eggs that butterflies had deposited on leaves in the vivarium and grows them into caterpillars, through four or five molts (called *instars*), until they form chrysalises. The lab was in a narrow building that seemed to be a pint-size trailer home. Along one wall was a long work counter and a small shipping area with cardboard boxes and Styrofoam; on the opposite wall were steel-wire racks. On the racks sat identical clear plastic boxes, each roughly the size of a file box and covered with a perforated plastic top. That day, Connie was raising only monarchs in the lab and, because January is a slow month for weddings, there were only fourteen boxes on the racks.

"It's a little cooler in here than usual," she said after taking up the first box on the lowest rack and opening it on the counter. "The ideal temperature for raising caterpillars is about eighty degrees, but I'm not interested right now in hurrying these guys along because I don't have many orders. A little lower temperature will slow down the whole process, which is fine by me."

She took the lid off the box. On the bottom of the box was a white plastic honeycomb, the kind you see covering overhead fluorescent light fixtures in offices. On top of the honeycomb, standing in a holder, was a test tube that was serving as a vase for a small bouquet of milkweed leaves.

Connie carefully separated the leaves.

"Can you see that?" she asked, touching her fingernail to a leaf.

She handed me a magnifying glass and I bent over and studied the leaf. Yes, I said, I could see something. It looked like a grain of rice.

"It's the newest little caterpillar born in captivity," she said proudly, "or at least one of them."

I saw other grains of rice. Altogether, there were about two dozen.

"And see over here?" She pointed to a triangle of leaf stuck into the heart of the bouquet. "That's the tip of the leaf the eggs were laid on. I just cut it off the plant and stuck it down here. This way, when the babies hatch, they can crawl right out onto some food. You can see there are a few eggs left to go." She closed up the box and put it back on the rack.

"Now, caterpillars shouldn't be on a diet of plant leaves in water very long because if they are, they're going to get diarrhea. And as soon as you get diarrhea, you get disease. And as soon as you get disease, you get dead. So, when all the eggs have hatched and the caterpillars are about a quarter-inch long, I clip off the pieces of leaf that they're on and transfer them."

She pulled out the next box on the rack and we looked in. Milkweed leaves lay directly on the grid. "This is where the caterpillars stay over the next two weeks or so. I just keep adding food and they keep getting bigger and bigger."

Every time Connie prepares a box with caterpillar eggs, she adds it to the left side of the bottom rack. The boxes move across and up the racks in a big S as the caterpillars inside grow. By the time a box reaches the right-hand side of the top rack, the caterpillars are grown, and in the last box they pupate.

Connie brought down the last box on the top rack and took off its green lid. I peered in reluctantly: insects with six legs are bad enough, arachnids with eight make me queasy, but show me a myriapod, which has eighteen or more, and I'm out the door. I didn't know exactly how many legs a caterpillar had, but I wasn't eager to get close enough to count.

I shouldn't have worried. The dozen caterpillars inside were—there's no other word for it—goofy looking. Each was about the size of my pinky. They were wearing white, puffy, down coats on which it appeared that some preschooler, with a clumsy hand and two blunt crayons, one black and one bright yellow, had drawn awkward stripes. Some of their stumpy black legs—there were eight pairs—were jauntily shod in white spats. They weren't creepy at all. They were cartoonish.

Connie lifted the green lid up above eye level so we could look under it. There were a half-dozen caterpillars dangling by their rear ends from the underside of the lid. She pointed to one that was partly doubled back on itself, as if it had a stomach cramp.

"You can see this guy is getting ready to pupate. He's attached his cremaster—those are the hooks on the end of his abdomen—to the lid, and he's put a little pad of silk there to attach his chrysalis. I know he's going to pupate soon because he's doing what we call J-ing." She urged me to take a closer look.

"Oh, are you in luck!" she crowed with such enthusiasm I thought maybe a lottery ticket was involved. "Just look at his antennae! See how they're all in a spiral?" The antennae, which normally are straight and fairly rigid, were drooping straight down from the caterpillar's head like two pieces of corkscrewed party ribbons. "That means he's just on the verge. Inside his skin he's pretty much all mush, which makes what he's going to do next all the more unbelievable."

As we watched, with our faces close to the lid, the J-shaped creature started to swing vigorously back and forth.

"How a sack of chemicals can move like that, I don't know," she murmured.

After a few minutes, he slowed and then stopped. I looked over to Connie to ask her a question, but she warned, "Don't take your eyes off him. This next part happens very fast."

Suddenly, the caterpillar's striped skin began to unzip, starting at the creature's upside-down front end and proceeding neatly up its back. Underneath, I could see there was another skin, a bright green one. In the next thirty seconds, the skin fully unzipped, gathered at the top, and shriveled to almost nothing. Gone was the cartoon caterpillar, vanished by the sleight of some unknown hand. In its place was a shiny, emerald pendant, a monarch chrysalis.

"Wow," I breathed. I had assumed that caterpillars created chrysalises around the outside of their bodies.

"I know," Connie replied, placing the lid back on the box. "I worked with them for months before I ever caught that moment, and no matter how often I see it, I'm amazed. But then, it's miracles every day in the butterfly business."

When all the caterpillars in the box had pupated, Connie would pick them off the lid, rinse them in a bleach solution, and take them inside. To see the next step, we walked across her backyard, through the kitchen, and into the small office where she does her bookkeeping and keeps the chrysalises during the ten or eleven days it takes for mush to construct itself into a butterfly.

Here, on a desk top, were more plastic boxes. One was labeled "Hatchery" and had a piece of cardboard as a lid. Connie took off the lid and tilted its underside toward me. A monarch was beating its wings rapidly while clinging to the empty, transparent chrysalis from which it had obviously just emerged. The lid, to which about thirty unhatched chrysalises were attached, looked like a jeweler's tray of polished nuggets of semiprecious stones. Each nugget was a different hue, all the subtle shades that jade, malachite, turquoise, and lapis lazuli could take. Each was encircled with tiny dots of what was surely pure gold. All I needed was a gold chain, and I could have worn any one of them.

"When I glue them on the cardboard," Connie said, "they're all that soft jade color and then they gradually shift toward blue. At the end, the chrysalis is nearly purple and almost clear, and I know the butterfly is about to come out." She touched her nail to an amethyst chrysalis. Inside I could see a bundle of orange-and-black wings.

The tour was over, and we wandered back to her kitchen, talking. I told Connie I had changed my mind, that I no longer wanted to buy butterflies. I wanted to buy caterpillars, monarch caterpillars, instead. M. Neumann was right about the brilliant lepidoptera, but he hadn't known the half of it. I wanted butterflies to do more than make a guest appearance in my tropics; I wanted them to colonize it.

Before I could have caterpillars, though, I had to have caterpillar food. While monarch butterflies will drink an artificial nectar, there is no fooling monarch caterpillars with substitute leaves. I would have to grow my own milkweed. Connie was sure I would be able to grow the plants from seed, but I had never planted seeds of any sort and had my doubts. Nonetheless, she zipped out to the garden, returning with a handful of seedpods, the long, thin seedpods of a milkweed. The pods were dry and split, and white feathery stuff poked out of the open edges. She opened one pod farther, and I could see that a tiny cocoa-colored seed clung to the end of each feather. She dropped the pods into a baggie, and we said our good-byes. By summer, she would expect to hear from me with an order for caterpillars.

I bought a seed-starting tray with seventy-two cells. Per Connie's instructions, I filled the cells with potting soil, wet the soil, dropped on several seeds, and then put the lightest covering of soil on top and gave it a good misting. I kept the trays under fluorescent lights and was careful to keep the soil moist. About a week later, to my great satisfaction, delicate green sprouts with two miniature leaves, some of them still wearing their seed coverings like little brown caps, pushed their heads above the surface. After three weeks, I decided my sprouts, which were about four inches tall, could rightfully be called seedlings. I patted myself on the back and wondered if I could join the 4-H.

Which was when trouble set in. My seedlings stopped growing. I called Connie. How many leaves did the seedlings have? she asked. Were there little roots poking out the holes at the bottom of the cells? I hadn't counted and hadn't looked. Six or eight, I reported, and indeed white threads of roots had found their way through the holes. Take the seedlings out of the cells, she directed, and plant three or four of them to a six-inch pot. The seedlings might be competing for light and nutrition and just need more growing room.

I bought ten small pots and transplanted my seedlings. I would like to report that all went swimmingly after that. After all, these were not delicate orchids but common weeds. But as a matter of fact, my milkweeds failed to thrive. They grew tall but ridiculously leggy, with undersized leaves clustered at the top of long, wavering stems, so that they looked like foot-high palm trees after a hurricane had passed through. By the end of April, my plants had hardly enough leaf material altogether to feed a single caterpillar, much less the substantial flock I had in mind. I tried pinching back their newest leaves to encourage branching, but they misinterpreted this gesture, taking it for a command to cease growing entirely. I was mystified. How could I fail at growing weeds, weeds that flourished without the slightest human care all across the country at neglected edges of parking lots and in roadside drainage ditches? I could understand why Leopold's Congo plants refused to grow for him, but what sins had I committed to merit such malice?

I finally gave up on my little milkweeds. In early April, I bought four *Asclepias incarnata* online. They arrived in six-inch pots, three stumps with a bit of new growth to a pot, and I put them outside in the sunniest spot in the backyard. They grew, as they say, like weeds, and by mid-May, I counted about twenty-five two- to three-inch leaves per pot. I called up Connie and ordered twenty caterpillars at $1 each plus one plastic butterfly box for $24.95.

The inch-long caterpillars arrived on a handful of milkweed leaves, which I observed were quite a bit larger than mine. After two days the caterpillars had eaten most of their leaves. With a disproportionate sense of satisfaction, I went outside and harvested a handful of my own milkweed leaves. I supposed that this was how other people felt about growing all their own vegetables, sewing their own clothes, or living "off the grid." What a marvel: I was self-sufficient in caterpillar food! I put the leaves on the plastic honeycomb on a Friday night and carefully arranged the remains of Connie's leaves, little green life rafts for caterpillars, on top.

The next morning, my caterpillars had disappeared. The new leaves were still there, but not one, as far as I could see, had even been nibbled. I took off the lid and rifled the leaves—maybe they were underneath?—but no one was there. Then I looked at the underside of the lid. There they were, all twenty of them. They clearly wanted out, out where they could find a decent meal.

I was dismayed. My leaves were inadequate. I had failed my first test of stewardship. Next thing I knew, my caterpillars would be lying on their backs, weakly waving their multitudinous white shoes as they starved to death before my eyes.

I looked more closely at the bits of Connie's milkweed

leaves that were left. Hers were definitely a lighter color than mine and fuzzier. I now recalled that Connie had spoken of feeding her caterpillars "giant milkweed." I googled the phrase and discovered that giant milkweed is not just well-grown milkweed, and not even a different variety or species of *Asclepias,* but a plant of an entirely different genus altogether. Giant milkweed (*Calotropis gigantea*) must be the filet mignon of milkweed. Clearly, what I had to offer was a stale bologna sandwich.

I called Connie, but it was the Memorial Day weekend and she didn't answer. I didn't know how long caterpillars could survive without food, but I imagined it wasn't long. I called Edie to see if Johnson's sold *Calotropis.* No, she laughed, it wasn't something people want in their gardens—it was a weed that grew to an unattractive shrub about ten feet high. But she thought maybe I could find some growing wild in Rock Creek Park. I should look in areas that got full sun.

I got in my car, armed with a plastic bag, clippers, and a photo of *Calotropis* from the Web. Not far from our house is a branch of the park, and I pulled off at the side of Military Road. Rock Creek Park is generally forested, but at this point, there was a large field of knee-high grasses and weeds. I started walking along the edge and, damn, if right there wasn't what looked like a giant milkweed. It was only about a foot high and had only eight leaves. I compared it to my photo: yes, this was definitely a fledgling giant milkweed.

I looked around to see who might be watching me. This was a federal park after all, and I was about to abscond with a piece of the national patrimony. A family of picnickers was spreading out a blanket nearby, but they weren't paying any attention to me. Ten feet away, though, I saw a waist-high sign, and I went, nonchalantly, to check it out. RESTORING NATURAL MEADOW: NO MOWING! it read.

Uh-oh. Where did clipping stand in relation to mowing? Surely to any individual plant, it was more or less the same. If the park police arrested me, would Ted, a member of the Nature Conservancy and a board member of the Earth Conservation Corps, bail me out? I imagined a stern-faced judge looking down at me from the bench and asking sarcastically, "And what, Ms. Kassinger, would happen if everyone 'just picked a few leaves'?" What were the penalties for destroying government property?

On the other hand, there were my starving caterpillars. My duty was clear; it was a matter of life or death. I clipped three leaves, which bled drops of a bright white milk from their amputated stems, and hightailed it for home.

With the handle end of a spoon, I coaxed each caterpillar onto a piece of the new milkweed and arranged my charges again on the bottom of the box. Nothing happened: maybe it was too late and they were too debilitated to eat. I couldn't watch and turned to other chores, leaving them to their fate. When I looked again a few hours later, the caterpillars were steadily munching. Maybe Maryland *Calotropis* wasn't quite up to Florida standards, but they had decided to make do.

Three leaves for twenty, skinny inch-long caterpillars lasted twenty-four hours. I made an early morning foray on Sunday. Afraid to clip more leaves from the first plant for fear of killing it, I broadened my search, heading deeper into the meadow. I didn't know how long clipped milkweed leaves would seem appetizing to caterpillars—experience suggested they were rather picky—so I cut only as many as I thought they would eat in a day. Of course, every day my charges got noticeably bigger and ate more. By the end of the week, I was clipping ten leaves and was eager for my now puffy brood to pupate.

Then one morning, about ten days after their arrival, I found them all under the lid, hanging in J-shapes. The next day, the clowns were gone and twenty jade green chrysalises hung in their place.

Most of the butterflies emerged on the ninth day, the remainder on the tenth. They hung from their transparent, empty chrysalises looking like bits of damp black-and-orange crepe paper. One fell to the grid and struggled, frantically and hopelessly, to return to its perch. I put my finger out to it and it clung with feet that felt like the scratchy side of Velcro. The crawling didn't bother me, I think because monarchs only have four working legs (two are tiny and tucked out of sight), so this fellow looked and felt more like a pet than an insect. I put it back on its chrysalis.

After the butterflies dried for a day in the box, I tried to feed them as Connie had. I had brewed up butterfly nectar according to her directions, soaked the sponges in nectar, and put the sponges into red plastic dishes that I'd cut down to shallow trays. I picked one creature out of the box by its closed wings—it was like pinching two pieces of slippery silk together—and held its feet on the sponge. Because my fingernails are very short, I couldn't manage Connie's trick of scooping nectar to its mouth, so I put a drop of nectar on a butter knife and held it to where I thought its mouth was. No tongue emerged. I tried a few of its buddies. Nothing doing.

My problem was there were now a lot of very active butterflies in what was suddenly quite a small box. They were battering one another in their efforts to crawl or fly free, and I was afraid they would damage one another. So I distributed my little butterfly feeders around the conservatory, opened the lid, and let them go, hoping when they got hungry they'd figure out where the food was.

They were a glorious sight, fluttering in and out of the tall shafts of sunlight that fall from the skylights. The orange in their wings glowed like embers against the black grate of their veins. They explored the up and down of the conservatory and the west and north windows. They rested momentarily on green plants. Several settled for a while on the orange and red spathes of the anthuriums, but moved on when they found no nectar.

They paid no attention to the red nectar dishes.

Instead, they gradually migrated up to the skylights and tried to fly through the glass into the beckoning blue. *Rat-a-tat-tat, rat-a-tat-tat* went their wings against the glass. The sound was an awful reproach. I reminded myself that these were insects. I wouldn't fret over twenty houseflies, would I? No, I'd be hunting them down with a flyswatter. These were simply houseflies wearing fancy ball gowns, I told myself. I was not convinced.

In the midst of this crisis, Evan, a young friend of ours and a recent Yale graduate, came over. He had had a part-time job at Yale's Peabody Museum, cataloging the museum's preserved butterfly collection. Evan urged me to call Dr. Lawrence Gall, a renowned lepidopterist, who had supervised his work at the museum. Feeling as though I was calling Steven

Hawking and asking him for the time of the next high tide, I telephoned Dr. Gall and explained my butterflies' situation. First, were they going to batter themselves to death up at the skylights? And how could I get them to eat?

Of all the butterfly species I could have picked for a conservatory, Dr. Gall told me, monarchs were the best. Although not all monarchs migrate, those that do need wings sturdy enough to survive a trip that can be thousands of miles long. So, as far as butterfly wings go, monarchs' were among the most rugged. Moreover, a monarch's body and wings taste of the milkweed poison sequestered there, which means that if a bird tries to eat one, it will usually release its victim without killing it. Because the monarchs' wings are so (relatively) large and durable, they are quite able to fly with beak-size sections missing from their wings.

As for the feeding question, newly emerged monarchs need at least a day before they are hungry, so they might not have been ready to eat when I tried to feed them with a butter knife. "You're going to have to force-feed them now," Dr. Gall said. "Soak a square of paper with nectar. Pick a butterfly up by its wings and park it on the paper. Then take a straight pin, uncurl its proboscis, and hold it down on the paper." The thought of taking a sharp pin anywhere near a butterfly's filamentary tongue made me uneasy. I have terrible fine motor skills; I don't even try to use mascara.

I waited until late afternoon as the butterflies began to settle down before I hunted down my flock, picking them off the tall plants and the grow lights. After I caught one, I sat down and rested my elbows on the wirework table, and with a pin in one hand and a butterfly in the other, managed to find and uncurl its tiny watch spring tongue and hold it on a nectar-soaked paper. Then I set it on its feet on the sponge in a nectar dish I had on the table.

The lesson seemed to take. My butterflies congregated on the sponge, a quivering cluster of black-and-orange beauties. Then, one by one, they flew off to find shelter for the night. The final test, though, would come the next day.

In the morning, I found that once again, they had made their way up to the skylights. *Rat-a-tat-tat,* they beat their wings, but I took it in stride. Later in the morning, they fluttered down again and, in that lackadaisical, haphazard way that butterflies have, found the nectar dishes. I regaled Alice with the story of my success and called Ted to report proudly that my brood was fully fledged.

For three weeks, the monarchs flitted about the conservatory. At breakfast once, we found one walking on the edge of an open jar of raspberry jam. Scotia, who adores chasing the big, lazy carpenter bees outside, left the butterflies alone. It seems that all of us agreed, there is nothing in the world like butterflies to lift your spirits, nothing at all.

Perfect Plants

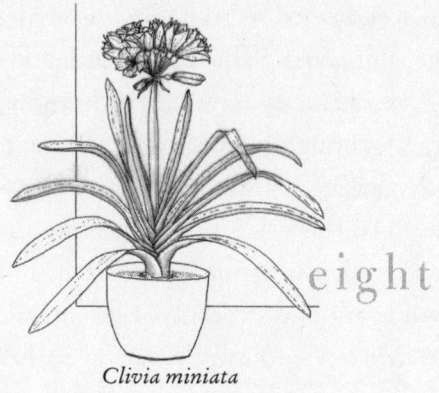

eight

Clivia miniata

I was in the throes of a bad case of the brown-thumb blues. Not only had I failed at growing *Asclepias* for my butterflies, my flowering hanging baskets in the bay window that had grown well through the spring were now, in the heat of summer, dropping their flowers by the dozens and spilling a confetti of petals into the pool. I couldn't seem to keep up with watering, and minor lapses proved deadly. A Chinese fan palm and several *Nepenthes* with their strange, pipe-shaped, insect-trapping flowers, both species that needed careful watering, were on their last legs. I felt particularly incompetent since I was failing at the height of the growing season.

Clivias were the perfect antidote. Clivias, take it from someone who couldn't grow weeds, are completely foolproof. Native to the shaded floors of South African forests, a clivia needs minimal sunlight, tolerates a wide range of temperatures, doesn't demand humidity, rarely needs repotting, and is divinely forgiving of inconstant watering. As a mark of its accommodating personality, you can pronounce its name *KLY-vee-uh* or *KLIH-vee-uh*, as you please.

Mature clivias in the wild are about three feet tall. Cousins of the amaryllis, they have similar long, strappy, deep green leaves that emerge in pairs from a central base. The leaves arc gracefully outward into two balanced stacks, like a fountain captured midcascade. Each flower is formed of six colored tepals. (Sepals protect the flower bud and can open to look like petals. When the sepals are indistinguishable from the petals, as they are in clivias, the petals and sepals are collectively called tepals.) The tepals of the most popular species, *Clivia miniata,* are trumpet-shaped and in the wild are almost always shades of brilliant red and orange. Modern breeders have developed a range of new flower colors, including soft yellows, creamy peaches, near whites, and, most recently, flowers that display a combination of those colors. The tepals of the other five species—*nobilis, gardenii, caudescens, mirabilis,* and *robusta*—have the same range of colors, but they are closely overlapping and pendant, so the flowers look like long skirts. The skirts have a slightly upturned hem of a contrasting color, a green hem, say, on a peach skirt. I like the pendant species best, but the *miniata* are by far the most popular. In all the clivia species, the flowers persist, unfading, for weeks. After a bloom finally falls, the ovary at its base—roughly the size of a raspberry, although it can be much larger—ripens and turns rich and variegated shades of maroon, red, green, and orange, an unexpected encore.

If you grow a clivia from seed, it will take four or five

years before it flowers. It takes that long for the plant to develop the fourteen leaves that can produce enough energy to put out blooms. When a clivia is mature enough to flower, it sends up a stalk, a *peduncle* (peh-DUN-kull) as thick as my thumb. From the top of the peduncle spring anywhere from ten to thirty short *pedicels* (PEH-dih-sells), which are delicate stalks of equal length—each of which gives rise to one flower. The flowers cluster together to form a floral sphere called an *umbel* (UM-bul).

I liked wrapping my tongue around these new words. Peduncle, pedicel, umbel. *Peduncle* is such a solid word, thanks to that internal "thunk," as solid as the stalk itself. (It takes a good-size bird to carry away the clivia's berries. The peduncle, not only sturdy but also ridged, is a perfect grab bar for birds' long toes.) A pedicel, as it sounds, is a more delicate construction. Both provide a *ped,* a botanical footing: the pedicel for a single flower, the peduncle for the entire umbel. *Umbel* is derived from the Latin *umbella,* which is in turn derived from *umbra,* meaning shade. Whoever coined *umbel* should have picked *umbella.* There's nothing 'umble about an umbel.

I was struck by how late the words for a flower's small parts came into English; they were all added to the language in the seventeenth century and later. The words for larger parts are Anglo-Saxon in origin and are older. *Blossom* was spoken before the year 900. The French *fleur* segued into *flower* soon after the Norman conquest. But *umbel* didn't appear until 1600, and *pedicel* was invented in 1670. *Petal,* remarkably, was not used until John Ray, the English botanist, came up with the term in 1700. *Peduncle* was coined in

1745, *sepal* in 1790, and the Swiss botanist Augustin-Pierre de Candolle invented *tepal* in 1827.

How could we have done without a word for petals until 1700? I suppose that before then, no one had a need to look closely into plants and identify their small components. While the names for small parts of a horse's foot originated before the Norman invasion, as reflected by Anglo-Saxon-derived words like *fetlock, hock, frush,* and *pastern,* plants were merely made of *roots* and *stems, leaves* and *blooms.* If something went wrong with the foot of the horse that pulled your plow, you needed to describe exactly where the problem was. But plant parts were interesting mainly when they were sown or eaten or used to treat an illness. Words like *husk* and *seed, graft* and *shoot, herb* and *stem* are Anglo-Saxon. Since no one ate a *calyx,* the collective name for sepals when they are closed around a bud, or used it to cure a cold, the word wasn't invented until about 1670, after plants had become of scientific interest.

The genus *Clivia* was named for Lady Charlotte Florentia Clive, the Duchess of Northumberland, although William Burchell, an English schoolteacher and amateur botanist living in South Africa, was the first European to collect it. In 1807, Burchell was a handsome, sleepy-eyed man—his engraving reminds me of Robert Mitchum—when he sent for his fiancée to marry him in Capetown. On the trip over, however, the young woman fell in love with the ship's captain and broke off her engagement when she arrived in port. In order to distract himself from his disappointment, Burchell set out on a journey of zoological and botanical exploration far into the interior of the continent, traveling in ox-drawn, covered wagons and accompanied by six native guides. When he returned to England after four years in the field, he had learned how to scramble an ostrich egg in its shell and gathered thousands of zoological specimens, over 40,000 dried botanical specimens, 2,000 seeds, and 276 bulbs.

Burchell spent the next decade talking with botanists about his finds and writing up his discoveries. One of the experts he consulted was Dean William Herbert, a well-born, Oxford-educated minister, former Member of Parliament, and respected botanist. Herbert recognized that one of the dried plants, a bloomless, strap-leaved one that Burchell had found near Grahamstown, might represent a genus never described before. He coaxed from Burchell the location where he had discovered the plant and convinced an army officer he knew in South Africa to bring home a live specimen. Herbert nurtured the plant in his conservatory, expecting it would flower. As the first expert to fully identify it, he would therefore have the right to name it.

Herbert was confident of his ability to bring Burchell's plant into bloom. The specimen appeared to him to be a member of the botanical family Amaryllidaceae, about which he was already an acknowledged authority and would later write a definitive book. This must explain why he felt safe in passing information about the unnamed plant to a dealer in exotics: he expected to have flowered the plant before any other specimens arrived in England. Unfortunately for Herbert, he put his plant in his tropical conservatory, which was kept warm all year. But clivias need at least six weeks of cool temperatures, as they experience on the South African plateaus, in order to generate their buds, and his specimen failed to bloom.

The dealer, meanwhile, had promptly collected a number of the plants and sold several to the Duke of Northumberland. The duke's gardener, a Mr. Forrest, placed them in the duke's new conservatory at Syon Park, which he kept cool in the winter. Forrest believed that the plant would prove to be a variety of *Agapanthus*, a South African plant with similar leaves but blue, lily-shaped flowers. So, when the flowers appeared in the Syon Park conservatory in October 1827—drooping, tubular, and bright orange with green hems—there were a number of surprised people.

Forrest sent a description and a painting of the plant to John Lindley, publisher of the *Botanical Register* and one of England's leading horticulturalists. Lindley named the plant *Clivia nobilis*, writing that the name was "a compliment long due the noble family of Clive," the family of the duke's wife. (There were ten illustrated botanical journals published in England in the 1820s, reflecting English fascination with exotic plants, and competition among the journals was cutthroat. The opportunity to flatter the highly influential duke was not to be passed up.) But on the same day, William Hooker, publisher of *Curtis's Botanical Magazine*, printed a nearly identical article and illustration of a plant, seemingly based on the painting of the one at Syon Park, and named the genus *Imantophyllum*. As a result, for several decades both names were used. *Clivia* ultimately won out, although if horticultural justice had been served, Burchell would have been immortalized in the plant's name.

(Poor Burchell never had any luck. He donated most of his botanical and zoological specimens to the British Museum, Natural History in London, but many were damaged in storage, which led to a quarrel with the keeper of the collection, John Edward Gray. One of the specimens that Burchell brought back was a zebra new to Europe, which Gray maliciously named *Asinus burchelli*. The zebra was later reclassified as *Equus burchellii*, but Burchell's bad luck still lingers. His zebra is now an endangered species.)

Clivias were well suited to the parlors of Victorian England, and they became popular houseplants. They were perfectly content to sit in a tenebrous corner, and it was all too easy before central heating to chill the plant in the winter. Over the years a single clivia would regularly send up a new offset or "pup" from its roots. Eventually, a single pot of clivias would produce dozens of umbels at a time, and some became family heirlooms, passed down from generation to generation. Alternatively, the pups could be separated, potted up, and given to friends.

Clivias, however, were never cheap, and after World War II, when the tempo of life speeded up, they more or less disappeared from European homes. From a commercial grower's perspective, clivias were not attractive. They used up greenhouse space for five years before they put up their first flower spike and were ready to sell. Besides, with the advent of central heating, they no longer flowered reliably indoors.

Although English nurseries largely abandoned clivias after the war, hobbyists in South Africa, Belgium, Japan, and China continued to grow and breed them. Japanese enthusiasts had begun collecting clivias in the mid-nineteenth century and bred them to meet the requirements of their smaller homes and distinctive aesthetics. They gradually reduced the tall and rangy wild specimens into much more compact plants with leaves no longer than a hand spread. Plants that carried a genetic mutation for striped and striated leaves held particular appeal and were bred for these variegations. In Japan, a clivia collection became, like a collection of bonsai, a sign of sophistication and wealth.

I had decided that the clivia was a potential candidate for my personal holy grail—the world's easiest, most beautiful, low-light tropical plant—and decided to make a study of them. To start, I contacted Dick Storch, the vice president of the North American Clivia Society. He urged me to come see his farm, and when I was visiting Anna at college outside Los Angeles, I made a side trip.

I drove south on a warm January morning, into the hills and past groves of avocado trees, to meet Dick at Clivia Hill Nursery in Fallbrook, which is about fifty miles north of San Diego. He greeted me at the gate to his four-acre hill-side farm, which has a sweeping view west across the valley toward a set of ochre hills sporting at this, the rainy season, a patchy green stubble.

Dick is seventy-one years old, with the sturdy frame and the straightforward manner of a former marine and the cal-lused, ragged-nail, dirt-lined hands of a farmer. He pushed open the screen door of his four-hundred-foot-long green-house. Inside, the ground was covered in gravel, which lent a companionable susurration to our tour. The clivias were neatly packed pot to pot on waist-high tables made of wooden pallets and stacked cinder blocks. There was nothing fancy about Dick's operation; there was no artificial lighting, no heating equipment, and only fans for cooling (despite the fact that it could get up to 120 degrees inside in July), and Dick and his wife, Quyen, watered and fertilized the plants with a hose. Altogether, he said he had about ten thousand plants, but he added that I shouldn't be too impressed because most of his crop was seedlings several years from maturity.

Dick was new to the clivia business, although he had always been interested in growing things. He grew up in Allentown, Pennsylvania, and as a teenager worked on his uncle's apple orchard and at a nearby dairy farm. In the Marine Corps, he moved around frequently, so he often had an opportunity to start a new garden and experiment with new species.

"I came out to California with the Corps in 1962 and was amazed at the way things grow here. I'm not sure where I got my first clivias, but I planted some in Santa Ana at the marine base at El Toro and then, when we moved to Encinitas, I planted more."

After he retired from the military, he went into the software business, and in 2003 was making a good living as a consultant. "I was in China in 2000 on an assignment in Dalian, way up on the northeast coast of the country. One day I was out for a walk when I found a woman with a pushcart selling what I could see were clivia plants. She told me that when the Japanese occupied China in 1937, the officers brought their clivia collections with them and trained Chinese servants in their care. When they retreated, they had to leave their clivias behind, and her father, who owned a nursery, developed a collection from some orphaned Japanese plants. But during the Cultural Revolution, people who cultivated ornamental plants, especially nonnative ones, became suspect, and her father saw the handwriting on the wall. He told her to move from Beijing to the country and take the best of the plants with her."

Dick brought back a hundred seeds, of which ninety-seven produced plants with variegated foliage. Four years later, just when his Chinese clivias bloomed, he was diagnosed with bladder cancer.

"I had to cancel all my engagements, and the word got out 'Storch is dying.' Long story short: operation, bladder cancer cured, ready to go back to work . . . no clients. Well, after a while, Quyen told me I was spending way too much time around the house, and I was going to have to do something.

"So," he said matter-of-factly, "I ordered five thousand clivia seeds from China, at around $1 a seed, and decided to start a clivia business at home. But I had two big problems. One, growing five thousand seeds is a heck of a lot different than growing five seeds. Two, I got advice from a grower out of state about how to speed up their development and blooming. He told me to clip the radical—that's the first root that comes out of the seed—before transplanting them. What he didn't realize was that I was talking about transplanting very young seedlings. By cutting that radical, I killed about four thousand of them."

Not one to give up, Dick bought replacement seeds, bought the land that is now Clivia Hill, and put up a greenhouse. When I met him, most of his crop was still a year or two from going to market. He did have about a thousand plants, survivors of his original crop, that he was selling to local retailers. That, however, was putting him into the transportation business, which was not a business he wanted to be in. Fortunately, a broker has contracted for his immature plants—all, that is, that turn out to be variegated—which he will then sell to nurseries on the East Coast.

"I've always liked the variegated clivias best; to me, they're the most interesting." We were leaning over a long table completely filled with variegated plants in six-inch pots. When I looked closely, I could see that every leaf on a given variegated plant was different, sometimes radically different, from its brothers. Some had yellow striations that looked drawn on with a fine-point pen, some had yellow tips that gradually shaded into green at the leaf base, one was neatly pin-striped, and another had a sharp, green racing stripe down the center of a yellow leaf. A few were evenly divided, solid green on one half and completely white on the other. The variety was infinite.

"Every time there's a new leaf, there's a new pattern of variegation," Dick said. "Each leaf is different from the last one—there's always a surprise. Unfortunately, only about 40 percent of seeds from variegated plants actually produce variegated offspring, so I end up composting a lot of my seedlings. And then, some variegated plants are too variegated. The white parts of the leaf can't photosynthesize, so the plant won't thrive, and I have to toss those, too.

"Growing vigorous plants is just as important to me as growing beautiful ones. Clivias are naturally the most forgiving, undemanding plants around, but some breeders," he growled, "are so focused on flower color or leaf form, they're breeding the hardiness right out of them. But my goal is to grow reasonably priced, compact, variegated plants that will thrive in the less-than-ideal conditions of an East Coast house."

Dick expected that his plants, "in spike" and ready to bloom, would retail for $75 each. If this sounds expensive, visit the website of White Flower Farm, a high-end nursery in Litchfield, Connecticut, and do a search for clivias. A 'Victorian Peach', which has broad green leaves and flowers in a range of peach shades, sells for $475. Or, at Shield's Gardens, you can buy a mature specimen of 'Sean's Peach', whose peach tepals shade into yellow and then green where they meet at the base of the flowers, for $1,400. There are unique, mature Chinese and Japanese variegated plants that sell for as much as thirty thousand dollars each. One seed (with no guarantees on its viability) from such a plant can run as much as a thousand dollars.

Yellow clivias are exceedingly rare in the wild, and the first one didn't reach Europe until 1897. The color results from several genetic mutations that reduce the production of anthocyanins, the pigments responsible for the orange-red color of the standard flower. Because the mutations are recessive and a number of genes are involved (mutations in different genes result in different shades of yellow), the yellow color was difficult to reproduce, except by waiting for a plant to pup. That made yellow clivias unusually valuable. In the 1950s, Sir John Thouron, a Scotsman transplanted to Philadelphia, began cultivating a yellow clivia in a greenhouse at his Glencoe Farms estate in the Brandywine Valley. In 1981, he donated a flowering pup to the Delaware Center for Horticulture for sale at its first rare-plant charity auction.

Steven Frowine, director at the time of White Flower Farm, coveted the spectacular yellow clivia and set about courting Sir John. I spoke to Frowine from his home in Jalisco, Mexico.

"Sir John's yellow had won best in show for three years at the Philadelphia Flower Show, which was just unheard of, and he was very protective of it. No one knows where he first got the plant, but I understand he gave the first division of it to Queen Elizabeth—Sir John had a lot of inside royalty connections. Within his family, it was understood that no one was to give that plant out to anybody. Supposedly, the one relative who did was completely ostracized by the rest of the family.

"It took me about three years of meeting with him at his estate to get that plant. I'll never forget him, this archetype of an English aristocrat in his fabulous gardens, in his impeccable greenhouses, walking around with his King Charles spaniels and dressed to the nines. Those spaniels ruled the house. When you ate there, they were put on the dining room table and they walked back and forth, taking their choice of what they wanted from your plate.

"Now, of course, Sir John didn't need any money, so buying the clivias from him was not really an option." Frowine knew his man, though. "First, I came up with the idea of naming the cultivar after him." Second, Sir John was a genuine World War II hero, an officer with Special Operations at Bletchley and a parachutist who was dropped behind German lines many times. Inspired by British-American cooperation during the war, he and his wife, the former Esther Dupont, had established an exchange program between the University of Pennsylvania and British universities. Frowine proposed that White Flower Farm would donate a percentage of the proceeds to the University of Pennsylvania. The two offers sealed the deal.

Sir John sent ninety young 'Sir John Thouron' to Longwood Gardens, the fabulous public gardens and conservatory near Wilmington, Delaware, donated by Pierre S. du Pont, which grew them to blooming size. Longwood kept half and shipped the other half to White Flower Farms.

"We got the entire batch at one time. We put the price at $495 apiece, which we knew was pretty outlandish, but we also knew the supply was very limited and we'd never get them again. Besides, the cost per inch of space in the catalog is high and we didn't have many plants to sell to recoup that expense. Then, I sent out a press release to all the garden writers. We were lucky, and the *New York Times* picked up the story. As soon as it ran, I could see we were going to have all kinds of interest. So we increased the price to $995 and said we would only sell one to a customer and the customer had to pick it up in person."

Frowine chortled. "We had people calling us from all over the country. We had all sorts of celebrities. Someone flew in by private jet to buy one. Others sent messengers. It was a frenzy! One person bought one and then snuck in her daughter for another.

"But frankly, even though those clivias each sold for a lot of money, I would not say they were highly profitable—there just weren't enough of them. From White Flower's point of view, the whole thing was probably more valuable as a promotional effort."

The price of clivias is driven in part by their biology. Unlike orchids and many other plants, clivias cannot be mass produced in a lab. Clivia growers are limited to pollinating their plants by hand, carefully dusting the stigmas of one plant with pollen gathered from either its own or another plant's anthers. If a breeder is working with seed, it will take at least three generations of inbreeding for the plants to breed true. A clivia requires at least four years (eight years in the case of 'Sir John Thouron') to flower and produce seeds. Even then, the first flowers often do not represent a plant's true genetic potential, and the breeder has to wait until the second or third flowering cycle. Establishing a true variety takes a minimum of fifteen years, and easily longer.

Alternatively, a breeder can wait until a pup develops and carefully cut it free from the mother plant. Some plants throw off pups in a couple of years, but others never do. Breeders need to wait for the pups to grow to two-thirds the height of the parent before removing them, and an independent pup will often require another few years to flower. Because the pups are the only way to be 100 percent certain of the form and color of the plant, those are the ones that command the truly stratospheric prices.

Dick occupies an unusual middle ground in the clivia world, with a foot in the world of the hobbyist breeder and a foot in the world of the commercial grower. Commercial growers are once again producing clivias, and larger-scale production has dramatically reduced the prices of certain varieties. It is now possible to buy a beautiful clivia at a retail nursery, supermarket, or Home Depot for ten or fifteen dollars. These plants—compact, nonvariegated, and the standard orange-red—are mass produced by West Coast growers. They can be planted outdoors or kept in pots or, since the price is so low, simply enjoyed as a winter bouquet and tossed out after the blooms fall.

The mass market clivia owes its existence to Belgian nurseryman Ernest de Coster who developed them at his nursery in Ghent in the early 1950s. The Belgians had been breeding clivias from the mid-nineteenth century and had already developed lines with shorter, broader leaves more suitable for indoor cultivation. De Coster set about to shorten the blooming time, which he recognized as a primary obstacle to profitable production. Eighty percent of de Coster's "Belgian hybrid" clivias bloomed in the third year, and a remarkable 20 percent bloomed in the second year, which meant he could double his production for roughly the same input cost. Modern, mass-produced clivias all descend from de Coster's genetic stock.

Hobbyist breeders also incorporate Belgian hybrids into their breeding programs, hoping to get a faster reproduction rate while pursuing their primary interest in developing new colors and leaf and flower forms.

Michael Riska, a snowy-haired, professorial man of about sixty, is the executive director of the Delaware Nature Society and also a hobbyist breeder. Mike agreed to show me his clivia collection at his home in Hockessin, Delaware. It was early April, and although many of his 3,000-plus clivias had finished blooming, the nights were still too cold to move them outdoors under the tall trees that provide the dappled sunlight that is ideal for the genus. So, to see the clivia collection meant a tour of the Riskas' entire house, a charming, whitewashed stone building constructed in 1790, because Mike had pots of clivias growing in every room of the house, including the attic, the basement, bathrooms, and hallways, as well as two garagelike additions where floor-to-ceiling shelves were filled with clivias. Clivias were everywhere, by every window and on every table, fountains of leaves with occasional bursts of umbels that hovered just above the cascade. I wanted to move right in.

Mike ended the tour at a cluster of large pots near the windows in his low-ceilinged living room. One of the pots was filled with the gorgeous 'Jean Delphine' variety whose flowers are a rich, brick color with undertones of chocolate and emerald green throats. There were also six generous pots filled with towering 'Sir Johns' still lofting dozens of four-inch, pale yellow flowers with their deep yellow throats. I asked what role Sir John had played in the renaissance of interest in breeding clivias.

"No doubt, Sir John had a lot to do with it, both by interesting his friends and by donating his yellows to the auction. But more than anything," he added thoughtfully, "I think the revival has to do with the Internet. I've been growing and breeding clivias for twenty-five years, but until the late 1990s, hobbyists like me were just puttering along on our own. With the Internet, I was suddenly able to see all kinds of plants and learn from people from all over the world. In 2002, I visited people in South Africa and California whom I'd met over the Internet, and I vastly expanded the stock I could experiment with.

"There's now a community of people—most of us are older—with a common interest and a common appreciation of this plant. The prices for these specialty clivias are outrageously high, but most of us rarely buy or sell anything. We share pollen, trade seeds, and exchange offsets."

I prodded Mike about the prices. Surely, he was tempted to sell offsets or seeds—couldn't he get many hundreds of dollars for a 'Sir John' pup?

"Sure, I could make a good bit of money on eBay. But these plants were gifts to me, given without any thought to their commercial value, just their value to me as someone who would love them.

"I do buy plants from time to time. Once, when I told one of my staff members that I paid $350 for a clivia, she told me I was crazy. But I asked her, 'Did you ever pay $350 for a piece of furniture? And how long do you think that piece of furniture is going to last or give you pleasure? Do you think you can take that $350 piece of furniture and pass it down for generations?' My $350 clivia will live forever, getting bigger all the time. And if I divide it, I could sell pieces of it for, for . . . for whatever, who cares?" he spluttered. "But if I wanted to get my $350 back, I could. And you can't say that about a $350 piece of furniture."

Of course, you can't kill a piece of furniture either, the possibility of which, I told him, would prevent me from ever spending $350, much less $3,500, for any plant. He countered that if I did spend that much on a plant, I would be best off spending it on a clivia.

"These plants are tough," he said. "You really have to work hard to kill one. A couple years ago, a guy gave me a plant that he'd left out too late in the season and it had gotten hit by frost. Then, he stuck it at the back of his basement, far away from the only window—a little, tiny one—and just left it there for sixteen months. The only time the plant got watered in all those months was once when his basement flooded. When he gave it to me to rehabilitate, its leaves were nearly white, it was so starved for sun. But it lived. In fact, I've still got it, and it flowers every spring just fine."

I figured Mike had to be telling the truth. Otherwise how could he take care of three thousand clivias and manage his very full-time job?

"I keep everything except my show plants in plastic pots, so they conserve water. During the year, I water no more than once every three weeks. I can go on vacation for a month with no harm. I fertilize a couple times a summer, with a 20–30–20 mix. On October 1, I clean up the plants and bring them inside. Then, I forget about them. Over the winter, they hardly need any light"—I had seen that the plants in his garage were in near total darkness—"and I don't water them at all. The only thing I've got to do is make sure the temperature gets down to at least 55 degrees for five to six weeks. After the first of January, I gradually warm them up to 58 to 60 degrees and water and fertilize them. Two weeks later, the flower umbels begin to emerge."

Starting clivias from seed is equally painless. Mike showed me a couple of flats of seedlings that had just germinated. The seedlings had emerged from seeds that had simply been placed on top of damp vermiculite. Some of their single roots were headed down, others were stretched across the surface. "In their natural habitat," he told me, "clivias will spread their roots laterally among leaf litter and the loosest soil. They can be epiphytic; you can even find them growing in the crotches of trees in South Africa."

Mike was glad to share his soil recipe with me, and when it was time to say good-bye, he insisted I take some clivias home. When he discovered that I had no miniatures and no variegated ones, he found me a young specimen of each. My only obligation was to send him an image of the eventual flowers. This was going to be a good number of years, but I knew clivia breeders are patient people.

I was grateful for Mike's gifts and glad that clivias were undemanding, especially when it came to watering. I was learning that the direction "keep evenly moist" was just another way of saying "guaranteed to die."

In theory, I should have gone around the conservatory every morning before breakfast, tested each plant, and watered as needed. That is the only way to ensure no plant gets parched. But I have always had difficulty following a routine. It should be easy—by definition, it requires little thought—but there's something in my nature that abhors a routine. For me, a routine feels like a sentence.

Even if I couldn't adhere to a schedule, my plants needn't have suffered so. I just had to pay more attention. But, just as I had suspected from the beginning, attentiveness was proving a problem. My children can recount—mostly with amusement rather than rancor—the times their mother was notably absentminded. When Austen was ten years old, she went away to summer camp. I bought the plane ticket, took her to Dulles airport, and put her on a flight to Boston where a camp counselor was to fetch her from the gate and add her to the group taking a bus to Maine. Shortly after the flight's expected arrival time, I got a call from the camp: Where was Austen? The counselor said she hadn't gotten off the plane. I panicked. This was every mother's nightmare. Every horrible possibility flashed through my mind. But how had it happened? I had watched her, anxious but resolute, disappear down the sky bridge, dressed in her baggy blue camp shorts and T-shirt, into the plane. Had she changed her mind and somehow returned to the airport? I had just called Ted to see which of us could get to Dulles the fastest, when the operator interrupted with a call from the camp. Austen had been found safe. I had put her on a U.S. Air, instead of a United, flight that left at the same time. She was in Boston, but at the wrong gate.

If only such a thing had happened just once. But I lost four-year-old Alice at a birthday party at Glen Echo Park, near a puppet theater heart-stoppingly close to a steep and wooded ravine above the C&O canal. Three-year-old Anna was retrieved by a neighbor as she headed to Bethesda on a pinecone-collecting mission; somehow she slipped out the door while I wasn't looking. Did I once leave a child in the shopping cart outside the grocery store, or was that just a constant fear? These are only highlights of a career of absentmindedness. The health forms not turned in, the carpools forgotten, the physician appointments written down for the wrong day or not written down at all. I didn't even try to remember the birthdays of any but my closest family members. The girls knew that if they needed cookies for school, they better make the mix themselves. I suspect they all had to forge my signature on a permission slip, and more than once.

I know I had, from their perspective, some redeeming qualities—no other kids got to test inventions for their mother's science books, and I was always available for conversation and pretty good down-to-earth advice—otherwise they might have disowned me. Today, they acknowledge that there was an upside to their mother's lack of focus. (To be accurate, I focus well but narrowly.) They learned early how to look out for their own interests and took on more responsibility than their friends whose mothers were more on the ball. My children never expected that I would wake them up in the morning or keep track of their assignments, belongings, lesson times, or sports practices. They learned how to take the bus and the Metro. They knew if they really needed me to be somewhere or do something, they could write a note and tape it to the front door—and put another one on my desk chair—and I'd, very likely, be there. And if not, they knew the telephone numbers of their friends' more organized moms, and weren't too shy to call.

It was a shame that I couldn't instill this sense of self-sufficiency in my plants. One morning, however, a story in the *Washington Post* caught my eye, and I thought my plants had found a way out of peril. It was a one-sentence squib about Singaporean college students who had genetically modified a plant so that it fluoresced when it needed water. I immediately turned to the Internet and ended up talking by phone to the effervescent Dr. Liew Oi Wah of Singapore Polytechnic Institute.

She was surprised to hear that her research had appeared

in an American newspaper, but was glad to talk to me. "Oh, yes," she said cheerfully in a lilting English accent. "The thing started when a professor from Nanyang Technical University asked me if I thought I had any use in my biotechnology lab for his sensor that measured color. Well, we know that when a plant is unhealthy, it usually turns yellow. But by the time your eye perceives yellow, it is already in quite a bad state, isn't it? So we wondered: could this instrument pick up very small changes in leaf color before our eyes could? And we found that the device could pick up optical signatures that indicated iron and calcium shortages long before we could see changes in the leaves.

"Then we thought, what about the water aspect? You know, we are quite keen to conserve water in crop production here in Singapore because our natural supply is very limited. Wouldn't it be nice, we thought, if a plant could tell us when it needs water rather than having us guess?"

Dr. Liew had one of her staff isolate gene switches that had been shown by Japanese scientists to be activated by water stress and found a number of candidate DNA segments. She then inserted a fluorescent protein gene from a jellyfish (*Aequorea victoria*) next to a water stress gene switch, hoping that when the plant was stressed, the fluorescent gene would also be activated. Sure enough, when Dr. Liew's students deprived the bioengineered plantlets of water, they fluoresced green after two hours, many hours before permanent damage would occur. Later, they tested potted petunias, which started to glow green six days after the watering stopped, which was seven days before the point of no return.

It sounded perfect to me. I had a vision of passing

through the dark conservatory in my nightshirt, watering can in hand, looking for glowing plants to water. I was ready to place an order.

It turned out there were a few problems that Dr. Liew and her students had left to solve. For one, the location of the fluorescence was unpredictable: sometimes the leaves glowed, sometimes the stems, but occasionally only the roots lit up, which was only useful if you happened to be a worm trying to read in bed. And she told me that I wouldn't actually be able to see the glow—the fluorescence had to be read by instrument. I said I could work with that. But Dr. Liew regretted that she couldn't send me any of her fluorescing plants: shipping plants, especially genetically modified ones, across international borders was next to impossible. Dr. Liew's technology was not going to rescue my plants from my inattentiveness.

Through my thirties and forties, I still had the illusion that I might, if I just put my mind to it and buckled down, better manage those elusive details at the margins of my life. But at fifty, I realized that my innate absentmindedness was now compounded by the forgetfulness of middle age. When I was preparing for our most recent family vacation, I forgot to make Austen a plane reservation at all. It was time to face the fact that I was not going to change.

Instead, the conservatory would have to change. All the little, exotic plants in four- and six-inch pots had to go. I didn't throw them out, but I combined three or four of them in a single, larger, but not much deeper, pot. (A relatively shallow pot means less wet soil beneath the plants' roots and, therefore, a lower likelihood of root rot.) I ended up with some odd-looking combinations, but all the extra soil held a lot more water. I experimented with adding water-retentive granules to the soil and ordered self-watering pots. They aren't cheap, but I especially like the ones that have a stick gauge that shows me how much water is left in the reservoir. I am still capable of letting a plant dry out, but because they need watering less frequently, I have fewer chances to do so.

My approach to the bay window had to change, too. Out with the flowering plants and in with large cactus and succulents. Edie ordered me a species of jade plant (*Crassula*), a pencil cactus like the one I'd seen at Glasshouse Works, an aloe, and an agave. My pineapple plant, which had thrown a pup that was sending up a new stalk, was another good bet. They all love the sun, but survive (I can assure you) with inconstant watering. I will never be a perfect gardener, but I at least have found plants adapted to my imperfections.

Ferns

nine

Nephrolepis exaltata 'Bostoniensis'

One autumn day in 1855, Miss Nona Bellairs set out for a hike along the southern coast of Wales between the villages of Tenby and Saunder's Foot. She was fern hunting, hoping to find an *Asplenium marinum,* a species that, according to the copy of *Moore's Popular History of British Ferns* in her bag, could be found there, growing on the damp face of the cliffs. Miss Bellairs—only her immediate family and very closest of friends would have thought to call her Nona—was thirty-one years old and a pleasant-looking woman with light-colored hair falling in corkscrews to her chin. The ninth of twelve children of the well-regarded and well-to-do rector of All Saints' Church in Bedworth in central England (and the model for the rector in George Eliot's *Scenes from Clerical Life*), she was unmarried and, like almost all single women of her class, she lived with her parents.

A party of fern collectors, 1871. *From Mary Evans Picture Library.*

We would hardly consider Miss Bellairs dressed for success in her undertaking. She would have been wearing a "walking dress," its outer skirt looped like the swags of draperies. The dress, sharply narrowed at the waist thanks to a laced, whalebone corset, was heavy and awkward. The outer skirt was supported with five or six layers of starched cotton petticoats, or a heavy horsehair crinoline, or perhaps the "Balmoral petticoat," a long woolen petticoat popularized by Queen Victoria. (The much lighter "bird cage" crinoline made of steel hoops wouldn't be invented until the following year.) She would certainly have been wearing a hat, trimmed with silk ribbon or possibly feathers—"Long feathers, even in the most tranquil scenes, are not inappropriate," advised *The Habit of Good Society: A Handbook for Ladies and Gentlemen* (1869). Gloves were mandatory; no respectable woman ever went out of doors without them. At least she might have been appropriately shod. Although it had been considered ungenteel to go walking in anything but soft leather shoes or, at most, "very slight boots," the queen herself had recently sanctioned the substantial "Balmoral boot."

In this cumbersome outfit, Miss Bellairs set out along a shore covered with huge and algae-slicked boulders. It was low tide and the boulders were surrounded by patches of stranded seaweed and pools of water teeming with tiny crabs. She was armed with a fifteen-foot bamboo pole with a knife tied to the end. With the knife, she would pry up ferns, and then pack them in the traveling bag she carried in her other hand. As she made her way, she scanned the cliffs above her, jagged and stark against the blue sky, and admired the trailing plants, tufts of grass, and the "tender weight" of pink and white morning glories that had found a foothold in the rock crevices. She was so distracted by the sights that occasionally the tip of her pole tilted down and the knife stuck in the seaweed, bowing the shaft and threatening to vault her off her feet.

When she spotted her prey, it was not on the open cliffs, but in a dripping sea cave, high on the cave wall, and out of the reach of her pole. Nevertheless, she climbed up on a ledge and had just begun, she wrote, "a sort of sky fishing, making desperate jerks to reach my object," when a voice suddenly boomed out: "Bless my soul, madam, you'll be killed! Hold on till I come." A little sailboat carrying a lady and a gentleman and steered by a sailor, stout and ruddy, approached. The sailor sprung from the boat, and with help from the gentleman, climbed the wall, and snagged the fern. Then, the little party in the sea cave gathered around the fern, "feeling we could hardly admire it enough."

(Intrigued by their enthusiasm for the fern, I looked it up, sure it would be something splendid. As a matter of fact, *Asplenium marinum* is a dwarfish, viney, completely unremarkable fern, about as attractive as its common name, the sea spleenwort.)

On a later outing, Miss Bellairs and a friend went to Somersetshire, seeking the *Asplenium ceterach* fern. They discovered it growing on the walls outside a village, but only on parts of the wall too high for them to reach. As they stood there wondering how to get a specimen, an old woman came out to offer them a chair and a knife. She knew what they were up to; other fern hunters had already cleared the lower stretches.

In fact, Nona Bellairs was just one of thousands of tourists who traipsed around the fields, woods, and shores of Britain in the mid- to late 1800s hunting down ferns. Ferns—collecting them in the wild, cultivating them inside the house in Wardian cases and outside in ferneries, drying and displaying them, creating prints and silhouettes from them, and decorating furniture and fabrics with their images—were a national passion. The craze was like a disease and, like a disease, it had a name: pteridomania.

Middle-class women in Victorian England were particularly susceptible to infection, for they were necessarily and conspicuously idle. For a man to claim middle-class status, he had to live by the work of his head and draw a salary large enough to support a nonworking wife. He had to employ at least one household servant: to have power over even one person's livelihood made him a master, one who ruled rather than was ruled. Together, these requirements had the effect of greatly increasing women's leisure time. Thanks to the success of British industrialization and imperialism, the middle class grew rapidly, and roughly two hundred thousand women were left to occupy themselves with suitably genteel hobbies, such as decorative needlework, music, sketching, gardening, and fern collecting.

But the mania for ferns was fed by more than leisure. Many in the middle class were only a generation removed from the working class. Insecure or eager to demonstrate their new status and fearful of betraying their origins, they strove hard to distinguish themselves from their social inferiors. If the rabble was noisy, uncouth, drunken, lascivious, and undisciplined, they would be the opposite. They would be "well-bred," with "refined," "correct," and "genteel" tastes. They would wear immaculate and modest clothing, display tasteful furnishings (there was no greater sin than vulgarity), pay rigorous attention to all rules of etiquette, refrain from displays of emotion of all kinds, and adhere to a rigid code of morality. There were dozens of conduct and etiquette books available to help the anxious middle class ensure that their dress, home, and manners never betrayed them.

It is not surprising, therefore, that Victorians fell for ferns. "I loved them," Miss Bellairs wrote, ". . . and brought to the study of Ferns a lover's heart." The plants epitomized Victorian sensibilities: they were simple, delicate, and elegant, and came in a restricted palette of shades of green and brown. The horticultural star of the Renaissance had been the flowered, scented, and fecund orange tree. Profligate Regency England loved pineapples and palm trees that evoked the exotic tropics. Victorians took to the fern, that most modest denizen of the cool shadows.

Shirley Hibberd, one of the great horticulture writers of the era, summed up the attraction when he wrote:

> *It is impossible for any one to give much attention to ferns without attaining to very correct and chaste notions of taste; and we might say that the love of ferns is always an accompaniment of correct ideas of embellishment. It must be a pure and simple taste which finds pleasure in the culture of plants which have no gaudy blossoms to attract vulgar attention.*

Here was a plant that Victorians, famously uneasy about sex, found acceptable. Ferns seemed to demonstrate that sex wasn't necessary. Unlike flowering plants, they had no phalluslike anthers or ovaries that swelled and ripened. Ferns seemed forever virginal. Or, if there was sex going on, ferns were extraordinarily discreet about it.[5]

Victorians had a general passion for collecting, and while aristocrats like the Duke of Devonshire collected first edi-

---

[5] People had been uneasy about the sexuality of plants since the late seventeenth century when the early botanists first proposed that flowers were sexual organs. Initially, plant lovers were outraged at the idea that these symbols of innocence in general, and of the Virgin Mary in particular, had anything to do with sex—and utterly promiscuous sex at that. It was not until 1848 that Wilhelm Hofmeister elucidated the life cycle of ferns, including their sexual phase of reproduction. Fortunately for the Victorians, that phase is invisible to the casual observer.

tions, Italian sculpture, crystals, and orchids, the middle class focused on birds' eggs, seashells, curios from abroad, and ferns. On weekends and on holidays, tourists like Miss Bellairs scoured the British countryside digging up ferns. During the week, nursery professionals were out, too. It was easy to spot the fern hunters: they carried a fern guide, a couple of trowels, a pick, and perhaps a shovel, and lugged along a carpetbag that they filled with layers of ferns covered up with damp moss. At first, fern collectors' goals were limited; they set out to accumulate one of every species of native *Pteridophytes* and their allied species, certain mosses and horsetails. Later, they tried to find all of a species' varieties and then unusual "sports" (onetime mutations) of those varieties.

There were so many fern hunters in the late-nineteenth century that some species were threatened with local extinction. Since ferns have shallow roots and mosses spread horizontally, collectors would simply peel off sections of ground cover, leaving swaths of bare soil, as if a giant had taken a razor to the land. "If the present rage continue," wrote Miss Bellairs in 1865, "I see no hope of any known species being allowed to remain in its old haunts. The poor Ferns, like the wolves in olden times, have a price on their heads." But her sympathy and concern did not restrain her hunting. She also wrote, without a pang, that "*Dryopteris* is a little difficult to pack, from its creeping roots; but I was unmerciful, cramming a whole heap of delicate little fronds and roots into one mummy case." The new railroads not only made it easy for collectors to get to the countryside, they also made it easy for ferns to travel in bulk to the city. One observer in Cornwall heard a collector boast that he'd sent a rail shipment of more than five tons of ferns at one time.

Where were all these ferns going? Ferns don't require a lot of light, but they do need high humidity. The atmosphere of the average drawing room of the era, which was not only dry but polluted with the fumes of gas and coal fires, was far from ideal. Fortunately, the Victorians had at hand Wardian cases, those glass boxes that in the 1830s had drastically improved the survival rate of tropicals in transit from overseas. One of the two plants that Ward had grown in his original case was a fern, *Dryopteris filix-mas*, and he demonstrated the efficacy of his invention by growing dozens of other fern species inside cases.

In the 1840s, the wealthy took up Wardian cases as a decorating device for their drawing rooms. Ferns were a natural choice for the cases: they liked low light, Ward had already firmly linked ferns and glass cases in the public mind, and there was a ready supply of tropical ferns in the estate conservatory. Wardian cases, which could be six feet tall and three feet long and often mimicked cathedrals, temples, and conservatories in their design, quickly became a status symbol. In what is surely the world's only ode to a Wardian case, Hibberd wrote:

> *In princely halls, and courts of kings,*
> *its lustrous ray the diamond flings,*
> *Yet few of those who see its beams,*
> *Amid the torchlight's dazzling gleams,*
> *As bright as though a meteor shone,*
> *can call the costly prize their own;*

Nevertheless, by the 1850s, the middle class, always quick to catch on to and adopt the fashions of the upper class, was buying Wardian cases, too, although theirs were smaller to match their smaller rooms and limited pocketbooks. They didn't fill them with tropical ferns: those were expensive and not widely available, and besides, tropicals would quickly outgrow more modest cases. Instead, they hunted the native ferns that were not only free for the taking but less delicate to boot. In 1855, Charles Kingsley, in *Glaucus, or the Wonders of the Shore,* grumbled to the fathers among his readers that

> *Your daughters, perhaps, have been seized with the prevailing 'Pteridomania,' and are collecting and buying ferns, with Ward's cases wherein to keep them (for which you have to pay) . . . 'Fancy-work' . . . has all but vanished from your drawing-room since the 'Lady-ferns' and 'Venus's hair' appeared.*

A Wardian case, however, could hold only so many ferns, a lot fewer than many fern lovers collected. Some people, including Miss Bellairs, lived where they could create an outdoor fern garden. All it took was a shady spot; a combination of rocks, broken tiles, and bricks to fashion a dell; and a source of water to keep it all moist. The ferns were anchored in a bit of loam, peat, or leaf mold, and settled in the gaps among the rubble. After they were planted, they more or less took care of themselves. Miss Bellairs's fernery at the rectory was a natural dell, shaded by an elm tree and backing onto a pond and a stream. Shirley Hibberd's outdoor fernery was completely artificial, made of a bank of builder's rubble and shaded by "tree loppings" and old beanpoles that he rested across tall tree stumps.

Hibberd was a working journalist, squarely in the middle of the middle class, who had wandered unintentionally into horticultural writing. In his *Rustic Adornments for Homes of Taste,* published in 1856, he noted in passing that it was possible to grow ferns in small glass structures, but he had no such building himself. The next year, he and his wife built a small conservatory in a sunny, recessed corner of their suburban house. Later, when a neighbor's construction and plantings blocked their afternoon sun, he took out the flowering plants and turned the glasshouse into another indoor fernery. By 1869, when Hibberd published *The Fern Garden,* he wrote that he "could mention hundreds of private gardens where I have seen beautiful ferneries under glass." The modest conservatory, for ferns and other plants, had become a common feature of middle-class English homes.

How did the conservatory conquer the middle class so rapidly? In the early 1840s, a conservatory had been exclusively a rich man's pleasure. The glass tax was still in place, making "hothouse building," according to *The Country Gentleman's Magazine* (January 1871), "too expensive for even moderately wealthy people to indulge in." For the most part, therefore, conservatories were tucked away from view on the grandest of country estates where ordinary Englishmen never saw them.

Although the Duke of Devonshire had always been generous in allowing visitors to tour the Great Stove at Chatsworth, it was not until 1849 when a railroad line was built to nearby Rowsley that tourists began to arrive in significant numbers, many of them on a "Cook's Tour." Thomas Cook, a former printer and lay minister, had started the packaged tour business in 1848, capitalizing on his experience arranging alcohol-free trips for his coreligionists in the burgeoning Temperance movement. He chose Chatsworth as one of his first destinations. Thanks to Cook's Tours, Chatsworth quickly became the most visited country house in England, introducing a steady stream of working- and middle-class people to the concept of the conservatory.

On May 20, 1846, the Royal Botanic Society of London opened the first public wintergarden in Britain in the eighteen-acre "inner circle" of Regent's Park. The glass building was constructed directly on the earth, which was covered with gravel and pulverized seashells. Visitors simply stepped through the ground-to-roof French windows. Inside, they followed paths through ever warmer regions until they reached the warmest "country of the palms." Afterward, they could eat and chat at little iron tables adorned with cut flowers. The structure could accommodate several thousand people at a time, and, especially because there was no entry fee, it was tremendously popular. An utterly novel and thrilling experience for Londoners, it was, Charles Knight wrote in his *Cyclopaedia of London,* "a veritable fairyland transplanted into the heart of London," and added, "birds singing in the branches make you again and again pause to ask, is this winter? Is this England?"

The Palm House at Kew Gardens, which opened in 1848, attracted even greater crowds. Kew had been a home to royalty since medieval times. In 1759, Princess Augusta established the Royal Botanic Gardens on a portion of the grounds. George III's fifteen children spent a good portion of their youth at Kew, an enchanted place where they played in the whimsical follies and visited the menagerie, which housed a mob of kangaroos. When the king was periodically struck by madness in the early 1800s, he lived at Kew where he could safely roam the grounds among the eleven thousand different botanical species by then naturalized in the gardens.

Botanists were welcome at Kew under Banks's leadership, but the public was not. "The science of Botany is best improved at a situation remote enough from the crowded populations of the metropolis to prevent the commerce of persons induced by idle curiousity alone to visit it," he sniffed in 1813. Commercial nurserymen and private gardeners weren't welcome either, at least when it came to obtaining duplicates, seeds, or cuttings of Kew's collection. The plants at Kew were as much the personal property of the Crown as the jewels in the Tower or the paintings on the walls of Windsor.

Both Banks and George III died in 1820. Neither George IV nor his brother and successor, William IV, took much interest in the palace or the gardens. They had no interest in spending royal funds on Kew, and the gardens' plant hunters were recalled from abroad. Private organizations, like the Liverpool Botanic Garden and the Royal Horticultural Society, wealthy individuals, and commercial nurseries took up the slack while Kew declined. When the Whigs, advocates of political and social reform and financial restraint, ousted the Tories from power in 1830, they questioned the cost and value of maintaining Kew's Gardens at all. After giving serious consideration to the idea of sending its plant collection to the Regent's Park wintergarden, the government did an about-face in 1840 and took over responsibility. Kew would retain a scientific mission, but it was to become, above all, a place for the public's recreation and education.

By this date across the channel, many of the grandest, private glasshouses had been taken over by national governments. There was no such structure at Kew; its only glasshouses were utilitarian ones used for propagation. National pride now required that something be built to reflect Britain's position as a great power and the world's leader in botanical explorations. The Palm House at Kew, completed in 1848, was 363 feet long and stirringly beautiful. On a sunny day, the shining glass skin of its curvilinear shells shimmered, and the image of the graceful building was mirrored on the surface of the large pond in front. In 1851, 328,000 people visited Kew Gardens.

It would have been the rare Londoner who was not exposed to at least one tropical conservatory by 1851, if not at Chatsworth, Regent's Park, or Kew, then certainly at the Crystal Palace in Hyde Park at the Great Exhibition, or as it was officially titled, the "Great Exhibition of the Works of Industry of All Nations." The six-month exhibition that opened in May 1851 was Prince Albert's pet project, and he headed the commission responsible for the event. After much discussion, the commission decided on Hyde Park as the site and announced a design competition for the host building. Architects submitted hundreds of plans in the initial round, but none could be built in the sixteen months left before opening day, at an acceptable price, or without sacrificing ten full-grown elms in the park that had become a rallying point for those opposed to the Hyde Park site. (Some opponents objected to the interruption of their daily horseback promenades. Others feared the exhibition as a general matter, believing it would introduce disease and revolutionary ideas from crowds of foreigners.) At the last minute, Joseph Paxton turned his attention to the question and submitted a design for a massive, three-tiered box of glass.

The building Paxton proposed was as revolutionary in its construction plan as it was in its architecture. Prefabricated, modular parts made in a Birmingham foundry would be sent by rail to London and assembled on-site. Paxton promised that what would be the largest building in the world could be assembled in an unbelievable nine months and at half the price of its competitors. He won the competition, and the building was finished three months ahead of schedule.

If the Palm House was a pirouette of a structure, the Crystal Palace was a swagger. More than ten stories tall at its highest point (high enough to accommodate the elms, which thrived under the glass), the palace covered roughly eighteen acres, was almost a mile in circumference, and was made of a million square feet of glass. By the time the exhibition concluded in October 1852, more than six million people (equal to about a third of the British population) had passed through. When it came time to dismantle the palace, its imminent destruction caused a popular uproar, even though it was never meant to be a permanent structure. The *Times*, originally an opponent of the Hyde Park location, led an editorial campaign to save it. Parliament gave the building a six-month reprieve, and in the interim, a group of private investors and lenders led by Paxton came to the rescue. The Crystal Palace Company bought the building for £70,000, deconstructed it, and shipped it off to a two-hundred-acre site in Sydenham in Kent, a short train trip from London.

The Crystal Palace Company did not simply resurrect the palace at its country home. Paxton reused the old parts, had new sections fabricated, and created a building that encompassed nearly twice the volume of space and was, according to the *Times*, "greatly enhanced in grandeur and beauty." The new palace was about the same length as the old one, but twice as wide and seventeen stories at its highest point. The original had one vaulted transept and a flat nave; the Sydenham version had three vaulted transepts and a vaulted nave. Fifty miles of underground hot-water pipes heated the building and twenty-five acres of glass covered it. If the panes had been laid end to end, starting in Washington, D.C., you could have walked a glassy path all the way to the Bronx.

The new Crystal Palace was a for-profit operation, and Paxton and his fellow shareholders required their enterprise to run in the black. To attract "the multitude," they provided a constantly changing program of entertainments of all kinds. The building hosted celebrations (of victory in the Crimea, for example), dancing and deportment classes, operas, and concerts; restaurants (ices, buns, and porter for the lower classes and lobster salad, *roulade de veau*, and fine wines for those with greater means); outdoor waterworks; "antediluvian reptile" (i.e., dinosaur) reproductions; and jugglers, acrobats, and fireworks displays. The seven Industrial Courts offered for sale the latest in manufactures. Behind the courts, a bazaar of small shops sold carpets, furniture, ribbons, porcelain, cigars, perfumes, clothing, scientific and surgical instruments, corsets, quack medicines, and soaps, among an ever-changing array of goods.

Educated Victorians subscribed to the theory that recreational activities for the masses should be instructive and "improving" ones that would advance the national character and prevent, among the working classes, such disruptive activities as strikes and Monday absenteeism. "Refined recreation, calculated to elevate the intellect, instruct the mind, and to improve the heart," the palace prospectus declared, "will welcome the millions who have now no other incentives to pleasure but those which the gin palace, dancing saloon, and the ale house afford them." Therefore, 858 reproductions of historical and contemporary sculptures (with fig leaves added as necessary) graced the palace and grounds. In addition, the portrait gallery offered 499 works and the picture gallery displayed 900 paintings for the visitors' edification. The ten spacious Architectural Courts illustrated historical styles by re-creating building interiors from ancient Assyria to Renaissance Italy.

But "however beautiful and perfect may be the works of art," none, according to the palace guide, could provide as much instruction as plants and flowers. The palace, therefore, was also the world's largest conservatory, with acres of spectacular tropical and temperate gardens to teach as well as delight. In the north transept, which was curtained off to create a tropical environment, a forest of palms towered over the visitors. The wide aisles to each side of the nave were filled with thousands of subtropical and temperate-zone plants, as well as full-grown trees, including *Fuchsia* forty feet high, *Acacia,* Australian paperbarks, rubber trees, cypresses, bananas, *Eucalyptus,* and 110 full-grown orange and pomegranate trees purchased from the estate of the duc d'Orleans. Chinese wisteria climbed the iron columns and crept along the girders, dangling clusters of lavender blossoms. More than three hundred four-foot-wide hanging baskets with spills of foliage and flowers hung over the nave and aisles. The flower gardens held eight thousand camellias, ten thousand geraniums, and more thousands of azaleas, tulips, lilacs, petunias, hyacinths, and other bedding plants. *Victoria regia* water lilies with pads nearly ten feet in diameter floated in an indoor pond that featured a crystal fountain at its center. Nathaniel Ward's original fern case with its original fern had a place of honor. Parrots paced along stands and brightly colored parakeets and weaver birds flew around wire aviaries.

The crowds came, and then came again. In the first ten years, more than fifteen million people passed through the palace's turnstiles. By the late 1860s, it is safe to say almost all Englishmen knew about conservatories, and the majority had been inside one.

Public conservatories inspired a demand for domestic versions, and by the 1860s, middle-class families could afford them. Glass had become cheap, thanks both to the repeal of the glass tax in 1851 and improved production processes. Several companies were manufacturing modular glasshouses using the methods Paxton introduced in constructing the Crystal

Palace. A homeowner could pick a design from a catalog—no architect, thank you very much—and the firm would assemble the ready-made parts at the person's house and even install heating and ventilation systems. *The Household* magazine claimed that half the new houses going up in England had conservatories attached.

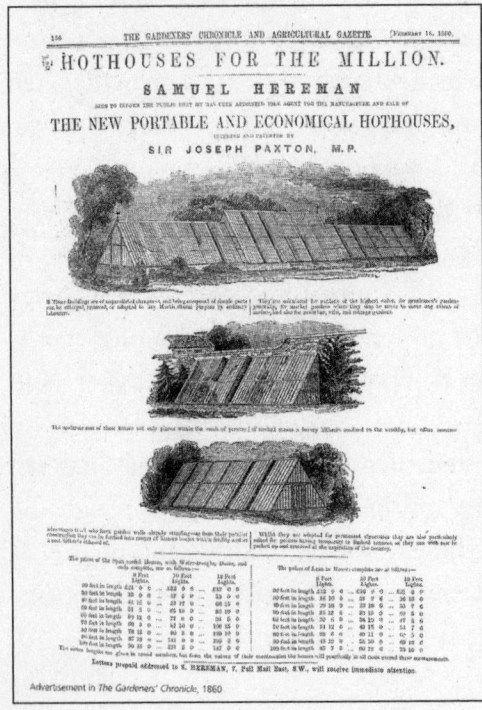

An advertisement in 1860 for Paxton's portable hothouses.
From The Gardeners' Chronicle and Agricultural Gazette, *February 15, 1860.*

That number certainly included collapsible versions, invented by Paxton in 1858, that even the lower end of the middle class could afford. "Hothouses for the Million!" exclaimed ads in *The Gardener's Chronicle* and other periodicals for Paxton's A-frame or lean-to glasshouses. There was nothing simpler, according to *The Floral World* in October

1860, than a portable. "There are no rafters, no framework, and there is no occasion for preparing a design and calling a council of carpenters and bricklayers." The family who didn't own a house could pack up its glasshouse and reassemble it in the garden of the next rental. These were no mean, cramped cold frames either. Erected over a two- or three-foot-deep excavation, they could accommodate vines growing across the glass ceiling, pineapples and vegetables along the sides, fruit trees toward the center, and even had room for "a delightful glass promenade" (albeit only in a straight line directly under the apex). Paxton priced his product at about £1 per linear foot—a serviceable collapsible conservatory might be fifteen feet long—at a time when a solid middle-class income was roughly £250.

Those families at the upper end of the middle class who were building new houses in the expanding English suburbs were able to afford a permanent glasshouse. They had little interest in growing fruit and vegetables inside; their glass rooms were places to socialize with family and friends in a tropical atmosphere. The conservatory often had an additional purpose, substituting a view of a neighboring house or an alley for a vista of greenery. For the family's breadwinner, a conservatory was a welcome antidote to the grimy city where he spent his days. For marriageable daughters, it could be a place for a bit of flirtation in a setting decidedly more romantic than the typical Victorian parlor freighted with heavy furniture and dark draperies.

It was the wife, though, who was assumed to have the most interest in the conservatory. Women—delicate creatures according to the prevailing wisdom—were considered to have an instinctive ability with hothouse plants, based, I suppose, on the idea that it takes one to know one. The care and study of tropical exotics, wrote one reader of *Gentleman's Magazine,* was particularly suited to women not only because it was "an elegant home amusement" but because "ladies can also more conveniently attend the regulation of the green-house sashes, which require closer attention than the ordinary concerns of gentlemen will allow." Men were meant for the wider world; women were constituted for home, garden, and greenhouse.

It was the responsibility of the middle-class wife to ensure that her family had the trappings and manners of its social position. She also instilled the social codes (no overt signs of affection, for example), established the proper relationship with the servants (distant), and stood as the model for the family's moral values. In that, the conservatory was a teaching tool.

"The pleasures of the garden," wrote Hibberd, "the tending and taming of household pets, the culture of choice plants in the greenhouse and the window . . . compel us to be students of the great out-door world, whence our noblest inspirations and most humanizing teachings are drawn." No student of nature, Hibberd claimed, had ever become a criminal. Nona Bellairs expressed the Victorians' belief that the study of plants had a religious value. "The Book of Nature is the Book of God," she wrote in *Hardy Ferns.* "It translates itself for every man into his own language, so that no error caused by man's defective wisdom can creep in." My favorite writer on the subject, however, was William Corbett: "It is the moral effects naturally attending a green house that I set most value upon," he wrote in *The English Gardener* in 1829. "How much better during the long and dreary winter for daughters and even sons to assist their mother in a green house than to be seated with her at cards or in the blubberings over a stupid novel."

Some women converted their interest in horticulture into a study of botany, the only socially acceptable science for a female. Botany was safe for women: it involved the contemplation of beautiful objects and strolls in the fresh air and did not involve noxious chemicals, unseemly dissecting, or too much abstract mental effort, which was deemed dangerous to the female brain. (If a woman engaged in too much mental exertion, according to prevailing medical theory, the energy available to her reproductive organs would be diminished.) Almira Hart Lincoln, an American, wrote *Familiar Lectures on Botany* in 1829, a textbook that went through seventeen editions and made her a small fortune. Jane Loudon, wife of John Loudon, after years of helping her husband with his books, became an accomplished and much-published botanist. In fact, by 1887, so many women had taken up the study of plants that *Science* magazine published an article entitled, "Is Botany a Suitable Study for Young Men?" Women's achievements in botany were all the more impressive because they were excluded from scientific societies and lacked access to herbaria, library resources, and the chance to learn from fellow botanists.

Conservatories came late to the United States. George Merritt built one of the earliest and largest private ones at his estate at Lyndhurst, New York, in 1869. James Lick, a California real estate mogul in midcentury, had an English-made glass-house sent by ship to San Francisco in 1876. (It stands today in Golden Gate Park.) Notable public examples included the New York Crystal Palace (1852), the U.S. Botanic Garden (1873), Baltimore's Druid Hill Park (1887), and the Phipps Conservatory in Pittsburgh (1893).

Lydia and John Morris built the first American indoor fernery at Compton, their summer estate in Philadelphia. The Morrises were brother and sister heirs to an iron-works fortune. Neither married and, in a particularly Victorian arrangement, they lived and traveled abroad together throughout their lives. Both were fascinated by gardens and wherever they went, they collected ideas and plants to take home to Compton. Inspired by the great English estates, they transformed their grounds into a perfect example of a Victorian park, with specimen trees from around the world, gardens, a greenhouse, and numerous follies. In 1899, John, who had an engineering degree from Haverford College, added an eight-sided, wrought-iron-and-glass fernery that he designed himself. Most other glasshouses of the era relied on interior columns to support the glass roof, but John braced the structure in such a way that eliminated the need for columns altogether. He and Lydia filled the space with more than four hundred different varieties of ferns.

In 1932, after John's and then Lydia's deaths, the University of Pennsylvania took over the management of what then became the Morris Arboretum. Operating funds were limited, however, and the fernery, neglected and near ruin, was closed. Then, in 1978, the trustees committed to its restoration and, in 1994, it reopened, fully returned to its

Victorian glory and named for Dorrance Hamilton, who donated $1.2 million toward the work.

The Fernery at Morris Arboretum, completed 1901.
From the Morris Arboretum Archives.

I drove up to Philadelphia to visit early one perfect spring morning. I went to see the building; I didn't go for the ferns. Despite having read several books on the subject, including Nona Bellairs's, I couldn't get interested in Pteridophyta. They didn't meet my basic criteria for tropical plants. First, they are generally not tolerant of neglect. Most grow near water because they need to be kept constantly moist. Second, although I could live without flowers, as a substitute I wanted leaves with color or, at least, interesting patterns. Fern colors range from dark green to grass green with an occasional detour to rust or gray, and they generally aren't variegated. I did relish the sight of my staghorn fern, which resembles a rack of fuzzy, green antlers, which I had hanging on a plaque, and my huge Boston ferns, but mostly because visitors erroneously presumed that their size was a reflection of my gardening talent. But in general, I found ferns uninspiring. They might be nice as background and space fillers, but they are too intolerant of a lackadaisical gardener.

When I pushed open the door to the Hamilton fernery, though, I began to have second thoughts. I found myself on a stone landing, like a cliff edge, looking down into a steep and intensely green dell. The dell was made of great, gray rocks—Wissahickon schist, I learned—but the rocks were largely obscured by ferns of every shade and every texture growing out of and over them. Some were like small trees, others shrubby, some cactuslike, some looked like vines, some seemed to have paws or claws that clung to rocks or hung out of hanging pots, and some looked as soft as velour. The greenery went right up the rocky slopes almost to the glass roof. Large fans turned overhead, stirring fronds that glistened from a recent watering. Unlike other conservatories where a canopy of palms shades plants at eye and ground level, the fernery, though sunken, was open to the glass roof, which seemed almost close enough to touch. At midmorning, the east slope was in shade, but the rest was sunlit and glowing. The sight was, as Andrew Marvell put it, "annihilating all that's made / into a green thought in a green shade."

There was no one in the fernery. To my right and left, sets of stone stairs led down about five feet into the earth. I took

the steps to the right, toward the sunny side, and followed
the winding gravel path. It bordered a little stream on one
side and hugged the steep, verdant embankment on the other.
As I strolled, I couldn't resist brushing my hand lightly over
the fronds—texture is the name of the game, I decided, when
it comes to ferns. The path crossed the stream with a little
wooden bridge. I stopped on the bridge, brushed a prickly
frond of a tree fern aside and looked down into a widening in
the clear water. Orange-and-white koi hovered, motionless
but for a wavering of dorsal fins and gaping mouths. On the
other side, the path was shaded, damp, and a little gloomy, so
I lingered.

It was only a minute before my guide, Dianne Smith,
joined me. Dianne, with a nimbus of auburn hair and a soft
and earnest voice, is the keeper of the ferns. This is not her
official title, which is simply "volunteer," but almost since
the day the fernery opened, she has been in charge. She has
always had a great deal of latitude, she said, in choosing plants.
The Morrises kept meticulous records of their tree and outdoor plant acquisitions, which the arboretum has continued
to do. But the Morrises enjoyed the fernery more as a folly,
not as a museum collection, and they never recorded what
they planted. As a result, Dianne has been free to buy what
she likes. Although she aims for an educational variety of
ferns, her primary goal has been to re-create the Victorian
spirit of the place.

Mystery and secrets were an essential part of that spirit.
In setting a fernery well into the ground, as the Morrises and
others did, they banished the outside world and disappeared
into their private Eden. The Morrises used other tricks bor-

rowed from British ferneries to heighten the hobbity feeling of the place. The pooling water at the bottom of the dell drew one into the fernery's depths. A grotto at the back, damp and fully shaded, sheltered the most fragile, sun-averse specimens like maidenhair and filmy ferns. At one point, the path, which seemed to have been trodden into place by unseen woodland animals, disappeared into a dark tunnel through the rocks. Starting through, I knew it could be no more than a couple strides long, but, still, it gave me a moment of suspense as I stepped into its darkness.

It doesn't take a psychiatrist to see why the fernery appealed to the Victorian mind—all those wild and damp and hidden places one could visit without a blush. But, since this was a creation of the Victorian subconscious, a fernery could only be just so wild. As Hibberd said, "Aim at wildness and apparent neglect *up to a certain point*" (emphasis added). Too much dirt and disorder might be construed as a reflection of the owners' morals. So Dianne's job was to re-create a neatened-up nature, one that didn't look as if humans had had a hand in it.

In fact, the fernery is completely dependent on the constant ministrations of its keepers. This is not a self-sustaining Wardian case on a giant scale. Without hand-watering as often as three times a day in summer, trimming twice a week, constant pest control, automatic venting and fan systems, water filters for the stream, food for the fish, shade cloth, and hot-water heating, the place could be a wreck in a matter of days in the summer or hours in the winter.

"It's a good thing you didn't come visit in January," Dianne said. "Oh my God, it was a disaster. I came in one

Friday morning and everything was dying. The ferns were turning black. I touched a plant and the fronds just fell off. I had never seen anything like it. It was a nightmare.

"No one here knew what the problem was, so I called my friend Bill Barnes, a plant broker who helps me find my ferns. He drove right over, took one look, and diagnosed it. We had just had the fish pond painted, three coats, and the paint was drying before we filled the pond again. I had been very careful with the paint, gotten all kinds of advice, and chosen one recommended by Sea World. Well, it was okay for fish, but one of its ingredients was ethylene, and as the paint dried, it released ethylene gas into the air. And that was absolutely deadly for the ferns.

"I was devastated."

Dianne looked so distraught recalling the situation that I was compelled to point out to her how wonderful and lush it all looked now, only five months later. Yes, she agreed, almost everything was on the road to recovery, and only a few plants had been completely killed. Still, it had been a close call. And she had had other close calls. When the fernery opened, she had overfertilized in hopes of jump-starting the little plants so that they would quickly cover the bare rocks. It worked; everything grew like crazy. But for insects, all that tender new growth was like an open bar at a frat party. You could practically hear them eating. For all its lush growth, a fernery—any conservatory—is terribly fragile.

Invaders

ten

Dizygotheca elegantissima

When I was forty-seven, my internist felt what he thought was a tiny lump in my breast and sent me off for a comprehensive mammogram. I was mildly worried, but I had had scares before, lumps that appeared and disappeared with the monthly tide of hormones. When the results came back negative, I forgot about the lump. Why not? I had breast-fed all three children, maintained a reasonable weight for my height, exercised, and, besides, a powerful technology in the hands of experienced specialists had told me I was in the clear. Eight months later, though, I felt a lump in what seemed to be the same place and went back to my gynecologist. He ordered a sonogram, which led to a needle biopsy, which led to a surgical biopsy. Then, the sand suddenly eroded from under my feet and I pitched into the sea of cancer.

The size of the lump was relatively small but, due to the eight-month delay, was now large enough to put me in a higher risk category and would influence my choices for treatment. I anguished about the first, negative mammogram. The national health-care company that owned the radiology center hit the news with a major accounting scandal. Had it cut corners by using an outdated machine? Were its mammographers or radiologists second-rate? My internist had seemed to think that a comprehensive mammogram included a sonogram. Was he wrong? Shouldn't he have noticed that no sonogram was done? But most of all, I berated myself. I should have researched the radiology center; I'd chosen it solely for its proximity. Why had I accepted a negative finding so blithely? Shouldn't I have asked more questions? And how could I have gone so long without checking for the lump again? I swore that if I survived, I would be more cautious, more vigilant in the future.

After a second surgery, I consulted three oncologists about the next step. All were clear that six weeks of radiation was essential. Then, they diverged: one was for chemotherapy, one thought I should do without it (or rather he thought that the decreased risk of a recurrence was more than offset by the increased risk of cardiac damage from the treatment), and the third said it was a toss-up. I agonized, but had to make a quick decision.

I thought of my daughters: I would do anything not to leave them motherless. What was six months of debilitating side effects compared with increasing my chances—even if by only a percentage point or two—of living?

I thought of Joanie, and how I had also failed to take her symptoms seriously. A lack of concentration? A faulty memory? Sleepiness? Pain in her wrists? It could happen to anyone. Then she had a seizure. In an astounding bit of wishful thinking, I convinced myself that she must have some mild form of epilepsy, which was certainly a bad thing, but surely could be managed with medications. I simply could not imagine that my sister, so lively and combative, with eyes that blazed with such a blue intensity, could be truly ill, much less incurably ill.

I thought of the blithe confidence I'd had nearly a year earlier that the lump was nothing dangerous. I hadn't been able to imagine that I could be seriously ill.

I decided to take every precaution. I would not be lulled into lying down in green pastures. I now knew what might lurk in the quiet grass.

So, every three weeks, I sat hooked up to an IV bag bulging with Adriamycin and cyclophosphamide, a bright red chemotherapy that dripped into a vein, making my head spin. My hair fell out in hunks, my mouth broke out in painful sores, and the smell of food sent me upstairs where I opened the windows, but I found an odd comfort as the side effects worsened. Surely, if the chemicals were destroying my hair and skin, they were destroying any errant cancer cell that might be multiplying in some lymphatic cranny. I read that some women were doing a more intensive chemotherapy, with higher-dose sessions and less recovery time between treatments. It was tough on the body, but also seemed to be more effective. Let me do that, I pleaded with my oncologist. I had mastered the lessons of caution. He firmly opposed the idea.

In the wake of treatment, I was absolutely rigorous about prophylactic checkups. Every few months, a physician—in sequence, my oncologist, internist, radiologist, and breast surgeon—examined me. I had mammograms and MRIs. I was determined never to be less than fully vigilant again.

That vigilance did not extend to my conservatory, however, or maybe I was too occupied keeping a watch on my internal goings-on. Or was I once again fooled by a healthy outward appearance? In any case, one December morning not long before I visited Dianne, when I was making an absentminded pass through the conservatory with my watering hose, I stopped to look more closely at one of my favorite plants, a handsome *Dizygotheca elegantissima* (false aralia) that has long and narrow, copper-edged leaves that appeared to have been trimmed with a pinking shears. That day I noticed what looked like bits of cotton stuck in some of the junctions of its leaves and stems. When I put my finger on the cotton, it stuck to me and melted, more like cotton candy. The stuff was odd but seemed innocent enough, so I ignored it.

A few weeks later, I noticed a lot more cottony bits, and I saw that the *Dieffenbachia* next to it had cottony bits, too. In fact, now that I was paying attention, I saw that nearly all my plants were similarly adorned. The citrus trees were particularly decorated, and some of their leaves were shiny and, when I touched them, tacky, like the backs of Post-it notes.

Then I saw them: bugs, about an eighth-inch long, powdery white, and oval-shaped. They were mealybugs, a type of soft scale insect that sucks the sap from plants. The cotton candy was the waxy material that the female exudes to cover the eggs she lays. In small numbers, mealybugs don't do too much damage. In large numbers, which inevitably result when small numbers are not dealt with, they cause leaves to drop off, and they can kill a plant. They also excrete a sticky substance called honeydew, which then develops sooty mold, unsightly and damaging in its own right.

Once I started looking carefully and consulting my books on pests, I could see I had other invaders. Those brown bumps on the stems of my citrus trees? I had assumed they were natural and ordinary excrescences, but in fact they were bugs, a kind of hard scale insect. The small black spots on the bird-of-paradise, which I thought were innocuous freckles, were another species of scale. That extraordinarily diaphanous spider webbing that wavered between the lobes of my two six-foot-tall *Alocasia*? The product of spider mites, which were also responsible for the thousands of pinprick yellow dots that I only then noticed. The pearly yellow or green bumps on the undersides of the *Schefflera* I identified as a species of sap-sucking, plant-killing aphids.

I was outraged. How dare bugs invade? This was my safe harbor, my personal Eden where there was to be no corruption, infection, and decline. How could I have overlooked them until—I feared—it was too late? I wanted to decimate them instantly and completely. I would wage all-out war, blast them with the strongest chemicals I could find. At least this time I could see my enemies, and I would annihilate them without mercy.

I raced off to Johnson's. Edie wasn't there, but I found a shelf of insect products at the back of the store. Nothing looked adequate to the task. The labels read "all-natural," "organic," or "pet-safe." I would need to make multiple applications. It would take time. What was this pussyfooting, namby-pamby approach to lethal invaders? I tried another nursery and then my local hardware store. There was nothing that sounded remotely deadly enough.

More toxic substances were available online, substances that actually sounded like the cancer drugs I had taken. I ordered a container of powdered dithiophosphate, otherwise known as Malathion, which promised to kill all of my pests plus dozens that I had never heard of, including rusty grain beetle, confused flour beetle, rice blast, Indian meal moth, and saw-toothed grain beetle.

The insecticide arrived packaged in a box that had warning labels on the outside. The actual bottle had a skull and crossbones. This was powerful stuff. But when I read in the accompanying booklet that "experimental studies reported increased numbers of liver tumors and a very small increase in the number of tumors in the nose or mouth in laboratory animals fed diets containing very high levels of Malathion for their lifetimes," I came to my senses. I put the bottle back in the box and sealed it up with packing tape, then washed my hands for a good five minutes. What had I been thinking? I had just endured hell to reduce my cancer risk by a percentage or two, and now I was thinking of increasing it? I went back to Johnson's.

Edie told me that there are several perfectly safe ways to deal with pests. Insecticidal soaps wash away their protective coating, so that their cells leak vital fluids. Soap sprays only kill about 50 percent of the insects touched by the liquid, so it takes several applications to get rid of a substantial majority of them. I had to be careful, though, she warned me, because too much spraying can burn the leaves. Neem oil, made from the seeds of the neem tree, works by interfering with insects' hormonal systems, so that their larvae remain immature or develop distorted wings, and their mating behaviors are disrupted. Neem oil also suffocates pests. It isn't an immediate killer and because it degrades quickly, it also requires repeated applications.

"Or," she said, "you could try beneficial bugs." I had read about beneficial insects, but adding bugs to get rid of bugs sounded improbable. Even if the beneficial bugs ate the pesky bugs, wouldn't I then have a beneficial bug problem? Aphids were bad, but would a horde of ladybugs be so much better?

Until 1867 farmers had few options when it came to controlling insects. They applied solutions of lime, tobacco, or a toxic plant called hellebore, but sending a child out to pick caterpillars or beetles off the leaves was about as effective, and cheaper, too. A farmer's best strategy was to diversify his crops to avoid devastation by a single pest, and cross his fingers.

But after *Leptinotarsa decemlineata,* a half-inch-long, yellow-orange beetle with ten black, lengthwise stripes, appeared in the potato fields of Nebraska, pest control would never be child's play again. Until 1859, this rather attractive little bug had been content to munch the leaves of weeds like nightshade and buffalo bur on the eastern slopes of the American Rockies. But settlers were moving west, clearing prairie and forest to plant their crops, some of which the six-legged locals found particularly tasty. On a farm a hundred miles west of Omaha, *Leptinotarsa* happened upon a field of *Solanum tuberosum,* the Irish potato. The beetles were in beetle heaven. Here were fields of plants of the same family as its familiar weeds, but these were tastier, more tender, and laid out as an all-you-can-eat buffet. They chowed down, and in short order produced children and grandchildren who tucked into the leaves with equal enthusiasm. Once they cleaned out one table, they spread their pretty pink wings and flew on to the next, leaving leafless stems, like empty plates, behind. When fall came, they dropped off the last leaves, and settled into basement apartments below their favorite restaurants for the winter. In the spring, they climbed out, hungry and ready to breed.

Colorado potato bugs, as they became known, spread east at the rate of about fifty miles a year, destroying crops as they went. Mr. J. Egerton of Garity, Iowa, wrote a letter to the *Prairie Farmer* in 1861, noting that the bugs "made their appearance upon the vines as they were up, devouring them as fast as they grew." The *New York Times* reported in 1867 that the "potato crops of Illinois and several other Western States were largely depleted by the ravages of the potato bug." They would reach the Atlantic Coast around 1875.

In 1867, an unknown midwestern farmer, desperate to save his crop, sprinkled his plants with Paris Green, a copper arsenic compound that had become a popular emerald green dye. It would seem to be an unlikely experiment, except that there were rumors at the time of people being poisoned by wallpaper and dresses dyed green with the compound. (The rumors were accurate.) In any case, the farmer was delighted to find that Paris Green killed the pests. Within a few years, farmers across America were using it not only on their potato vines, but, dissolved in water or mixed with kerosene, on many other vegetable and fruit crops and on cotton plantations. In the mid-1870s, another arsenic-based dye, London Purple, became even more popular. It was even cheaper and easier to dissolve, and it stained foliage purple, so a farmer could easily see when it had worn off and he needed to apply another round. Over time, however, farmers discovered that London Purple weakened the plant as well as killed the pest, and Paris Green again became the insecticide of choice.

The gypsy moth, a veritable plague in parts of New England in the 1880s, inspired the next development in chemical pest control. The caterpillars were so numerous, one observer in Medford, Massachusetts, wrote in 1889, that "the trees were completely stripped of their leaves, the crawling caterpillars covered the sidewalks, the trunks of the shade trees, the fences and the sides of the houses, entering the houses and getting into food and beds. . . . In the still, summer nights the sound of their feeding could be plainly heard, while the pattering of the excremental pellets on the ground sounded like rain." The caterpillars were more than a domestic nuisance; they were a commercial disaster for orchardists. New England apple trees were defoliated and harvests declined precipitously. London Purple and Paris Green were only partially effective. Someone tried lead arsenate in 1892. It proved highly effective, and farmers were soon applying it to vegetables and to other fruit crops.

By the end of the 1930s, hundreds of millions of pounds of these pesticides had been spread on American food and cotton farms, and people were slowly awakening to the dangers inherent in incorporating such lethal substances into their lives. The frequent poisoning of the workers handling insecticides was a given. During the gypsy moth plague, a study issued by the state of Massachusetts blandly reported that about 10 percent of the men employed spraying suffered from arsenic poisoning.

Consumers were affected, too. British authorities nearly embargoed American apples in the mid-1920s for sky-high levels of arsenic residue, although that information was kept from the American public. In the United States, chemical companies dismissed rumors of consumer poisonings as "sensational reports." Some experts made the case that arsenic in the body was natural, maybe even beneficial. The first questions about the effects of the pesticides on consumers' health did not appear in the American press until the late '20s, when newspapers began reporting increasing numbers of cases of illness and death attributable to arsenic poisoning. In 1933, a girl in Billings, Montana, died after eating a fruit with arsenic residue. The same year, dozens of cases of gastroenteritis in Los Angeles were attributed to arsenic from pesticides. Other people were reported falling ill from eating arsenic-tainted asparagus, and an outbreak of severe illness was attributed to coleslaw made of cabbage that had thirty-five times the amount of arsenic deemed safe. Dermatologists reported infants with eczema due to arsenic in their mothers' milk. In 1935, the *Journal of the American Medical Association* editorialized that "spray residues must constitute an important menace to the public health." Two influential books, Ruth deForest Lamb's *American Chamber of Horrors* and Kallet and Schlink's *100,000,000 Guinea Pigs,* which would go through more than two dozen printings in 1933 alone, drove home the point.

Contributing to the massive overuse of these chemicals was the unhappy fact of insecticide resistance, which develops when a species evolves physiological characteristics that protect it from a chemical. Although an insecticide may kill 99.9 percent of a species, there are always some individuals blessed with a genetic mutation that allows them to survive. The survivors then reproduce, repopulating the environment with individuals perfectly designed by natural selection to survive the poison. The potato bug was particularly quick to develop resistance to insecticides, perhaps because it has coevolved with its host plants in the family Solanaceae, many of which have high concentrations of toxins.

The Colorado potato beetle again inspired innovation in pesticides. Although European governments had banned the import of American potatoes in an attempt to exclude the pest, it crossed the Atlantic as a shipboard stowaway as early as 1876. After an outbreak in England in 1901, authorities burned potato crops and plowed the soil with kerosene to make sure they killed the potato bug. The bug spread to France before World War I. (A German cartoon shows the kaiser granting a potato bug an Iron Cross for its work destroying French potato crops. The Nazis would later accuse the Allies of dropping the beetle over German soil.) The Swiss chemical corporation J.R. Geigy S.A. had developed DDT (dichloro-diphenyl-trichloroethane) in the late nineteenth century, but it was not until one of its chemists tried out the compound on infected potato plants in 1939 that anyone understood its insecticidal potential. Two years later,

Geigy was selling the compound to Swiss potato farmers and to the Swiss Army for topical use on the large number of lice-infected refugees who were arriving in the country. Geigy's U.S. subsidiary then offered samples to the U.S. Department of Agriculture, which discovered the compound was effective against mosquito larvae (particularly important in protecting troops from malaria in the Pacific theater), scabies, and bedbugs. By the end of the war, experiments proved DDT and its related chlorinated hydrocarbons were astoundingly good at killing all kinds of agricultural pests. Even better, the new insecticides were markedly persistent, adhering to crops for months after application. The component chemicals were readily available and cheap. DDT and related compounds were touted as the "Killer of Killers" and the "atomic bomb" for insects. By the late 1940s, they were replacing most of the old insecticides.

Early-nineteenth-century entomologists knew that certain entophagous (insect-eating) insects attacked destructive phytophagous (plant-eating) insects and kept them under control. No one, however, applied that knowledge in the field until 1868, when the cottony-cushion scale made its first appearance in the citrus groves of California. The scale, named for the cottonlike sac the hermaphroditic insect makes to protect its eggs, degraded the fruit, caused leaves to drop, and killed twigs. It spread quickly and was unaffected by applications of the insecticides of the day. By 1887, California citrus growers were burning their trees to get rid of the pest, and the very existence of the young industry was in question.

Growers begged the USDA for help. Luckily, the Division of Entomology was headed by Charles V. Riley, one of the few entomologists in the country who had an interest in biological control of insects. Riley discovered that while the pest was rampant in New Zealand, it was somehow under control in Australia. He reasoned that the scale was native to Australia where some natural enemy kept it in check, and he sent an explorer, Albert Koebele, to bring back whatever was eating the pest down under. At first, Koebele had trouble finding any scale at all, they were so well controlled, but ultimately he found scale pupae in Melbourne and Adelaide that had been parasitized by *Vedalia cardinalis,* the vedalia lady-beetle. He cut off branches covered in the beetles, packed them in wood and tin boxes and in Wardian cases, and sent them, at various times, on the monthlong journey to California. By January 1889, a total of 514 surviving vedalias had arrived in Los Angeles, which were then placed on a caged tree on the property of grower F. W. Wolfskill. By April, the heavily infected tree was almost entirely clear of pests. The cage was removed, and the bugs obligingly moved to the surrounding trees. Within six months, all of Wolfskill's trees were clear. By the end of the year, after the release of ten thousand vedalia in 208 California groves, the cottony-cushion scale was gone. At a cost of about $1,500, the California citrus industry was saved.

Biological control of insect pests (or *biocontrol*) had other successes, but the weapons of choice in the battle against bugs remained chemicals. Chemicals were easy to apply and cheap, whereas hunting down the biological predator of a pest, cultivating it in sufficient numbers, and figuring out how and when to distribute them took time and effort. Besides, just because an accidentally imported pest was thriving in its new American environment, it didn't mean its purposefully imported predator would do so well. Unusual weather conditions, local insect predators, or even road dust could impede a beneficial bug's progress even if it was, in general, well suited to the task. In addition, to keep the beneficial adults fed and generating larvae, which generally do the predating, farmers had to provide the right plants for the adults to eat. A farmer couldn't just dump a bunch of good bugs in a field and walk away, as he could with chemicals.

But there were even bigger obstacles, commercial ones, to biocontrol. The fundamental problem was that beneficial insects were not patentable. Anyone could breed them. And, if a particular entophagous bug worked well and the adults reproduced in the field, they might prove to be a one-time sale or, at best, only an annual sale. On the other hand, profits from chemicals were protected through patents and, thanks to the inevitability of resistance, there was a never-ending demand for new (patentable) chemical products. In sum, there was tons of money to be made with chemicals and hardly any to be made from beneficial bugs.

It was not surprising, therefore, that little research was done on nonchemical pest control. After World War II, when chemical companies like Dow, Monsanto, and Union Carbide were making huge profits on DDT and its cousins, they poured funds into their own research departments and endowed positions and funded projects in university entomology departments. Naturally, that research was directed toward chemical pesticides. Everett "Deke" Dietrich, who would go on to found Rincon-Vitova Insectary in Ventura, California, the first commercial producer of beneficial bugs, wrote that after the war "there was no consideration in any of my undergraduate or graduate entomology classes or from any of my mentors about the possibilities for biological control." In one of the classes he took as a PhD candidate at the University of California, the students were advised to collect the labels of current DDT-related insecticides: together, these would constitute their primary reference book for pest control, one the professor assumed would last their careers.

Dietrich eventually found an intellectual home at the university's Division of Biological Control, which was headquartered at Riverside in Southern California. The division was an anomaly, the only research institution in the country devoted to biological control at a time when almost everyone believed that synthetic, broad-spectrum pesticides like DDT had ended pest problems forever. Nonetheless, Riverside entomologists developed a method of mass-rearing *Macrocentrus ancylivorus,* a parasite of the oriental fruit moth whose larvae had been decimating peach tree crops. Massive releases of the parasites in 1944 to 1946 were so effective that by 1947 hardly a single moth could be found in the targeted orchards. At the same time, Riverside was involved in clearing two million acres of California rangeland of Klamath weed, a toxic Australian invasive that had shut down cattle ranching in the area, by introducing an Australian beetle, *Chrysolina quadrigemina.* Still, throughout the 1950s Riverside researchers were considered antediluvian and eccentric, if harmless, and the division's budget was periodically threatened with cuts or elimination.

The outlook for biocontrol began to improve in the 1960s. DDT was proving less than miraculous. As early as 1948, dairy farmers on the East and West coasts found that flies had become resistant to it. The first cases of resistance among agricultural pests, among them the apple-eating codling moths, cabbage looper moths, and tomato hornworms, also appeared in the United States in the late 1940s and early 1950s. By the early 1960s in the lower Rio Grande Valley of Texas, the cotton bollworm and the tobacco budworm, secondary pests that had burgeoned when DDT temporarily eliminated the boll weevil, had become resistant to all available insecticides. Cotton farmers were desperately spraying their fields, as many as eighteen times a year. Public health was endangered, with an epidemic of pesticide poisonings in crop duster pilots, aircraft loaders, and farm workers. It looked like the end of cotton in the valley.

The cotton farmers were not alone in their troubles. Rachel Carson pointed out in her 1962 book, *Silent Spring,* that sixty-five species of phytophagous insects had become DDT resistant, including the Colorado potato bug. Spider mites were killing hundreds of thousands of acres of western forest after DDT eliminated their natural enemies. The Louisiana sugarcane crop has been devastated by borers that proliferated after their predators were killed by DDT applied to eradicate fire ants. Illinois farmers lost their corn crops to a borer similarly unleashed after insecticide treatment for Japanese beetles. As scientists gained a deeper understanding of the genetic basis for resistance, a growing number of entomologists, beyond the Riverside group, warned that reliance solely on chemical technology would never work. The genetic plasticity of insects meant they would always evade a single angle of attack; natural selection and evolution would triumph.

In 1970, a cultural and political shift occurred. Congress established the Environmental Protection Agency, the first Earth Day took place, and hearings on Capitol Hill were leading to a phaseout of DDT and new pesticide laws. In 1972, the "Huffaker Project" was funded by the national Science Foundation and the EPA. This project involved eighteen universities and three hundred researchers who studied the management of cotton, alfalfa, citrus, soybeans, stone fruits, and pine forest with an ecological approach and the least use of chemical pesticides and became the prototype for integrated pest management (IPM) programs worldwide. These programs involved improving planting methods to avoid infestations and attract beneficials, constant monitoring of fields to identify precisely what pests and beneficials were in the fields and at what density, supporting pests' natural enemies or adding them, timing any chemical applications to avoid killing beneficials, and other environmentally friendly techniques. Today, many universities have IPM departments, and the concept is well embedded in the horticultural and agricultural communities.

I decided to institute my own IPM program in the conservatory. On a sunny Saturday in June, Ted and I emptied the conservatory of most of the plants, carrying (or dragging) them to the backyard where I could hose them down. The bird-of-paradise were the most satisfying patients to attend to; I blasted the mealybugs off their leathery leaves with water shot out of the sprayer attachment to the garden hose. Next came a heavy spraying of neem oil. I used three bottles of the stuff and wore out both hands squeezing the bottle trigger. After the plants dried, we took them back in. The effort took much of the weekend, but a month later the plants still looked clean to me.

In November, however, a month after I'd brought the citrus trees in for the winter, I began to notice the cottony bits, the webs, and the tiny barnacles of hard scale. It was too cold to take the plants outside again, but I knew that in the crowded conditions of my winter conservatory, the pests would spread quickly. I couldn't use neem oil without making a slick mess on the floor and walls.

It was time for reinforcements. I called up Rincon-Vitova, the insectary that Deke Dietrich had helped found four decades earlier and spoke to Jan, his daughter who now runs the company. She suggested green lacewings as the best all-around predator. I ordered five thousand eggs of *Chrysoperla rufilabris,* a species she said was well suited to the warm and humid conditions of my conservatory. Five thousand lacewings were clearly overkill, since each lacewing larvae could eat dozens of prey, but I was taking no chances.

The eggs came glued to thirty cardboard strips, along with a supply of moth eggs. (The moth eggs provide food for newly emerged lacewing larvae, preventing them from cannibalizing unhatched lacewings eggs.) The strips had a hole at one end for hanging on twigs or leaves so I festooned the conservatory from one end to the other. Within three days, the eggs turned from green to gray, which meant they had hatched. I never saw the little larvae, though; they just disappeared into the leaves like invisible guerilla warriors on a mission. After two weeks, Jan suggested I add a second round of lacewings that could clean up any mealybugs that had hatched after the first attack.

I wasn't sure for a long time if the lacewing larvae had done their work. I saw only a few adults, which was too bad since they are quite beautiful, about a half inch long with a slender green body, pale green cellophane wings, and golden eyes. But as the husks of scale insects, mealybug bodies and nests, and the spider mites' webs disappeared, I finally concluded that my campaign had been successful.

I now try to be more vigilant about pests. Every houseplant guide will tell you to deal with them as quickly as possible; they never just go away. Dianne Smith swears by a prophylactic treatment of two tablespoons of Listerine mixed in a gallon of water, so I have mixed up a batch and whenever I remember, I spray. But I know the bugs will be back. New ones will ride in on Scotia's fur or on someone's sleeve or in the soil of a new plant. Open the door and there is a chance a mite or a fungus will waft along on a current of air. I wish my conservatory were sacrosanct and I could fully protect the life inside from external dangers, but it isn't and I can't.

I'd like to think I can prevent all dangers myself, as well, but I know I am no more inviolable than the glass skin of my conservatory. I no longer revisit the missed opportunities of those early months of cancer. Maybe that's because, as the years go by without a recurrence, I think I have it beat. Or maybe, I have accepted that perfect vigilance is an illusion. I cannot have a mammogram every day; it is not possible to look under every leaf every day. The fact is, pests are destined to get in, no matter how watchful we are. We just deal with them as best we can.

Apopka

eleven

Anthurium

No tropical plants sold in the United States are actually grown in tropical jungles. U.S. Department of Agriculture regulations prohibit the importation of plants in soil because soil can harbor insect larvae, fungi, and bacteria that could wreak havoc in American agriculture. Any plants imported from the tropics arrive as inch-long, soil-less, "microcuttings" grown, as they are here, in laboratories. Fortunately for those of us who like houseplants, the climate in the southern half of Florida is a passable substitute for the tropics for at least nine months out of the year. Two Florida locations—the area around Apopka, just north of Orlando, and around Homestead, south of Miami—are home to many of the wholesale growers that supply the garden centers on the East Coast. The Apopka growers have come to specialize in the smaller plants, those that are sold in three- to eight-inch pots and grown in greenhouses. The nurseries near Homestead buy much of their stock from the Apopka nurseries and then raise it outdoors in the ten-inch and larger pot sizes favored by interior and outdoor landscapers. I decided I'd make a visit to Apopka where undoubtedly my foliage plants had, so to speak, their roots.

Midday in mid-July was not the best time to arrive in central Florida. As I left the Orlando airport, the radio reported the temperature at 100 degrees, and the air over the asphalt highway was gently simmering. Apopka is forty minutes northwest of the airport, past the billboards for Sea World and Universal Studios and out along Route 429, a new highway that speeds commuters from their Orlando jobs to the ever-spreading bedroom communities. But where the highway ends just outside Apopka, I found myself in a decidedly rural world where only a few tendrils of suburban cul-de-sacs have begun to explore the flat countryside.

Apopka. It is not a name to conjure with, unlike nearby Winter Garden, Winter Park, Winter Springs, or Kissimmee, a flirtatious Seminole word that means "heaven's place." Apopka, another Seminole word, means "potato eating place," a fact that leads locals to refer to their town, with wry affection, as "The Big Potato." It's an appropriate moniker. Apopka is a down-to-earth kind of place, where people have always made their living from the land.

Various native American tribes hunted and farmed in the area and fished in fifty-thousand-acre Lake Apopka for nearly ten thousand years before the Spanish arrived in the sixteenth century. Smallpox and war so decimated the original Timucuan tribes that by 1730, only a few dozen individuals remained. Seminoles moved in from Georgia and

Alabama, only to be defeated by the U.S. military in the Second Seminole War. The last members of the tribe were transported to Oklahoma in 1841. In 1842, Congress passed the Armed Occupation Act that gave 160 acres in eastern Florida to anyone (anyone white, that is) willing to clear, enclose, and cultivate at least five of those acres and live there for at least five years. Settlers also had to be willing to bear arms and choose land at least two miles beyond any military post. The coast soon attracted settlers, but it was not until the mid-1870s that Orange County, including Orlando and Apopka, was occupied in any numbers.

The climate seemed propitious for growing oranges, and boosters lured northerners with the promise of a salutary climate and riches from citrus cultivation. The editor of the *Apopka Citizen* boasted in 1879 that there had not been a single funeral in the community for an entire year, a remarkable situation, he wrote, given that "we see about us everyday numbers of people who came here mere skeletons, hardly able to crawl, who are now hale and hearty, recuperated in both health and wealth." But the truth was that freezes, hurricanes, insect infestations, and yellow fever made health and wealth more elusive than promised. Still, citrus growers persisted, and by the mid-1890s, growers were shipping around five million boxes of oranges, and area wineries were using millions more to make orange wine. (I discovered that it is still possible to buy orange wine made in Florida and ordered a bottle from the Florida Orange Groves Winery. All I can say is that it must be an acquired taste.) Entrepreneurs also drained thousands of acres of the marshy southern side of Lake Apopka, revealing fertile muck ten feet deep, and farmers made good money shipping winter vegetables north. One of the few crops that didn't flourish, ironically, was potatoes: deficiencies of potash and phosphorus in the muck lands caused them to rot in the ground.

At the turn of the century, the mania for ferns that gripped the English middle class traveled across the Atlantic. The craze got a big boost in America in 1894 when F. C. Becker, a Boston florist, ordered a shipment of two hundred *Nephrolepis exaltata* and discovered one mutant whose fronds, instead of growing straight up out of a pot, swooped gracefully over the sides. *Nephrolepis exaltata* 'Bostoniensis', or Boston fern, was an immediate hit.

In 1910, Harry Ustler was a twenty-one-year-old order clerk at the Springfield Floral Company, a flower wholesaler in Ohio that also grew Boston ferns. Ustler and his boss, a Mr. Powell, were well aware of the demand for Boston ferns and realized that the largest factor in their price was the cost of heating the northern greenhouses where they were grown. They figured they could make money raising them in a southern climate and shipping them north. Ustler quit his job and went to central Florida to find an appropriate site, only to have Powell—who was supposed to finance the venture—drop out. A stubborn fellow, Ustler stayed on, taking a job as a waiter at the Altamonte Springs Hotel while he figured out how to start a business without any funds and no knowledge of growing ferns outdoors in a subtropical climate. He must have been a remarkably persuasive young man because in short order he managed to talk one of the hotel guests, a visitor from New Hampshire named W. P. Newell, into going into business with him. Newell would supply the capital and Ustler would do the work. After leasing a shade-house in Orlando for a year, in 1911 the partners moved the business to land Newell owned in nearby Apopka.

Within a few years, Ustler had more orders for ferns than he could fill, and he convinced his brothers and a dozen Apopkans to grow ferns that he would market. By 1923, Apopkans were calling their town "Fern City," never mind that the population had yet to reach fifteen hundred and pigs and cattle still roamed the streets. In 1927, Ustler employed about a third of the population of Apopka and shipped out more than a million ferns, essentially all of Apopka's production. Many of the plants were sold to five-and-dime stores like Kress, Kresge, and Woolworth. The result, according to the *Mayflower* magazine, was that "no other fern ever attained such widespread popularity in the cities of the country at large, and the city florist decorators and plant dealers find the demand for it seemingly unending."

Apopka growers gradually diversified to other foliage plants, adding heartleaf philodendron (*Philodendron cordatum*) in the late 1920s, Chinese evergreen (*Aglaonema modestum*) and rubber plant (*Ficus elastica*) in the 1930s, and many more species in the 1940s. Entry into the business was easy. Sunshine and water were free, shadehouses made of slats left over from broken orange crates were cheap, and even glasshouses were not a huge investment. An initial stake of seed or cuttings could be had for pennies per plant. As more growers arrived, suppliers of fertilizer, pesticide, and equipment moved to their customers. In the 1950s, Fern City proclaimed itself "The Indoor Foliage Capital of the World," and it was.

By the 1960s, more than a hundred varieties of ornamental plants grew in Apopka greenhouses, and nearly a quarter of Apopka's population was involved in their production. The back-to-nature movement of the 1970s created a sharp upsurge in the demand for houseplants; twelve hundred new foliage plant businesses opened in Apopka in that decade. Laboratory tissue culture techniques in the 1980s sent production costs down and sales up, and the labs produced hundreds of new hybrids. According to the USDA, in 2007 the wholesale value of foliage plants (not including poinsettias and African violets) was $630 million, and Florida produced 74 percent of those sales. At an average wholesale price of around three dollars, that meant Florida nurseries grew and sold more than 150 million foliage plants.

There was no better place to start a visit to Apopka than with Tim Landers, owner of Benchmark Foliage, an eighteen-acre nursery on Hogshead Road. Benchmark is typical of Apopka's medium-size foliage businesses, neither one of the dozens of mom-and-pop operations nor one of the handful of large-scale, high-tech operations with dozens of acres under glass. I pulled up to the nursery at ten o'clock on a blazing morning when the air was already as moist and thick as a dog's breath. Six white-painted greenhouses, each of which enclosed about a football field of space, stepped back in two rows from the road. Nine plastic-covered hoophouses covering about a quarter acre each stood to the side. I didn't see any office, so I headed for the broad opening of the shipping dock.

Tim Landers, a lean man with a deep tan, a soft Alabama

drawl, and a gentle manner, greeted me as I climbed the small stairway at the side. Stacks of paper-wrapped, boxed plants lined the walls. Two Australian shepherds, stretched out on the floor and panting, slapped their tails a few times against the concrete, the canine equivalent of the laconic southern "hey." A young woman drove a forklift around us, moving boxes to the edge of the shipping dock, while Tim gave me an overview of his business.

"I bought this place in March of '93," he said, "and I was just at the point of purchasing it when what they call 'The Storm of the Century' came through. The nursery was slammed, completely wrecked. Broke every pane of glass. Fortunately, the owner had good insurance on the glass, although I suspect he took a big loss on the plants, which weren't part of our deal."

Tim repaired and restocked the greenhouses, and he now employs eighteen people, most of whom have been with the company ten or more years. Each year, he ships about six hundred thousand plants worth about $1.8 million, mostly *Croton, Dieffenbachia,* and several varieties of ivy, plus smaller numbers of *Neanthe bella* and *Areca* palms, various ferns, orange jasmine, *Ardisia,* and *Ficus elastica* 'Burgundy'. About 40 percent of his plants go to brokers and another 40 percent go directly to the garden centers that, like Johnson's, contract with a trucking firm to make regular pickups. The remainder are sold to the drive-in trade and to regional garden center owners and florists who scout out the best deals and send their own trucks. The plants he sells to brokers might go directly to retail outlets or they might be bought by growers in Homestead or elsewhere to be grown into larger specimens. Brokers keep information about the ultimate buyer to themselves, and Tim is very careful when he encounters potential direct customers: if he unwittingly poaches one of his brokers' customers, he runs the risk of alienating the broker, a serious matter.

We headed outside into the hammering sunlight, followed by the dogs, and down the broad dirt path that runs between the two rows of greenhouses. Tim stopped in front of one, and with two hands slid open the big greenhouse door that screeched mightily as he did. Suddenly, we were in a cool-green world. Before us, at hip height and suspended in midair, was a vast green sea of foliage flecked with bits of creamy foam. Six feet above the sea hung a cloud cover of ivy plants, their stems trailing. The horizon, the far end of the greenhouse, was so distant that the plants were just a verdant blur. The roof of the greenhouse, painted a translucent white, radiated a diffuse light that cast no shadows. Even the air, refracted and reflected, was a watery green. A low roar emanated from a dozen or so five-foot-diameter fans lodged in the greenhouse wall.

"*Dieffenbachia* 'Parachute'," Tim shouted above the fans, as we approached the plants. They were not, in fact, levitating, but growing in pots on seventy-foot-long, five-foot-wide tables—"benches" in the business—that were completely obscured by leaves. I now could see that there were a number of distinct, rectangular patches in the sea, each one composed of plants at a different stage of growth. I looked more closely at the plants near us. The elongated green leaves that shot straight up from the soil on slender stems had a long, creamy patch down the center. Tim gathered up several bushy, two-foot-tall plants in his arms so I could see the bench, Styrofoam covered and stained by algae, beneath.

Benchmark uses two methods of watering and fertilizing: flooding and dripping. The *Dieffenbachia* are flooded: the bench they sit on is really more of a tray that about twice a week is filled from a pipe below with a water and fertilizer mix and then, after eight minutes, drained. The pots of ivy overhead are fed and watered by a drip line that runs along the rod from which they hang. One slender black tube snakes from the line into each pot. Both methods not only efficiently put water and nutrients directly into the soil, they also avoid wetting the leaves, which could lead to unsightly spotting or, worse, fungal disease.

Running lengthwise down the benches between each row of pots were half-inch-wide, white plastic pipes—there were about ten miles of piping in this greenhouse alone, Tim said—that circulated warm water from a boiler. Although Apopka gets only a couple below-freezing nights per year, Tim has to run the boiler—a big expense—when temperatures dip below fifty or sixty degrees, depending on the species. The pipes apply heat where it is needed; there is no sense wasting energy to warm the entire volume of air in the greenhouse. Plants with woody stems—his ivy, for example—are more tolerant of cold, but soft-tissued species, as most of his plants are, would be ruined instantly in a freeze.

"My biggest problem, though, isn't weather," Tim said, "but cash flow. I've got to pay my workers every week. That means I've got to make a little money every day, and that means I've got to have a certain number of plants ready for sale every week or as near to it as I can get. It takes me fourteen weeks to get dieffs in three-inch pots out the door. The larger pots, the eight-inch ones, take twenty-six weeks or longer. The six-inch ivy pots take twenty-two weeks, and the six-inch *Crotons* take about twenty-five weeks. That's an average; it depends on the season. The palms can take up to two years." He showed me Benchmark's current price list. It was organized into categories by pot size. Plants in three-inch pots sold for under fifty cents while eight-inch pots ranged from about five dollars for ivy to about six dollars for a *Neanthe bella* palm. Clearly, the profit is in volume.

The trick, Tim said, to the nursery business is to have the right plants at the right size at the right time all the time. The trouble is that he has to make decisions about what will sell, and therefore what to plant, anywhere from fourteen weeks to two years in advance. Those decisions are complicated by a host of variables. For one, it takes longer for plants to grow in the winter months because there are fewer hours of daylight. He has to get the mix of plants right, growing new and unusual varieties while at the same time making sure he's got enough of the tried and true. There are fads in the tropical plant business, but he has to be careful about committing to what's hot at the moment. Other growers are likely to hop on any trend, which can mean that six months or a year down the road, the market is glutted and the price is too low to make a profit. In addition, although growers can produce tropical plants in Florida year-round, demand for them is seasonal.

I wondered why that would be. Wasn't the point of indoor plants that you could have them year-round?

"Think of your garden center in winter," Tim prompted me. "What is it you're going to see there from October until

January? Mostly mums in late fall, poinsettias in December. Lots of retailers just don't have room for foliage plants in those months. Most of my customers don't want to talk to me until January." To deal with this problem, he has been expanding into *Crotons*, which, with their red, orange, and yellow leaves, are becoming a big fall crop; last year he sold fourteen thousand and could have sold a lot more if he had had stock. He also is expanding into ivy trained on hoops for the Christmas season. Still, winter is slow for everybody.

"But what's really scary about this business is I've got a perishable crop. I can't just put my plants on a shelf and wait if I can't get a good price. If my plants aren't moving out the door as soon as they're the right size, all I'm doing is wasting growing space and throwing away expensive fertilizer and water. In the winter, if it's a bad winter, I've got to add the cost of heating. And the longer the plants sit, the more likely they're going to get disease or just plain go south."

We moved on to a glasshouse devoted to ivy. Tim introduced me to Miguel, "my most valuable employee," who stood in an aisle between benches. (The aisles, unproductive space in a greenhouse, are so narrow I had to lift my elbows above my waist and angle forward.) Miguel was making cuttings and planting the eight-inch hanging pots of ivy that I had seen in the first glasshouse. He had a pile of two-foot-long vine cuttings to one side and pots filled with soil in front of him. I watched as he took a long cutting in one hand, a secateur in the other, and in one motion clipped off a short bit of vine with one leaf on it and stuck it in the soil. He did this thirty-five times for each pot, filling one pot with evenly spaced bits in less than ninety seconds. Miguel, paid by the piece, earns as much as a thousand dollars a week. Not bad, Tim said, for an immigrant without a high school education.

We spent another hour walking through all the glass-houses and the airy hoophouses, home to fields of *Spathiphyllum*, *Ardisia* (a small-leafed plant that Benchmark grows from stock originally collected in local bogs and then raised from seed), *Dracaena* boldly striped in white and green, several varieties of ferns that go to florists for filling out bouquets, and *Areca* palms, slow growers that he starts from seed. Wherever we went, we were surrounded by elevated fields of ideal plants, all radiant with good health and working at maximum efficiency turning sunlight, water, and nutrients into lush vegetal material.

Others might have been encouraged by seeing such perfection, but the sight inspired worry for me. Just look what it took to create these marvels of plant growth. The conditions in the Benchmark greenhouses were perfect, with the ideal mix of light, humidity, food, and water provided in precisely calibrated times. The plants were constantly monitored, regularly repotted, and, as they grew, frequently respaced on the benches by people who were totally attentive to and knowledgeable about them. Of course, these plants flourished grandly. But, I asked Tim, could I or any northern homeowner, with an environment in every way unlike his, keep plants looking anything as beautiful as these?

Tim considered for more than a few moments before answering.

"Well," he said, dubiously, "it is certainly possible. It can be done. And some species are definitely easier than others.

The *Dieffenbachia,* ivies, and palms are pretty easy." If the plants, he added, had been raised in a greenhouse with 80 or 85 percent shade as his were, they would have a better chance in a home. That was one of the problems of buying larger plants that had been raised in Homestead outside in full sun. Those plants had to be gradually transitioned to the lower-light conditions inside a house, but most homeowners wouldn't know to do that.

Some tropicals just aren't suited to interior use. He pointed to a *Croton petra* with its tricolored leaves. "If I took this plant and put it in my house, it would live for about six or eight months and then deteriorate. Look, these plants come from the rain forest where there's near 100 percent humidity. The chances of keeping a rain forest plant in a house . . . Well, let's just say it's chancy."

He considered some more. Mine was a question he clearly hadn't given a lot of thought to; no more, I suppose, does a corn farmer think a lot about whether his crop is going into fritters or chowder.

"I tell you," he said, "I've seen some people, just general laypeople, who are real good with houseplants. But I've probably seen more like my wife who can't grow a damn thing."

I laughed. "How about you? Can you keep them alive at home?"

"You know, I don't know. I never tried. It's like being a plumber. Last thing a plumber wants to do at the end of the day is fix the kitchen faucet."

After we left the last greenhouse, we headed slightly downhill toward the shadehouses where I could see acres of simple wooden frames covered with a dark mesh cloth and open on the sides. As we walked, Tim explained that the mesh allowed rain to fall through while reducing the strength of sunlight by about 80 percent. Sometimes, he used two layers to cut the light even further. The plants in the shadehouses were set on the ground on black plastic that prevented insects from burrowing into the plants though the pots' drainage holes yet allowed rainwater to seep away.

We walked into a dense, hip-high thicket of *Croton petra*. Each plant mimicked a Caribbean sunrise: the lowest leaves of each plant were a deep red, and as the leaves grew higher on the stem they shaded through orange to yellow to yellow with bright green veins. En masse, they were stunning.

I asked Tim about pesticides. He rarely has to use anything in the greenhouses, he said: washing the surfaces and tools regularly with bleach keeps the environment clean. Even outside—and I would hear the same thing from every grower I met—plants in excellent health are able to resist insects and disease without chemical assistance. Only if they are stressed by too little water, sunlight, or nutrients do they became vulnerable. The fact is, pesticides are expensive—one, he said as he shook his head, costs more than $1,000 per gallon—and using them cuts deeply into profit margins.

We were about to head back up the slope when I asked Tim what he saw in the future of the Apopka foliage plant business. Tim, who until now had spoken at a languid tempo, suddenly grew animated.

"Here's my problem with this industry right now. There's not a lot of kids that can afford to get in it. Not by the time they go out and pay for the land, build the structures, buy the plants and soil and seed and all, then wait ninety days for the first crop to grow, sell it, and wait another thirty days to get their money. Costs are going up on near everything. Only thing that's gotten any cheaper is plastic pots.

"The biggest issue, though, is that housing developers are driving the cost of land up—looks like Apopka's going to be the next suburb of Orlando. And insurance is sky-high. I have to insure each of my glasshouses separately and that means a $5,000 deductible on each one. There's government insurance on my crop, but it only covers 50 percent of a loss. Also, there's a ton of regulation and paperwork that eats up a lot of my time.

"In fact, one of the reasons I'm hanging in here is because the mom-and-pop operations are going under and no one's coming in to take their place. I figure that's got to be good for me." He paused. "I'm just a dirt farmer. This nursery is my life savings. I don't have any IRAs. Every dime I made, I've plowed it back in here. This eighteen acres is my retirement."

He pointed down the hill, where I could see that the scrubby land dropped off more steeply. "You see down there about five hundred yards? Someday that's going to be the shore of Lake Apopka."

Tim explained that twenty thousand acres of Lake Apopka had been drained in 1941 to create more land for vegetable farming. Then, in the mid-1990s, the water authority changed its approach to the lake and bought out all the muck farmers, with the goal of returning Lake Apopka to its original footprint. After the purchase, the authority discovered that the land was heavily contaminated with organophosphates and other chemicals, but was in the process of a massive cleanup.

"Even if no one wants this place as a nursery, I expect a developer'll buy it. This property is going to have a lake view." Tim was philosophical. The beautiful plants were just a crop and the farm was a just way—the only way he happened to know—to make a living.

Harry Ustler, the man who started the Apopka foliage business, may have gathered some of his original stock from the wild ferns that grew in the shady scrub around Apopka, but he would have taken cuttings from his best plants to create the next generations for sale. Today, a commercial grower is far more likely to call up a tissue culture lab (or, as some call it, a micropropagation lab) and order microcuttings of the species he next plans to grow. Depending on a specie's habits and the market conditions, a grower might order Stage II microcuttings, which are bare, inch-long stems with two or three leaves and just a hint of root growth; Stage III microcuttings, which have roots; or, for a little more money, three-inch-high Stage IV plants rooted in a plug of soil about the size of a man's thumb. The plugs are usually sold in a "liner" of seventy-two plugs that sells for about a dollar; a plastic bag of several hundred microcuttings might go for half that. All of the tiny plants will be clones, exact genetic copies grown from the same small piece—maybe even a single cell—of a parent plant. All of them will have started life in the world's smallest greenhouses: glass test tubes.

If the idea of cloning makes you queasy, relax. Cloning comes naturally to plants; cloning is simply asexual (or *vegetative*) reproduction, and plants do it all the time. Strawberry plants send out stolons that grow along the top of the soil, send down roots, and become new plants. When a blackberry branch comes in contact with the soil, it sends out roots and starts a new plant. Grasses produce underground stems that will periodically produce roots and send a new aboveground shoot. Potato plants reproduce through buds on the underground tuber. All of these new plants are genetically identical to the parent. Besides, some of our favorite fruits are cloned by humans: bananas, seedless grapes, and seedless oranges were once mutations that, sterile, would have vanished if we hadn't cloned them.

To make a clone in a laboratory, a technician starts by removing a tiny piece of *meristematic* tissue from a plant, usually from its growing tip, although in some species the tissue can also be harvested from leaves, as in begonias, or roots, as in carrots. The meristematic cells are analogous to stem cells in animals: they are largely undifferentiated and have the ability to divide indefinitely and become all kinds of plant tissue, depending on their location and exposure to light, nutrients, hormones, and other environmental factors. The extracted tissue, called an *explant,* is chemically disinfected to eliminate any fungi or bacteria growing on it and is placed on a sterile cultural medium in a test tube.

The composition of the medium is all-important. It contains not only all the inorganic chemical nutrients, amino acids, vitamins, and sugars a plant needs to develop, but also a variable mix of growth-regulating hormones. At the first stage in the tissue culture process, the medium is enriched with *cytokinins* that send signals to the explant to produce multiple tiny juvenile shoots, each with two or three leaves.

A technician can further multiply those shoots by cutting off the side or *axillary* stems and transferring those to additional test tubes to create more new shoots. Or she can transfer them to another medium rich in another class of hormones, *auxins,* that induce the shoots to branch and develop roots and, over a period of weeks, become young plantlets ready for the greenhouse. By taking advantage of the totipotency of meristematic cells, tissue culture can theoretically produce an infinite number of genetically identical plants from one explant. New explants, however, are regularly taken and cultured to avoid the occasional mutations that occur in repeated cell division.

Dr. Robert Hartman, now president of Classic Caladiums, a commercial caladium production company in Avon Park, Florida, has been an innovator in the tissue culture industry since its beginnings in the mid-1970s. The tissue culture industry took off in Apopka, he explained to me, as a response to a disease problem. Viruses and bacterial diseases were a major issue for nurseries that specialized in aroids, the family of plants that includes such popular indoor species as *Dieffenbachia, Syngonium, Philodendron, Caladium, Colocasia,* and *Aglaonema.* A nurseryman might leave his greenhouse full of thousands of apparently healthy *Dieffenbachia* on a Friday afternoon, open the doors on Monday morning, and discover that all his plants, every single one, had turned to mush over the weekend. The *Erwinia* bacterium was usually the problem. It could lie dormant and undetectable for months and then, in response to an increase in greenhouse temperature or some other environmental change, break out overnight. If all of the grower's stock was grown from cuttings of a few infected mother plants, he would have unwittingly infected every plant in the greenhouse. Losses could total hundreds of thousands of dollars.

Hartman, who had studied plant virology and tissue culture in graduate school and was the first to tissue culture aroids for commercial production, started a company to produce plants that he could guarantee to be free of known viruses when they left the shipping dock. His lab, and the many others that jumped into the business in the 1980s, couldn't entirely eliminate diseases from Apopka greenhouses. But infections tended to be localized to one area of a greenhouse (where, say, a worker had used nonsterile clippers) and could be eliminated before they became catastrophic.

Tissue culture started as a means to eliminate disease, but Apopka growers quickly realized there were other advantages to using the technique. Tissue-cultured plants, they discovered, grow more quickly than seed-generated plants, and they are stunningly uniform, a highly desirable quality for growers promising to deliver a particular product. They are also more likely to reach healthy maturity than plants grown from cuttings because the process of taking a cutting creates a wound through which all sorts of pathogens can enter. And tissue-cultured plants give growers a unique commercial advantage: if a grower discovers he has a promising mutation or an interesting hybrid, he can create new stock in a matter of months rather than slowly building his inventory through generations of cuttings.

But best of all, micropropagated plants are juvenile plants, plants whose biological clocks have been turned back to nearly zero. A plant made from a cutting is a bit like Dolly, the cloned sheep, who developed arthritis at five and died of a lung disease typical of a much older sheep. Dolly's problem was that she was created from the multiplication of an adult mammary gland cell and she was, in part, the age of that original cell. In a similar way, a cutting creates what is essentially a smaller and newer, but only slightly younger, version of an old plant. Older plants have accumulated cellular damage, just as older people do. Older plants have different growth habits, too, than juvenile plants. They tend to be tall and leggy rather than compact and full (if women were plants, fashion models would be sixty instead of sixteen), and their cuttings tend to grow leggy, too. What Hartman and others found was that tissue-cultured plants are rejuvenated versions of the parent plant: more vigorous, bushier, more vibrantly colored, and altogether more salable.

Tissue culture changed the Apopka nursery business dramatically, driving down the costs of production and vastly increasing the variety of available plants. Some plants, like *Spathiphyllum,* that had been difficult to reproduce by seed or cutting and were notoriously variable suddenly became uniform, easy to replicate, and therefore more inexpensive to grow. It is thanks to tissue culture that you can buy inexpensive orchids in grocery stores and choose from among thousands of hybrids.

Tissue culture, Tim said, has revolutionized his business. Traditionally, propagation—getting seeds to sprout and grow and getting cuttings to root—has been the hardest, riskiest part of the business. An uncertain and significant percentage would fail to thrive. Now that he can buy microcuttings of many species, he can estimate more precisely how many market-ready plants he will have for sale. It has become much easier to schedule production.

But there has been a downside. The almost unlimited supply of inexpensive microcuttings has meant that the prices for his products have dropped. And while the drop in prices has expanded the market for tropical houseplants, it has also changed the structure of the foliage plant business significantly. Until the 1990s, most houseplants were sold through garden centers or florists. Now they are cheap and plentiful enough to be sold through mass-market merchandisers like Wal-Mart, Home Depot, and Lowe's. (Retailers now work to convince consumers that they should purchase a flowering potted plant when traditionally they would have bought a bouquet of cut flowers. The potted plant, they point out, is about the same price but can last for weeks with no more care—adding water—than a bouquet. Potted plants are, in essence, bouquets with benefits, the benefits of roots.) In recent years, well over half of the indoor plants in the United States were sold through "big box" stores.

Selling to big box stores, however, is not for small and medium-size businesses like Benchmark Foliage. As several smaller growers explained, on one hand, there is an attraction to growing to order for a big box. Any order would be big, commanding all the grower's space and eliminating the uncertainties of the marketplace. On the other hand, the big boxes can impose difficult payment terms, including allowing themselves ninety, rather than thirty, days to pay. The chains also give their retail customers money-back, no-questions-asked guarantees on their purchases, but any returns, whether justified or not, are often charged to the supplier.

Worse, a small grower becomes dependent on the big box, giving up his or her relationships with other buyers, which means in turn that the grower is very vulnerable to downward price pressure. As one grower said, "Doing business with a big box is like being in a ring with an eight-hundred-pound gorilla. You better be a damn big gorilla yourself."

If anyone can get into the ring with a big box and come out unbloodied, it is Hermann Engelmann Greenhouses, Inc. Engelmann is by far the largest grower of foliage plants in Apopka, with nine locations and three million square feet (or sixty-seven acres) under glass. In 2008, its 250 employees grew and shipped out fifteen million plants of four hundred different species. About half of Englemann plants were bought by the customers that Tim Landers avoids: home improvement chains, national discount merchandisers, and supermarkets.

Bisser Georgiev, vice president for sales and marketing, took me on a tour of three of the vast greenhouses. Instead of a single species under one roof, there were dozens, growing in great blocks of color—pink, purple, red, and shades of green—in a gigantic quilt. Men and women in floppy hats and sunglasses—the glass roof was painted a translucent white so it was bright inside but not sunny—moved slowly along the edges of the waist-high benches, clipping as they went. In one area, five tiers of terra-cotta hanging baskets of ivy, all trailing vines in exactly the same artful way, were attended by a man on stilts. Elsewhere, thousands of *Nepenthes* (pitcher plants) hung from the ceiling over a field of *Helxine soleirolii* (baby's tears). I marveled at a runway of spiky red *Cryptanthus* and what must have been an acre of pink-veined *Fittonia*. Misters went off periodically, spreading veils of vapor over green carpets. A little orange tractor went by pulling a train of wheeled benches filled with potted plants. No dirt floors here. The greenhouses were spotless, perfectly pristine. I could have had a minor surgical procedure on one of the empty benches.

The disparity in scale is actually the least of the differences between the operations of Hermann Engelmann and Tim Landers. When a Home Depot, Lowe's, or Wal-Mart buyer places an order with Engelmann, she chooses among nine different "models," which are assortments of plants in a tray. Engelmann chooses the species in the assortment. The buyer's options are strictly limited: she can choose between hanging baskets or pots and she can choose the color, style, and size of the pots. There is no ordering a case of *Pilea glauca,* much less nineteen pots of it.

On the other hand, she gets the benefit of Engelmann's extensive research on consumer purchasing trends, as well as its experience of what mix of plant colors, habits (upright versus spreading, for example), leaf pattern and shape, and pot type will make a display that will inspire a customer to pick up a plant and put it in her shopping cart. Bisser knows that more than 75 percent of indoor foliage plants are purchased on impulse. Very few people make a trip to a big box with the goal of buying a houseplant. Consequently, Engelmann's treats the foliage plant business not primarily as a farming operation, but as a consumer goods business and, in particular, as a home decor business. As Bisser put it, Engelmann is the Procter & Gamble of the indoor foliage industry. And, if as is likely the case, the big box buyer and its salespeople have no more expertise in houseplants than they do in mouthwash, then the Engelmann model is a very attractive proposition.

Just because Engelmann recognizes that a big box customer buys a plant in the same way she buys a throw pillow does not mean she gets an inferior product. Brokers and even other growers agree that Engelmann's products are excellent. Given the Engelmann business model, that is not surprising. As Bisser explained, because the product is branded—every Engelmann plant carries a prominent and distinctive "Exotic Angel" tag—consistently high quality is essential. The company has every interest in producing plants that make consumers happy, not just the day they bring them home, but over the long run. To that end, Engelmann uses soils that are custom mixed to match the aeration, pH, and water retentiveness requirements of each species. Its plants are acclimated to light levels found in homes, even though that can slow growth and extend production time. The Exotic Angel tag details the plant's needs for light, water, and fertilizer, and notes whether the species is suitable for novices or more experienced growers. There is no benefit in selling someone a plant he or she is going to kill within a week. The success of the business model depends on customers who associate quality and success with Engelmann and make another purchase.

Bisser said retailers do not reduce his bills if there are customer returns, and he has successfully resisted the "pay by scan" proposals—where the company pays the supplier only after the product has passed through the checkout scanner—that the companies push. It seems that the volume purchasing leverage exerted by the big boxes is matched by the vast production capabilities of Engelmann. Home Depot and Engelmann are an ideal match: a high-quality mass producer paired with a mass retailer.

What does Engelmann's and Home Depot's success mean for smaller growers like Tim Landers and for independent garden centers like Johnson's? Much of the answer lies in the creativity of the garden centers and the adaptability of the small growers. The successful garden center has to provide more attentive and experienced salespeople to attract the more sophisticated and demanding consumers who make a special trip to buy plants. The garden centers also have to stock larger, more expensive, and more unusual specimens than the big box is willing to carry. The successful small grower has to be flexible, willing to fulfill small and special orders, and propagate unusual varieties that command higher prices, at least until the large producers can gear up to produce en masse. Some would even argue that Engelmann and Home Depot have been a positive development for small growers and garden centers. By inspiring that first impulse buy and providing an inexpensive, high-quality, and successful plant, Engelmann and Home Depot initiate the casual consumer—who would never have ventured into a specialty garden center—into indoor plant culture. The impulse buy is repeated, the plants flourish, the consumer needs more advice and is willing to spend more for a larger specimen, and he finds his way to the specialty garden center.

At least, speaking as someone who always roots for the Davids against the Goliaths, the Edies over the Engelmanns, I hope so.

Paradise

twelve

Ficus Carica

After three years, my conservatory had evolved. I had started off with a one-of-everything approach, trying to figure out which plants could survive in my north-facing site, which had the most interesting leaf colors or patterns, and which required the least effort on my part. As I developed my list of favorites, I slowly arrived at what I suspect for most gardeners is an instinctive understanding: a mass of many individuals of a single species is more pleasing than a hodgepodge of single specimens of many species. So, in the center of the conservatory I now had a thicket of anthurium with spathes in peaches, oranges, and reds. I rooted goldfish plants (*Nematanthus*) cuttings and set six pots of these drooping, deep green, orange-flecked beauties on a tiered bench along the north wall. Four bird-of-paradise plants, which proved to be surprisingly tolerant of low light, formed a jungly thicket behind the anthurium. My specimen cacti and succulents were happy in the western bay window.

In the third summer, a friend gave me a large, fruiting pineapple. I also discovered the Edible Landscaping Company outside Charlottesville, Virginia, and ordered a half-dozen fruit-bearing plants: an English brown turkey fig, a coffee plant (which bore white flowers and red berries in quick succession), a strawberry guava, a pineapple guava, a pomegranate, and a loquat. At the end of the third autumn, after I had moved the new trees and my collection of limes, oranges, lemons, and kumquats inside under the grow lights, I found I had to exile my more shade-tolerant plants to windows in other parts of the house. There were ferns in the bathrooms, *Spathiphyllum* in the dining room, *Aglaonema* on the landing, *Dracaena* on the kitchen counter and in the living room, and a tree-form *Schefflera* was the first thing I saw when I opened my eyes in the morning. I didn't expect them to grow, I just hoped they'd survive the winter. The long-leaved clivias that had spent the summer under the oak tree in the backyard went to the basement to work on their flowers. Only when they started to bloom would they get a space upstairs.

When all my charges were settled into their various winter digs, I looked around and realized that my conservatory was looking less like the understory of a tropical jungle and more, with its fruiting trees surrounding the clear and shining pool, like a medieval vision of the Garden of Eden.

For a very long time—roughly 1500 B.C. to the eighteenth century—for those in the Judeo-Christian world, the word *paradise* was synonymous with the Garden of Eden. According to

Jean Dulumeau in his comprehensive *History of Paradise*, the word itself derives from the Old Persian *apiri-daeza*, which meant "orchard surrounded by a wall." The Old Testament description of the Garden of Eden in Genesis 2:9–10, bare as it is, derives from that ancient idea.

> *The Lord God planted a garden in Eden, in the*
> *east; and there he put the man whom he had formed.*
> *Out of the ground the Lord God made to grow*
> *every tree that is pleasant to the sight and good for*
> *food, the tree of life also in the midst of the garden,*
> *and the tree of the knowledge of good and evil. A*
> *river flowed out of Eden to water the garden, and*
> *there it divided and became four rivers.*

God put Adam in the Garden "to till it and keep it," added "every beast of the field and every bird of the air," and finally Eve. And that is about all the description we have of the biblical Eden.

So why do we have such a rich vision of the Garden? We owe the details to the ancient Greek and Roman writers. They had their own paradisial gardens, which were far more imaginatively furnished than the ancient Jewish one. The Greeks believed they were living in the fourth and much degraded iteration of the world, and they looked wistfully back to a vanished Golden Age. Plato described it in *The Statesman* as a place where people

> *had fruits in plenty from the trees and other*
> *plants, which the earth furnished them of its own*

*accords, without help from agriculture. And they
lived for the most part in the open air, without
clothing or bedding; for the climate was tempered for
their comfort, and the abundant grass that grew up
out of the earth furnished them with soft couches.*

Theocritus, a Greek poet of the third century B.C., was more expansive:

*A wealth of elm and poplar shook o'erhead;
Hard by, a sacred spring flowed gurgling on
From the Nymphs' grot, and in the sombre boughs
The sweet cicadas chirped laboriously.
Hid in the thick thorn-bushes far away
The treefrog's note was heard; the crested lark
Sang with the goldfinch; turtles made their moan,
And o'er the fountain hung the gilded bee.
All of rich summer smacked, of autumn all:
Pears at our feet and apples at our side
Rolled in luxuriance; branches on the ground
Sprawled, overweighed with damsons.*

Ovid, the Roman writer of *Metamorphoses* (about A.D. 8), embellished further:

*Men, content with food which came with no one's
seeking, gathered the arbute fruit, strawberries from
the mountainsides, cornel-cherries, berries hanging
thick upon the prickly bramble, and acorns falling
from the spreading tree of Jove.*

Then Spring was everlasting, and gentle zephyrs
with warm breath played with the flowers that
sprang unplanted. Anon the earth, untilled, brought
forth her stores of grain, and the fields, though
unfallowed, grew white with the heavy bearded
wheat. Streams of milk and streams of sweet nectar
flowed, and yellow honey was distilled from the
verdant oak.

Other Romans—Pindar, Homer, and Horace—added their own flourishes and, more important, imagined that such a place still existed, either as the Elysian Fields in the after-death underworld or in the Happy Isles. The latter, according to Horace, rose far out at sea where "ever blooms the vine unpruned, and buds the shoot of the never-failing olive; the dark fig graces its native tree; honey flows from the hollow oak; from the lofty hill, with plashing foot, lightly leaps the fountain." These were places well worth pining for.

Early Christian writers in the Mediterranean world absorbed these lush descriptions of pagan paradises, and hung them, like colored lights and ornaments on a bare Christmas tree, on the sparse Old Testament image. Prudentius, a Roman Christian poet born in 348, put Adam and Eve in

Leafy bowers in pleasure garden fair:
Where spring's scents did always blow
And four stately streams did flow
O'er meadows pied with blossoms rare.

Writing at about the same time, St. Ephrem, a deacon, teacher, and poet in Syria, added fig trees, the flowers of the eternal summer, lambs unthreatened by predators, and soil that yielded wine, honey, milk, and butter.

Most of the earliest Christian philosophers assumed that Eden had been a real place. St. Augustine, whose convictions deeply influenced Western Christians for centuries, made it clear in *The Literal Meaning of Genesis*, written about 415, that the tree of life in Eden was "a real material tree" and the rivers were "true rivers," although they also had some figurative meaning. The Venerable Bede (673–736), one of the most learned and respected Christian scholars during the Middle Ages, wrote: "Let us have no doubt that the paradise in which the first human being was placed is to be understood as a real place." Thomas Aquinas was equally certain in the thirteenth century that the earthly paradise, Eden, existed in an absolutely literal sense. The French priest Vincent of Beauvais, in his popular encyclopedia of the thirteenth century, even pinpointed the exact times that Adam and Eve sinned (noon on the very day God created them) and were expelled from the Garden ("shortly after, around the ninth hour"). And Eden, they were all convinced, not only had been a real place, but it was still extant.

Medieval cartographers were far from agreed on the precise configuration of the Garden. Some imagined it was enclosed by a wall with a single gate guarded by fire or angels within a sort of Greater Edenic Area. Others placed the Garden on a mountaintop far above the clouds—almost to the moon—where the air would be pure. Still others pictured it as an island separated from the rest of the sullied world by unbounded ocean. But no matter how they imagined it, Eden was real enough that they located it on their world maps.

The fifteenth- and sixteen-century explorers who embarked on their treacherous voyages were drawn chiefly by the prospect of winning gold and glory, but the hope of running across the long-lost paradise was a real incentive. Latin America with its year-round warm climate, lush landscapes, parrots, and trees with strange fruits seemed like it might well be the outskirts of the Garden. Christopher Columbus had a unique vision of the layout: in his view, Eden was shaped like a pear and the unattainable Garden was at the top of its stem. After his third voyage in 1498 when he explored the northeastern shore of South America, he conjectured that the Orinoco River, which empties into the Gulf of Paria between the mainland and Trinidad, had its source in Eden. That made the east coast of Venezuela the front yard of paradise. No one could enter the Garden itself because mankind had not yet been redeemed, but it seemed possible that people might get near enough to catch a bit of the glow.

Luther and Calvin believed that, thanks to Adam's sin, all his descendants were therefore condemned to a state of depravity that deprived them of the ability to achieve, either through acts or faith, reconciliation with God. Only those preordained for salvation would make it to heaven. The reality of Eden was a foregone conclusion and of great interest, of course, to those who thought they might be among the elect, and Calvin's commentary on Genesis was accompanied by a map that included Eden, which he placed east of Babylon. The map then appeared in copies of the popular Geneva Bible, the mass-produced Bible first printed in 1560.

Seventeenth-century religious philosophers and poets, Catholic and Protestant alike, devoted much ink to the importance of paradise and continued the debate about its precise location. John Milton, in his epic poem of 1667, *Paradise Lost,* put the garden in Assyria. Luis de Urreta, a Dominican priest, thought that equatorial Africa in general and Mount Amara in Ethiopia in particular was a better bet. But even as priests and poets speculated, natural philosophers were raising some discomfiting questions about the reality of an earthly Eden, now or ever. Nicolaus Steno, an Italian anatomist who lived from 1638 to 1686, tried to answer the question of how seashells came to be found at the tops of mountains. Even if one assumed that the biblical flood had deposited ancient seashells on mountaintops, how did the shells come to be inside rocks? Genesis was clear: Earth, which certainly included rocks, was created first; living things, like sea creatures, came after. Was there something not quite right about the biblical chronology of Earth's history? Was the Bible to be taken less than literally? And what did that mean about the earthly paradise?

In the eighteenth century, as Enlightenment natural philosophers turned to data collection and hypothesis testing to understand the world, they found no evidence for an extant Eden. Explorers were filling out the contours of the world map, and it became harder to posit where a secret Eden might lie. Those who believed that the Garden had once had a literal existence came to assume it had been swept away in the flood. By the end of the century, scientists were concluding that Earth and life on Earth were much older than once thought, and that the Garden of Eden was allegory, not history. Today, even Christian inerrantists who believe that the Bible is accurate in all respects, and that the Garden of Eden was historical fact, do not expect to stumble upon it on a Caribbean vacation.

Dreams of an earthly paradise well up from the depths of the human psyche, and one can argue that every utopian community has been an attempt to re-create our lost Eden. In 1984, a group of idealists devoted to the philosophy of synergism made a unique effort to establish an unsullied oasis of natural and human harmony. They set out to construct a three-acre model of Earth's biosphere—that is, its life-supporting crust, waters, and atmosphere—inside a hermetically sealed, high-tech conservatory. The location of this Eden was neither an island, nor a mountaintop, nor an ancient site. It was in an isolated sixteen-hundred-acre plot in the desert outside Tucson, Arizona.

What they called Biosphere 2 (Earth itself they termed Biosphere 1) would contain miniature versions of a rain forest, a desert, a savannah, a marsh, an ocean, and farmland. There would be animals and insects, fish and fowl. And there would be people: eight synergists who would tend the five biomes, husband the animals, and till the arable soil. Biosphere 2 would be completely self-sufficient. No air, food, water, or any other substances would go in. No waste of any kind would come out.

Amazingly, they made it happen. Ed Bass, a Texas multibillionaire, a self-styled "ecopreneur," and a believer in synergist ideas, backed the project with $200 million. On September 26, 1991, four men and four women stepped through an airlock into their glass-enclosed Eden, not to emerge, if all went according to plan, for two years. John Allen, who also calls himself Johnny Dolphin, was their charismatic, mercurial, manipulative, and paranoid leader who directed operations from outside.

I can't explain synergism or why the philosophy led to this particular project, which was variously described as a re-creation of an earthly paradise, a prototype for living on Mars, a "refugia" for sustaining the survivors of a nuclear war, and an endeavor to advance the science of ecosystems. I can pass along that synergism is related to Buckminster Fuller's desire to "understand the methods that Nature actually uses in coordinating the Universe (both physically and metaphysically)" and to William Burroughs and Brion Gyson's book, *The Third Mind,* a very peculiar book of interviews, short fiction, and cut-up and rearranged pieces of unrelated texts. Synergism's adherents believe in harnessing the energy of social groups, using theater to explore one's inner life, and making money from "ecotechnics," a term that is less than helpfully defined as "the ecology of technics, and the technics of ecology."

But never mind the whys and the what-fors. By September 1991, a 539-foot-long glasshouse with stepped glass pyramids on either end, nine glass vaults above its midsection, and a mushroom-shaped tower had risen in the foothills of the Santa Catalina Mountains. The structure was a frame of seventy-seven thousand white, tubular-steel struts that held sixty-six hundred glass panels. Workers spent months sealing an underground stainless steel liner to the frame and then sealing sixty miles of seams between the frame and the glass panels. During construction and with the help of dozens of experts in the fields of entomology, ecology, botany, agronomy, animal husbandry, oceanography, soil geology, and climatology, the future inhabitants of Biosphere 2 filled the interior of their future home. The Missouri Botanical Gardens donated mature rain forest trees. A whole section of marsh—mangroves, soil, crabs, snails, and everything else in the water and soil—arrived from Florida. Corals were sent from a Yucatan reef devastated by a hurricane, and tropical fish from the Caribbean were added. The savannah grass was local. In addition to thousands of plant species, there were dozens of different soil types. Animal life included two dozen insect species, lobsters, snakes, goats, small pigs, chickens, tortoises, skinks, and several six-inch-long tropical primates called bushbabies.

The five wilderness biomes were contiguous in the long central trunk of the Biosphere, which was more than eight stories high at its highest point. The rain forest had a thirty-foot cascading waterfall and a pond. The savannah was modeled on South American grasslands. Coastal Baja California provided the cacti and succulents for Biosphere's desert, which had similarly dry soil and periods of high humidity. The hundred-foot-long Everglades marsh included three swamps with increasing levels of salinity, and the ocean, which contained nine hundred thousand gallons of salt water, had a coconut palm beach and a coral reef. The farm, officially the Intensive Agriculture Biome, was housed on a half acre in a glass structure with vaulted roofs connected at a right angle to the wilderness biomes. Behind the farm was the Human Habitat, with separate bedrooms and shared kitchen, dining, and common rooms. The tower housed a library.

Thousands of sensors, "sniffers and sippers," gathered data on air, soil, and water quality. Sprinklers provided rain. Three pumps sucked about ten thousand gallons of seawater into a hollow wall at the back of the ocean and then released it, sending waves surging to the shore while pushing food to the coral. The Technosphere, the level below ground, covered two acres and was filled with 117 pumps; two miles of pipes; dozens of air handlers; water storage tanks; heating and cooling exchangers; desalination systems; plumbing, composting, and water and air scrubbing equipment; machine tooling and woodworking shops; and storage areas. Nearby were two domed metal buildings, each more than fifty yards wide and connected via underground tunnels to Biosphere 2. In the mornings, as the air in Biosphere 2 warmed and expanded under the desert sun, it flowed out of the conservatory and into the two "lungs." In the evenings, as Biosphere 2 cooled, it rushed back.

Fundamentally, the experiment worked. The marsh reeds and savannah grass grew luxuriously; the animals multiplied; bananas, guavas, and papayas ripened in the tropical rain forest; fish and crustaceans swam in the sea; peanuts, rice, lablab beans, sweet potatoes, and other crops flourished, in rotation, in the fields. The air was breathable and urine was turned into drinking water.

But, if this had been the original Garden of Eden, Adam and Eve would have made their exit long before the ninth hour. In the biblical Garden, the First Couple exerted no effort in growing their food. Farming in the Biospherian Eden, however, was tremendously hard labor. Every morning, all the members of the crew worked on the farm, planting, weeding, combating pests, or harvesting, and several continued into the afternoon. The half-acre farm had been sized with the expectation of using highly productive hybrid species, as well as chemical fertilizers and pesticides, but the actual farm used none of those. Even with every inch planted and with pots of sweet potatoes perched in every available sunny spot in the Biosphere, the crew could barely grow enough food to survive. The Biospherians lost, on average, 14 percent of their body weight, and like underfed people everywhere, they struggled for the energy to work and thought obsessively about food. Bedeviled by proliferating cockroaches that competed for their crops, they contemplated killing two birds with one stone and eating the roaches for dinner.

Only months after the doors were sealed, carbon dioxide levels rose to dangerous levels. The years 1991 and 1992 were El Niño years, when weather systems over the Pacific Ocean resulted in more cloud cover over Arizona. With clouds blocking the sun, plants grew more slowly in Biosphere 2 and failed to soak up sufficient carbon dioxide inside. The crew had to pour bicarbonate of soda into the ocean to keep the pH levels high enough for the fish and other creatures to survive. To remove excess carbon dioxide from the air, they resorted to a mechanical scrubber, and they grew and harvested as much savannah grass as possible. Soon, though, they had tons of slowly rotting grass and other biomass, as well as calcium carbonate sludge from the scrubber, piling up in the basement.

At the same time, oxygen was disappearing from the atmosphere inside Biosphere 2, and no one could figure out where it was going. The air inside grew thin. After a year, the crew was living at the equivalent of fifteen thousand feet. Several crew members suffered from sleep apnea, and everyone felt dizzy walking up stairs. Essential labor in the farm slowed as the Biospherians became too weak for the physical effort. The doctor on the crew found himself so confused with hypoxia that he had to hand off his responsibilities. At fifteen months and again at twenty-three months, oxygen had to be injected into the Biosphere.

There were technological fixes for slow starvation, excessive CO_2, and oxygen deprivation.[6] If the synergists had had a series of trial runs with time between trials to analyze data and incorporate modifications, these and a host of smaller problems could have been identified and resolved. But such a stolid and incremental approach was not for visionaries who held "galactic conferences" and were intent on making "something new not only in the limited realm of greenhouses and human technology but also in the larger domain of Earth history." John Allen and his deputy believed unreservedly in their superior understanding of how to organize human interactions to accelerate science. Even when the project was foundering, they rejected the

---

[6] Finally, they figured out that the excessive CO_2 resulted from too much organic matter in the soil and that oxygen was disappearing into chemical bonds within the structure's curing concrete. Simply using less microbe-rich soil and sealing the concrete might have solved the problem. And if there had been only seven Biospherians, the food supply would have been adequate.

advice of the distinguished scientific advisory committee that tried to rescue them.

In fact, the managers of Biosphere 2 understood almost nothing of human psychology. Suspicious and secretive, they alienated the press and the scientific community almost from the first day of operation. They also fostered what became an insuperable schism in the crew. On one side of the divide were those who objected to Allen's public denial of oxygen, CO_2, and other problems in the Biosphere, his failure to implement the advice of the advisory committee, and his refusal to allow crew members to seek the help of mental health experts to deal with depression and the overwhelming internecine tensions. On the other side were those who viewed the scientists, the press, and then their colleagues as enemies out to destroy the experiment. Both factions, underfed and oxygen deprived, screamed furious accusations at each other. Eventually, the "pragmatists" and "disciples" (my terms) could no longer bear to speak to or even look at each other directly. They ate in silence and averted their eyes as they passed. Although no blows fell, the prospect was real.

For Jane Poynter, one of the pragmatists, the accusations of betrayal made by the disciples, Allen, and his deputy were devastating. Allen, whom she met when she was twenty, became an "infallible" father figure to her, and her fellow synergists were a kind of family. She had spent ten joyful years at the synergists' communelike ranch outside Santa Fe and in training on a research vessel in the Indian Ocean and the Red Sea. But eight months into the Biosphere 2 adventure, her life had turned into a hell under glass, and although she was committed to the intellectual promise of Biosphere 2, she longed for September 26, 1993, the day the doors would open.

A second crew stayed only six months. Columbia University took over the facility and converted it to an unsealed research lab and a museum of Biosphere 2. In 2007, the University of Arizona took on the management of what is now called simply the Biosphere. When I toured the building in 2008, there were a dozen cars in the parking lot. Inside, the place was as quiet as the desert outside. There was a research project in the savannah—designed to gather data on how global warming affects piñon trees—which consisted of a bunch of dead and half-dead trees. The work could be done as well, the guide admitted, in an ordinary lab.

In 2006, thirteen years after the Biospherians walked out through the airlock, Poynter published a thoughtful and candid book on the experience, *The Human Experiment: Two Years and Twenty Minutes Inside Biosphere 2*. It took her so long to start the book, she wrote, because it took that long to sort through her experiences and memories, to come to grips with the metamorphosis of such intimate and inspiring friendships into shattering distrust and perilous anger.

I was surprised how Poynter's book resonated with me. Synergism seems to me to be a grandiose and essentially meaningless concept, and its structure and practice decidedly cultlike. Nonetheless, I fundamentally sympathized with the audacity of Biosphere 2, such a monumental project so improbably undertaken by amateurs. Against all odds, the place worked, and if John Allen hadn't rejected the experts' offers of assistance, it might be operating today, when a sealed, miniature biosphere could provide experimental data on climate change. But as much as any other aspect, I empathized with the anguish Poynter felt about the transformation of her relationships and her long reluctance to unpack her box of memories.

Joanie was living and working in San Francisco when, after her seizure, her internist sent her for an MRI. When I answered the phone in the kitchen early that afternoon, she told me the results of the procedure calmly: the MRI had revealed a massive tumor. I still can hear my "no!," shrieked as if the news were an assailant I might fight off. The next day, she was on a plane to Johns Hopkins Hospital in Baltimore for a biopsy of her brain. Before she came out of the anesthesia, the surgeon told us the tumor was inoperable. He could no more remove it than he could excise water from a wet sponge. She would, however, gain time from a course of intensive radiation.

At one of Joanie's many medical appointments, the examining doctor speculated that the tumor had been growing for a long time, probably years. Suddenly, I realized the disease explained personality changes in my sister that I had noticed but mostly rationalized away. Four years earlier, not long after Joanie had moved to California, she had joined Ted, me, and the girls (then three, seven, and eight) in Hawaii where we rented an apartment for a week. But somehow we hardly saw Joanie; she was always running an hour or two behind us. Just as we were returning from the beach, struggling with our collection of rafts and floaties, juice boxes, bags of Cheerios, and plastic buckets and shovels, she would be blithely making her way there with a towel and a book.

Then, as I was cleaning up from lunch, vacuuming crumbs from the floor and wiping peanut butter off the kitchen table, she would wander in, wondering what there was to eat. I was disappointed and annoyed that she didn't seem to care to intersect with us. Did she think I had gotten too domestic? Maybe I had. How much fun was it for a single woman to hang out with us? But then why had she come? When I tried to talk to her about it, she was vague.

Over the next few years, we continued to talk regularly on the phone. There was no one I could speak to with more candor; we were sisters, with all that shared history, and the most intimate of friends. Her visits, though, were less successful. She seemed to be in a lower gear than I, cruising with the top down while I was maneuvering a timed road rally, reading a map and steering at the same time. I decided that she had become a laid-back Californian, no longer adapted to the East Coast buzz. She teased me for my frenetic pace, especially when, inevitably, I clipped a metaphorical curb and a hubcap went rattling off. Maybe it was unavoidable, I concluded, that our lives were diverging, but at least our conversation was unchanged.

With that MRI, Joanie's life as she had known it for forty-one years ended. Wide-area radiation of her brain combined with strong chemotherapy reduced the tumor, but the side effects were devastating. She slept twelve hours or more at night. During the day, she was often hit by an irresistible urge to sleep. Her sense of time was lost, as was her ability to concentrate. It might take her an hour to dress in the morning, but she had no idea of how she had spent those minutes. She walked slowly, and made her way down the front steps carefully, her hand gripping mine in case she lost her balance. Getting into a car was a gradual process. Nonetheless, on her visits, she walked to the bookstore in Bethesda with Austen, went to the movies with Alice, and was still available for long confidences with Anna. The radiation thinned her hair drastically, but that, she said serenely, was the least of her problems, and she amassed a collection of hats from around the world. Her favorite was a black pillbox elaborately embroidered with a rainbow of silk flourishes, but she looked good in all of them. She was still pretty and funny, and when her health insurance provider rejected a medical bill, she did battle against injustice with indignant fervor.

Her boyfriend, Tony (St. Anthony, to my mind), with whom she lived, sometimes came east with her and was good-humored and patient with her limitations. I was furious with fate and, at some bedrock level of my psyche, unable to accept the changes in her. I must have asked her a dozen times whether she thought drinking coffee might keep her awake longer. I jiggled my foot impatiently waiting for her to get ready to go out, as if she were purposefully holding me up. I sent her every article on advances in brain tumor treatment. See, I was telling myself, science will save us. Joanie knew better.

There are two moments I particularly regret. Once, when she came along with us on a vacation near Mt. Tremblant in Canada, we took the girls to a river to slide down some smooth rocks. Joanie asked me why I hadn't brought my bathing suit, and I explained. A minute later, maybe less, she asked me exactly the same question in exactly the same tone of voice. The precision of the repetition was eerie, and I must have done a double take. Joanie instantly understood. She was embarrassed and no doubt frightened: this was another step toward oblivion. Then, months later when she was visiting for a few weeks, I came home one day to find her in our kitchen, rearranging the contents of the cabinets, moving plates and glasses, spices and cookbooks, from one side of the kitchen to the other. I cried out in protest. She stopped and turned to me with a breaking voice, "But, Ruthie, I can't think anymore. I just wanted to be useful." I could have bitten off my tongue. Rearrange everything, toss it all out for all it matters.

I finally got it. She was not going to recover. I was going to be left without her.

She had a couple of reasonably good years, but then the drugs stopped working and her condition worsened. Her stays became more difficult as her forgetfulness increased and her tempo decreased. She had a few bouts of paranoia; she could no longer read; and all she could follow on TV was golf. I was caught between going fast enough to keep up with my family and work and going slow enough for Joanie. I began to edit what I said to her, in part because she had trouble following a complex story, but more because I couldn't bring myself to talk about the various this-and-thats of my life: she was dying, for God's sake, and I was not. In the face of these facts, everything was impossibly trivial. She felt the loss of candor and hated it. She demanded more honesty from me and accused me of withholding.

But there was more. She also seemed to want deep revelations from me, the unmasking of essential truths. We needed, she said, to "really talk." But I had nothing to reveal. All I had was ordinary talk, which seemed—which was—inadequate. I promised to do better, but only became fearful of disappointing her, and so I avoided occasions when just the two of us would be together. One afternoon, she erupted at me, shouting, sobbing her accusations—I was heartless and had no time for her—and she threatened to leave. I sobbed, too, pleading with her to stay, promising again to do better. I suspected that some part of her rage was the disease, the terrible pressure of the tumor expanding in her skull, but that was no help. I was failing my beloved sister when she needed me the most.

She and Tony moved to a ground-floor apartment in Florida, near my parents' condo, and I visited her there. She was valiant as her cane gave way to a walker. She lost more and more control of her body and needed twenty-four-hour care, and in January, she announced it was time for hospice. We found a place with the kindest nursing staff, and she settled in. Then, one afternoon in early February, in one final display of her independent, contrarian spirit, she declared, in a halting but determined voice, that she was leaving the hospice and going home. This was no idle expression of a wish; somehow, she got out of bed and stood, demanding her clothes. It took Tony, me, my parents, and the hospice staff together to convince her to stay. Any one of us would have bent to her will. Two days later, she went into a coma; four days later, the night before her forty-sixth birthday and with Tony at her bedside, she died.

When our daughters were small, Joanie decided that we needed to say a grace before dinner and found a simple, ecumenical prayer of thankfulness that she taught us. We started reciting it every night, and we have continued to say it every evening, whether it is just Ted and me for dinner, the girls, or guests. I can say with certainty that I have thought of Joanie at least once every day since her death.

But thinking is not feeling, and it has taken years for me to see through the traumas of our last years together, back to the days of carefree, sisterly camaraderie. For many years, I couldn't find the good memories. When I went to find one, it was as if I were shuffling through a pile of old photographs glued, with time and humidity, together: the good ones I wanted to look at were stuck to the bad ones, and I couldn't bring myself to try to peel them apart. Maybe they weren't separable at all.

In April 2009, as I was finishing the manuscript of this book, a box arrived from Tony, who was moving to a new apartment. He wrote that inside was a collection of Joanie's photos that had been taken before he met her and would have more meaning for me. I wasn't sure I could open the box; certainly I couldn't do it by myself. I slid it under a chair in the corner of the dining room. I would wait for Anna and Austen to come home from college, and then they and Alice could open it with me.

On a Sunday evening, we cleared the table in the conservatory and opened the box. Inside, there were several dozen envelopes of photographs and stacks of slides. A half dozen or so of the envelopes were from her high school and college days and her job at the bicycle company. There was Joanie, always slim and fit, but with different hairstyles: first, the long, straight hair parted in the middle of her high school years; later with blunt bangs, in a chin-length Anna Wintour style; and, finally, in an elfin cut with a wispy fringe.

A few old boyfriends turned up. (She was never without a boyfriend, I explained to the girls, and never parted from any except on friendly terms.) There was a thick packet of portraits of a luminous, thirtysomething Joanie taken by someone who was clearly in love with her. The girls gasped at her beauty. The photograph at the very bottom of the box was of the two of us, practically nose-to-nose and grinning, at my wedding.

But the surprise was that most of the photos in the box were of her young nieces, taken when she lived nearby and from the many vacations she shared with us. There were hundreds of pictures of Anna, Austen, and Alice that I had never seen, from the days of newborns to grade school. She was a good photographer, fearless, naturally, about getting up close to her subjects. There was an eight-year-old Austen in overalls sticking out her tongue, a three-year-old Anna dismayed at her dirty hands, a four-year-old Alice holding up a worm and looking as if she couldn't wait for Joanie to turn away so she could drop it down a sister's shirt, and hundreds of other moments that made us roar and giggle and hoot. I was stunned with the evidence of Joanie's delight in and love for our daughters. And it dawned on me that Joanie, if she had been well, if she had lived, would have understood and forgiven my failings during her last years. I, too, was a beloved sister.

Two hours later, my head aching with a potent mix of grief and laughter and full of memories recovered, I headed for bed. Tomorrow, I would make an album of the best photos. Each of the little girls, now young women, hugged me and shared her thoughts about Joanie. And that was the closest I've come to paradise in a long time.

Living Walls

thirteen

Living Wall

Biosphere 2 was like a Hawaiian island, a beautiful and fragile tropical garden perched atop a massive underwater mountain. Except the substructure in Tucson was not lava rock, but steel and aluminum, generators and pumps, cables and I-beams, subterranean pipes and ducts, and room-size machines. Biosphere 2 was a terribly vulnerable garden. It gobbled energy. If the power had failed at midday, the temperature inside would have rocketed to 130°F in less than an hour. That power required a torrent of annual funds. Ed Bass had expected his venture to become self-sustaining through tourist revenues and technology spin-offs, but, due in large part to the cost of energy, Biosphere 2 turned out to be a financial drain. On which Bass pulled the plug in 1994.

Glen Kertz, on the other hand, is betting that his greenhouses can be used to *make* energy. Kertz is the CEO of Valcent Products in El Paso, Texas, and inside some of his greenhouses he is farming algae, algae that can then be turned into oil to power cars or jets or heat homes. In other greenhouses, he has a vertical farming system that produces more food in less space with less fertilizer and water. Valcent is betting that oil from algae will prove to be an economic alternative to burning fossil fuel and that urban vertical farming will be an economic alternative to trucking produce across the country. If he is right, glasshouses will help save our planet, not serve as escapes from its ruins.

I arrived at Valcent on a cool but sunny December morning when the wind was blowing so hard that the palms' fronds streamed out horizontally and wraiths of desert dust shot in streaks down the drive. Kertz, a man built on the Daddy Warbucks model, with candid, light blue eyes, greeted me outside the company office. The Valcent buildings—a collection of greenhouses and corrugated aluminum buildings—ranged in a row behind the office away from the street.

Turning algae into fuel is not a new idea. Algae are primitive, aquatic organisms that photosynthesize like plants. Like plants, they convert sunlight and carbon dioxide to organic material, and in the process transpire oxygen. Algae don't develop roots, stems, leaves, and flowers, but they do produce bio-lipids—in other words, oil—which they store inside their cellular walls. In some species, as much as 70 percent of an alga is oil. Much of the oxygen on Earth was created by stromatolites, a kind of algae that thrived three billion years ago. A high proportion of the fossil fuel we burn today was formerly—very formerly—vast mats of algae.

Algae have a lot going for them as a source of fuel. They

can grow almost anywhere where there is sunlight and water, from the Arctic Ocean to boiling sea floor vents. The water can be fresh, brackish, salty, sulfurous, or polluted. Algae are the fastest-growing forms of life on Earth: some can double their volume in a few hours. Compare that with a corn crop that takes months to mature. Better yet, huge volumes of the stuff can grow in small spaces. Theoretically, Kertz told me, we could grow all the algae needed to supply America's transportation needs for a year on a small piece of the south-western desert. And because each species—of which there are hundreds of thousands, if not millions—synthesizes a different kind of oil, growers can produce jet fuel, heating fuel, or gasoline of different grades, and quickly switch species to meet market demand. The green icing on the cake is that algae sops up CO_2 while liberating oxygen, both at a terrific rate. Scientists estimate that algae sequester about half the world's CO_2 emissions and produce between 73 and 87 percent of atmospheric oxygen. There are no living things more essential to life on Earth than algae.

Valcent's first order of business has been to identify those species that produce the most oil and figure out what nutri-ent mix, pH levels, temperature, and other variables make them grow best. So we started our tour in the lab building where I saw a series of rooms full of microscopes, incuba-tors, refrigerators, growth chambers, freeze dryers, robotic pipetting machines, and centrifuges. In one room, steel shelves lined the walls. On the shelves, Erhenmeyer flasks, full of liquid and backlit by fluorescent light strips, glowed in eerie shades of yellow, gold, chartreuse, and green. On a table was what looked like a post office scale, except that its platform was moving, gently swirling the varicolored contents of the dozen or so flasks onboard.

"When we find a species that we think has potential," Kertz explained, "we grow it out on petri dishes and then in these flasks. As you can see, each species has a slightly different color and of course other biological characteristics. We run further tests, and those that show the most promise, we grow on in vats." He showed me several large glass carboys in which deep green opaque liquid was burbling gastricly. "When we find a species worth trying on a large scale," he continued as he strode out the door, with me hurrying to keep up, and into the greenhouse a few feet away, "we introduce it into the bioreactor."

The bioreactor was a long row of clear plastic panels, each four feet wide by ten feet tall and three inches thick, with a serpentine channel running through each one. Brilliant green water—a mix of algae, air, and fertilizer—bubbled through channels. It was a remarkable sight: as Kertz said, it's the top three inches of a scummy pond hung vertically.

The panels connect to an underground tank, and the algae solution circulates from sunlight to the dark tank and back again. In the tank, the algal cells process the photons they've captured into new cellular material, including oil, and reset themselves to do it again. Once a day, half the bioreactor's contents is siphoned off and pumped to a tank in the next room. There, it enters a powerful centrifuge that spins the water out of the algal soup. What remains is a thick, black algal paste. But as fast as the centrifuge spins—and it whines along at a force of 30,000 G's—it can't spin the oil out of the algae. That fact surprised me. Surely, an alga cell wall is vanishingly thin. How tough could it be to rupture that?

The answer is very tough. An alga's cell wall is constructed of microscopic fibers of cellulose intertwined and crisscrossed in layers, like a sheet of plywood. Some cell walls incorporate crystals of silica, the famously hard mineral also known as quartz; others contain calcium carbonate, the material of bones and reefs. These are hard nuts to crack. It takes a supercritical fluid extraction (CFE) process, the same process that extracts the caffeine from coffee and the flavoring components from hops. CFE reactors pressurize carbon dioxide to 10,000 pounds per square inch while heating it to 1,000°F. The oil inside the algae is volatilized and passes through the algae's sheathing. The CO_2 is then separated out and the oil is further processed—fractionated—into different end products.

Before Kertz got interested in growing algae vertically, he was already busy growing vegetables vertically. "I had been working in greenhouses for many years when I was struck by how inefficiently they used space. I was growing everything on a single, shallow horizontal plane, but heating the entire cube of space. At the time, energy was becoming a greater component of greenhouse expense, and it seemed to me we ought to use that vertical space. That meant growing food up, not just out.

"Energy was also becoming a big issue in food transportation. Here we were, flying food thousands of very costly miles from across the country and all over the world. I really thought we needed to produce food where the people are, which means in cities. Which is exactly where there is no farmland. But, if you could put your vertical farm in city greenhouses near your consumers, you could reduce your costs significantly and save the planet, too."

Kertz took me through the vertical farming greenhouse, which is a related business called VertiCrop. The basic growing unit of the VertiCrop system was a white, open tray made of what looked like—and turned out to be—a piece of ordinary downspout sliced lengthwise and chopped into four-foot-long sections. Ten trays hung one above the other at one-foot intervals in a rack. The racks were attached to an overhead conveyor, one that looked like—and turned out to be—the kind that dry cleaners use to retrieve your clean sweater for pickup. As I stood there, trays of young buttercrunch lettuce, spinach, and carrots passed by at a steady five feet per minute. Several thousand plants were snaking along a 710-foot path through the greenhouse.

"Not only do we save energy," Kertz said, "we save on water and fertilizer." He showed me a station where nozzles sprayed liquid fertilizer and water on the plants as they swung by. "What we apply goes directly onto the plant, not to soil between plants or soil between rows. As you can see, we can spray it in precisely controlled amounts exactly where we want it. Whatever doesn't go on the plants falls to a drain at the bottom. We can capture it, sterilize it with UV light—to eliminate any chance of biological contaminants— and recycle it. And, because we're in a completely controlled environment here, there are no insects or weeds so we don't need to spend money on pesticides or herbicides."

Kertz says he can grow practically any crop anywhere. "About the only crops not suited for a vertical farm are large grain crops like wheat and corn. We're working on growing rice." All he needs is sunlight. Plenty of technical issues about algae oil remain and a commercial product is years away, but the vertical farming system is a reality. Paignton Zoo in southwest England recently installed a VertiCrop system to help supply its reptiles, birds, and mammals with year-round fresh vegetables and fruit.

I was enthralled with the idea of a vertical farm. It has been a tenet of my secular faith that although the world might seem headed for shortage and loss, despoliation, and maybe even doom, opportunity is actually just ahead. That dead-end wall that looms at the end of the swimming pool will turn out to be the place where, thanks to our species' extraordinary creativity, we make a last-second flip-turn and launch ourselves anew.

For a while, I daydreamed about creating a vertical farm in my conservatory. I'd buy a dry cleaner's conveyor and run it around the perimeter, power it with algae oil, and send trays of lettuce, tomatoes, herbs, and rice circulating slowly around. I'd grow bananas in the center of the room and print out my drafts on banana paper.

I ran this by Ted, just for the sake of seeing his brow furrow. In fact, he only asked if I would please start with strawberries. I suspected conveyors would be pricey, so I decided instead to channel my energy into a stationary vertical garden.

The photograph of a middle-aged man staring out from hooded eyes below a high forehead crowned with a back-ward sweep of green hair would have been unsurprising in

Rolling Stone. But the magazine I was reading was the *New Scientist.* The man was not wearing a lab coat but a Hawaiian tropical shirt. His left hand sported a thumbnail long enough to fillet a fish; his other nails looked like they would come in handy for spearing hors d'oeuvres.

I had to read on. Patrick Blanc, the subject of the story, *is* something of a rock star, albeit in the world of plants. Trained in botany and employed by the French National Center for Scientific Research for a quarter century, Blanc specializes in tropical plants, particularly those that flourish without soil and in shaded places like the understories of jungles and the shadows of cliff faces. He travels six months out of the year researching and collecting plants around the globe. When he isn't in the field, he is busy designing and installing "murs végétaux," a term that is variously translated as green walls, plant walls, living walls, or vertical gardens. His creations are huge artworks, dense and varied tapestries composed of hundreds of species and thousands of individual plants that grow on frameworks of plastic and irrigated felt. They entirely cover the interior and exterior walls of museums, concert halls, stores, office and commercial buildings, hotels, and a few private homes. Blanc works primarily in France, but also elsewhere in western Europe, southeast Asia, and, more recently and in a limited way, the United States.

Interesting idea, I remember thinking at the time, but my curiosity extended only to wondering how Blanc managed to climb through a jungle canopy with his nails intact while I couldn't zip my pants without nicking one.

Three years later, I was looking at the seven-foot-by-four-foot section of wall in my conservatory that I had been trying to cover with *Ficus pumilla,* the "creeping fig" that I'd admired at Logee's. The vines had gotten off to an excellent start and had covered the lowest three feet of the wall in leaves in six months. But I must have done something wrong—no doubt, too much water or too little—because although the stems had climbed over the wall clock and a return air vent and were headed toward the ceiling, their upper sections were leafless. In fact, some of the leaves on the lower section had turned brown and fallen off. My carpet of green was looking threadbare. It was then that I remembered Patrick Blanc, the guy with the green hair and the green walls. A Web search turned up a host of articles and even a film, by Christoph Schuch, about him. He had just written a beautifully illustrated book, *The Vertical Garden,* about his walls and how they work.

Born in 1953, Blanc grew up in Paris where as a child he became enthralled with aquariums and tropical fish. As a teenager, his interest shifted from the fauna in his aquarium to the flora. One day, after he had come to an understanding of the role of aquatic plants in purifying the water, he decided to root a clipping from his mother's potted philodendron into the layers of synthetic wadding in the filter system of his aquarium. The plant happily established itself in the wadding, sending out long roots into the water and stems and leaves out above the tank. He took the tank off its table and put it on the floor, added more species to the filter, and hooked up artificial lighting. As the plants grew, he trained them up a six-foot trellis attached to a wood board. A simple aquarium pump pushed water up from the aquarium through a garden hose to the top of the board. Where the hose ran across the top of the board, he pierced it with a series of holes so that the water dripped out, down the board, and back into the aquarium. He had created his first living wall.

As a student at the Pierre and Marie Curie University in Paris, Blanc began traveling to the tropics to study how forest understory species survived on vertical surfaces. Thousands of species, he discovered, were capable of living without significant amounts of soil, including species that we're accustomed to seeing growing horizontally in the ground. He found them growing instead in the crevices of cliffs rooted in a bit of leaf litter, clinging to the damp surfaces of rocks, gripping tree bark, and flourishing in the spray behind waterfalls. Back in Paris, he wrote up his findings for his doctoral thesis.

He also applied his insights to improving the ever-expanding living wall in his apartment. Biological substances—mosses, coco fiber, and cotton cloth—inevitably decomposed, causing the plants to lose their grip and fall off, as well as creating unpleasant odors. Ultimately, he settled on a synthetic textile. In 1994, Blanc created his first public vertical garden in Chaumont-sur-Loire, and in the next ten years went on to create dozens of commissioned projects, chiefly for public spaces.

All of the projects featured in Blanc's book, whether indoors or out, on flat or curved walls or wrapped around pillars, use an enormous variety of understory foliage plants—about a hundred species on a hundred-square-yard wall—of all textures, shades, and forms. Blanc tends to grow them in swathes at least a yard long, often with a diagonal orientation, as if they were growing along the lines of sloping strata in the landscape. From a distance, the walls look like abstract expressionist murals in shades of green, gold, and russet paint that the artist has dolloped on thickly with a trowel. They are full of visual energy.

I was well beyond intrigued. I was entranced. There are only three Blanc walls in the United States and two of them are in Manhattan. The larger of the two is at the Phyto Universe spa at the corner of Fifty-eighth Street and Lexington Avenue. One Saturday morning, I took the train up to see it. For one, I wanted to see a wall up close. But I had also decided that I would try to create my own version of the wall where my creeping fig was slowly perishing.

I walked east from Penn Station over to Park Avenue and strolled north to Fifty-eighth, where I turned right toward Lexington, so that I came upon the corner building from the broadest vantage point. Phyto Universe, a day spa that features plant-based products, is on the top floor of a three-story building sheathed in glass. There, like a leafy crown on the building's brow, was a ten-foot-high, solid band of jungle greenery that stretched across both its Lexington Avenue and Fifty-eighth Street façades. Nothing of the spa was visible behind the wall. When the stoplight changed, I crossed Lexington, passing a vendor selling hot dogs from under his orange umbrella at the corner and in front of a phalanx of yellow taxis, and looked for the entrance to the spa. It wasn't immediately evident, but I poked around the building's exterior and found the door to a tiny lobby on Fifty-eighth.

When I got off the elevator, I could see the interior side of Blanc's wall beyond the front desk. I had talked by phone to Ted Hanson, a professional gardener and the caretaker of the wall, who had agreed to meet me and tell me about it. By the front desk was a small man, perhaps in his midsixties, with shaggy brown hair, even shaggier brown eyebrows, deep-set eyes, a lined face, and a grizzled stubble. He was wearing a wrinkled button-down shirt over a red T-shirt. We eyed each other, and just as I concluded that he couldn't possibly be a spa employee (and might be a hobbit), he must have concluded that I (in khaki pants and a sweatshirt and devoid of makeup) couldn't possibly be a spa patron. We approached each other, and he asked, shyly and in such a low, whispery voice that I strained to hear him, if I was Miss Kassinger.

With little further ado, he led me on a tour of the lush inside wall, pointing out species as we walked along it. Hanson had helped plant the wall two years earlier, supervised by Blanc's colleague Sylvain Bidaut who had flown over from Paris. Like all of Blanc's walls, Hanson said, this one was built on a metal frame that holds the plant wall at a small distance from the building surface. A layer of expanded PVC paneling, lightweight but rigid, was fixed to the frame, and a sheet of waterproof plastic covered the PVC. On top of the plastic were two layers of purplish-pink synthetic felt attached to the PVC with steel staples. To plant the wall, the installers cut horizontal slits in the top layer and, following Blanc's detailed map, slipped young plants, whose roots had been washed of most of their soil, into the slits. They shot a staple into the felt on each side of the plants to keep them in place until they rooted. It had taken their crew about a month to anchor roughly twenty-five thousand plants—four for every square foot of felt—into the wall. An irrigation system across the top of the wall sent water containing a dilute fertilizer dripping onto the felt for a few minutes five times a day. I saw that the water dripped in a shallow metal tray at the bottom of the wall. Somewhere, it emptied into a drain.

The elimination of soil in Blanc's system makes a large living wall possible. It's a question of weight: a square yard of quarter-inch wet cloth weighs about 17 pounds; a square yard of four-inch-deep wet soil weighs about 220 pounds. Large soil-based living walls require a much more substantial framing system or they will pull the building's skin right off the underlying structure. Soil-based systems—and there are two North American companies that make small systems for the consumer market—also require containers to hold that soil. That means, however, that plants will eventually become root-bound in their containers and need replacing. In Blanc's system, the roots wander anywhere they please, insinuating themselves ever more securely into the damp felt.

Hanson led me through the back of the spa through a passageway to the exterior side of the living wall. We sidled sideways down the sleeve of space about a foot wide that separates the plants from the outside glass. Looking over my shoulder, down over the wobbly waist-high letters that spelled PHYTO UNIVERSE, I had a falcon's-eye view of Lexington Avenue. The cacophony of honking horns was surprisingly loud, almost as if there were no glass. One look was enough, and I turned my attention to the plants.

Hanson was telling me about the problems he has with the outward-facing side in the winter, and he pointed out sections that he'd had to replant. There is no heat on this side of the wall, and some of the foliage suffered badly from the proximity of the freezing glass. He had been slowly replacing a number of the original species that couldn't adapt to a New York winter. Some plants that survived had become infested with spider mites. These he was pulling out. He replanted according to Blanc's design, but with what he considered more practical species. He wanted plants that didn't shed, were hardy and resistant to bugs, and didn't need frequent pruning. He was taking out the begonias (too fragile) and the hibiscus (too prone to bugs.) I tried to convince him to cut off a little sample of the pink felt for me—I wanted to compare its absorbency to other materials—but I might as well have asked him to clip me a small piece of The Ring. He told me this felt was available only in France; the manufacturer was Blanc's secret.

I decided to create my own wall to suit a small space at home and with materials that I could easily find. Ted helped me construct a wood frame and cover it with lightweight PVC panels (see Appendix B). Of course, I couldn't find Blanc's pink felt, but I did find white capillary mat at an online greenhouse supply store and bought enough for two layers. It wasn't nearly as feltlike as Blanc's, but I hoped it would simulate the perpetually damp cliffs where Blanc finds many of his plants growing.

The irrigation system was easy to put together. I wanted to recycle the water, so I wouldn't waste water or fertilizer. I bought a four-foot-long window box, lined it with a piece of rubber pond liner, placed it at the bottom of the wall, and filled it with water. In the window box, I placed a submersible fountain pump not much large than my fist, which was capable of lifting water to eight feet, and I attached it to a garden hose that ran up the side of the wall. At the top of the wall, I connected the hose to four feet of drip tape, which I capped at the end. Then I secured the tape between the two layers of my planting material. A timer turned on the pump four times a day for five minutes at a time, just long enough for the water to run through the materials and start dripping back into the window box. After soaking myself and the floor a few times, I had what I thought was a working wall.

I started confidently and bought ten three-inch pots of four species—*Calathea ornata,* a dashing variety with pink slashes on its dark green leaves; a *Philodendron* with mottled green and yellow leaves; maidenhair ferns; and a species of *Selaginella*—and planted them according to Blanc's directions. They filled about a quarter of the wall. I looked for a liquid fertilizer and found a two-part kind called Sensi made for hydroponic situations. Because Blanc wrote that he used fertilizer at a 10 percent concentration, I did the same.

All was well for about six weeks. Then, I noticed that the *Calathea* were looking a little pale. The *Selaginella* were browning around the edges. The delicate leaves of the maidenhair were withering, leaving bare black stems. Only the *Philodendron* seemed healthy, although its new leaves were decidedly smaller than the old ones. I took a few plants out to check their roots: they looked all right and there was no bad odor, a sure sign of rot. Maybe, I thought, they were too dry or maybe they were getting fertilizer burn. I increased the flow of water and cut back on the fertilizer.

Three weeks later, they looked worse. The maidenhairs were goners. I found spider mites on the *Calathea*—a sign of stress—and sprayed them heavily with neem oil. I hadn't used stainless steel staples, and I wondered if maybe iron was leaching into the water. I was throwing away little plants, trying to remember that plants were not puppies. Nearing despair, I called the 800 number on the back of the fertilizer bottle.

A man named Roy, with a gravelly voice and a fatherly attitude, answered. He had me describe exactly how the leaves looked. When he heard that the leaves were either yellowing at the edges or were yellow all over, he immediately diagnosed nutrient deficiency. Far from adding too much fertilizer, I was starving my plants. When leaf tips and central veins turn yellow, brown, or black, the problem is overfertilizing; discolored edges and overall yellowing are signs of undernourishment. When I described the condition of the ferns and their location at the particularly saturated area at the bottom of the wall, he said it sounded like they'd died from lack of oxygen.

Roy calculated that for a seven-gallon window box, I'd need to add one-third cup each of both parts of the fertilizer every week. And I would have to test the pH level regularly: the water had to be 5.6 for the plants to properly absorb the nutrients. Since tap water is 7.0, I would need to add a little phosphoric acid to acidify the water. In summer, when the temperature of the water exceeded 68 degrees, I was going to have to watch carefully for root rot. Warm water would be less oxygenated, an excellent environment for the anaerobic bacteria that are responsible for root disease. I would need to add hydrogen peroxide weekly. And, he added, I had to get rid of the capillary mat: it was too water retentive and my plants were drowning. I needed to find a material that filled with water, but then drained rapidly.

It was back to the Web to search for a better medium. One possibility was rock wool, a porous material manufactured by melting basaltic rock, spinning the melt into fibers, adding a binder, and compressing the stuff into slabs. The drawback to rock wool is that the fibers get loose and not only pierce and irritate the skin, but may be dangerous to breathe. To work with rock wool, you need to wear protective gear. That wasn't for me.

Fortunately, in researching rock wool, I stumbled across a new product, an artificial rock wool. "Sure To Grow" (or STG) is made of spun polyethylene and is no more hazardous than the fluffy material you find in a fiberfill pillow, which, it turns out, is pretty much what the stuff is. I took out the remaining plants, pulled out the staples, and took down the capillary mat. Then I stapled down a one-inch layer of STG. On top of the STG, I stretched and stapled some light plastic netting, a material I found on the Internet used to prevent children from falling off outdoor decks. I thought the netting might provide an anchor for the roots, like the crevices in tree bark or the rough surface of rock faces. On top, I stapled a half-inch layer of STG.

Hydroponic growing, I realized, might involve a bit more than simply substituting soil with fiberfill and using a particular fertilizer. I consulted Brian Rubin, owner of Maryland Hydroponics in Laurel, Maryland, who told me I had to replace the water in my hydroponic system once a week. When I moaned about the work involved, he pointed out that I could simply detach the hose from the drip line and use the pump to empty the window box, either out a window or into the sink. He sold me a little bottle of SUPERthrive, a plant hormone that encourages root growth, a pH test kit, a small bottle of phosphoric acid, and Physan (instead of hydrogen peroxide) to kill bacteria and fungi. I was ready to try again.

My approach this time was more cautious: I would get more species, but fewer specimens of each. Tom and Ken at Glasshouse Works thought *Pilea* would be particularly well suited to a wall that was generally moist and sent a half-dozen varieties. Edie suggested three species of those hardiest of genera, *Philodendron* and *Pothos,* as well as ponytail palms and *Chlorophytum* (commonly known as spider plant). Friends at Longwood Gardens thought *Fittonia* would be good, so I added white-veined and red-veined species. I found a mini *Spathiphyllum* from Joshsfrogs.com. Dianne Smith suggested staghorn ferns. *Sansevieria* (mother-in-law's-tongue), *Aglaonema,* and *Hedera* (ivy) are hardy, so I got one specimen of each. *Alocasia* like wet feet, so two of those went in, as well as two polka-dot plants (*Hypoestes phyllostachya*) and a *Dracaena warneckii*. I found a variety of miniature *Anthurium* ('Smalltalk') to try. For the bottom of the wall, I tried *Anubias,* a plant that can live happily in an aquarium, and *Juncus spiralis*, a corkscrew marsh grass.

This time I washed my plantlets clear of all soil and soaked them in SUPERthrive before I transplanted them. (Root systems, I discovered, are highly varied and interesting. Some are so delicate that I could slip them behind the netting, eliminating the need to staple them in place. Others, like the *Anthurium,* are stiff and brittle and hard to transplant. My *Dracaena* species had roots the color of carrots. *Chlorophytum* roots turned out to be tuberous, which helps them survive inconsistent watering.) I had discovered that even stainless steel staples corrode. Worried about the effects of excessive iron in the water, I found some plastic staples and a staple gun that accommodated them.

This time, the wall worked. Water saturated the STG, but then it drained quickly, allowing the roots to get air. The higher dose of fertilizer kept the plants green and growing slowly. After three months, I actually had to prune back the *chlorophytum* and philodendron. I still smile whenever I notice the wall watering itself, always right on schedule. At last my watering problems are solved.

There has been tweaking to do. I had to drill more holes in the drip tape to eliminate some dry spots in the wall. I'm still working on the mix and location of the plants. I placed the ponytail palms too high; they make an unfortunate shadow directly below their grassy fronds. The polka-dot plants got leggy (they needed more light), and none of the plants liked the bottom of the wall, which stays saturated (the pooling water probably lacks oxygen.) I wish I'd used half-inch STG for the bottom layer as well as the top because it is hard to staple through both layers. And I may need to hang a grow light at the top of the wall this winter.

The wall is now a smashing success. Not only is it beautiful and more lush by the day, there is something about seeing the plants in this way, straight on and close up, that appeals to me. It is like lying down in a tropical jungle without getting your knees dirty. Visitors are immediately drawn to it, even before they notice the blooming citrus. They stand only inches away, peer into it to find the treasures—five *Cryptanthus* 'Earth Star' that look like red sea anemones are a favorite—and stroke the fuzzy staghorn fern.

One of the wonderful things about the living wall is that it never breaks my heart, unlike my Calamondin orange tree that for some reason this past winter, sighed, shrugged her delicate shoulders, and dropped all her leaves on the floor. The wall is made of dozens of little plants, so while I'm always a little saddened when a plant dies (I try to remember that there are tens of thousands of identical ones growing in Apopka), I know I can replace it for a few dollars or just wait a bit for its neighbors to grow over the empty spot.

But best of all, the living wall is an ongoing experiment. It's hard to know what will grow best in it. Ponytail palms, for example, shouldn't do well—they prefer high light—but in fact they're quite happy. Maidenhair ferns flourish on the Phyto wall in New York, but they shrivel almost instantly for me. I'm considering trying sweet flag (*Acorus americanus*) in that difficult spot, the lowest six inches of the wall. Or maybe I'll just float lotus or water lilies in the window box. What I really want to do is create another vertical garden on the north side of the conservatory where, in the summer, southern light streams through the skylights and lights up the wall. I could try growing strawberries there; Ted, steadfast and generous man that he is, certainly deserves them.

When I started the conservatory, I wanted a perfect green refuge, an unchanging paradise where I would be cocooned from decline and loss. In fact, what I've come to love best about the conservatory is its constant alterations: the comings and goings of family and friends; the now annual arrival of butterflies; old plants that need to be pruned or repotted; new plants that catch my eye at Johnson's; a new generation of bugs to be battled; the rearrangement of the landscape from summer, when the fruit trees move outside, to winter when they come back in; the clivias coming into bloom; and now my evolving living wall. The conservatory reminds me every day that I can live with life's inevitable losses, both small and large. A real paradise, it turns out, is not a quiet, immutable refuge, but a place where there is always something new under the sun and I wonder each day: "What next?"

Acknowledgments

So many people generously gave me their time, telling me the stories of their businesses, their conservatories, or their passions for particular plants. In addition to those individuals mentioned in the book, I thank Bill McLelland and Jim Shields for information on clivias; Jan Dietrick and Ron Whitehurst of Rincon-Vitova Insectary; Holly Shimizu and Bill McLaughlin of the U.S. Botanical Garden; Paul Meyer and Robert Gutowski of the Morris Arboretum; Bill Barnes; Robert Bowden of the Harry P. Leu Gardens; and Bob Ustler, Jack Christmas, and Randy Strode for information about the Apopka foliage industry. I give special thanks to Tony Underwood and Ken Bradley who shared their memories about Joanie.

I owe much to Kenneth Greif who has encouraged me for decades and offered wise counsel and thoughtful comments on the manuscript. Ellen Roberts, too, has been a great support and adviser. Thanks go to Lizzie Thorne for ad hoc research help, Jane Phillips for editing, and to Ben van Dusen and Desmond Hall, architects extraordinaire, for the conservatory sketches. The book wouldn't have been possible without the wisdom and expertise of Jennifer Brehl, Emily Krump, and Michelle Tessler.

Sometimes, it takes a neighborhood. Linda Button, whose painting graces the cover, and Eva-Maria Ruhl, whose line drawings illuminate the text, entered into the spirit of my horticultural and literary endeavors, and I am profoundly grateful to them. They are wonderful artists and fine friends.

Always, it takes my family, and from the depths of my heart I thank Anna, Austen, and Alice, my in-house consultants, researchers, and editorial staff, and Ted, always supportive in all ways.

Appendix A
PRONUNCIATION GUIDE

Carl Linnaeus, the eighteenth-century Swedish botanist, established a binomial system for naming plants. For the most part, the casual gardener will come across the name of the plant's genus, followed by the name of its species (*Clivia miniata,* for example). The species name often is descriptive (*miniata,* for example, means reddish). Sometimes a plant also has a variety name (*Clivia miniata* 'Lindley'). A variety is defined as a naturally occurring or selectively bred group within a species that has minor distinctive characteristics.

I have found that over time, as I learned the pronunciation of Latin names of my plants, they have come to serve as unconscious templates for unfamiliar names. I also keep W. T. Stearn's wise observation in mind: "Botanical Latin is essentially a written language. . . . How [the words] are pronounced really matters little provided they sound pleasant and are understood by all concerned." So, with those two thoughts, I offer the following guide[7] to pronouncing the names of plants in this book.

---

[7] From Davesgarden.com.

Acalypha pendula (ak-uh-LY-fuh PEND-yoo-luh)
Acorus americanus (AK-or-us a-mer-ih-KAY-nus)
Aglaonema modestum (ag-lay-oh-NEE-muh mo-DES-tum)
Agapanthus (ag-uh-PANTH-us)
Allamanda (al-uh-MAN-duh)
Alocasia cuprea (a-loh-KAY-see-uh KUP-ray-uh)
Aloe (AL-oh)
Ananas comosus (A-nan-as kom-OH-sus)
Anthurium (an-THUR-ee-um)
Anubias (an-YOO-bee-as)
Aphelandra (af-el-AN-druh)
Ardisia (ar-DIZ-ee-uh)
Areca (a-REEK-uh)
Aristolochia (a-ris-toh-LOH-kee-uh)
Asclepias incarnata (ass-KLE-pee-us in-kar-NAH-tuh)
Aspalathus (as-pal-ATH-us)
Aspidistra (ass-pi-DIS-truh)
Asplenium marinum (ass-PLEE-nee-um MAR-in-um)
Asplenium ceterach (ass-PLEE-nee-um KET-er-ak)
Aucuba (AWK-yoo-bah)

Bignonia (big-NO-nee-uh)
Billbergia pyramidalis (bil-BER-jee-uh peer-uh-mid-AH-liss)
Bougainvillea spectabilis (boo-gan-VIL-lee-uh speck-TAB-ih-liss)
Brugmansia (broog-MAN-zee-ah)

Caladium (ka-LAY-dee-um)
Calathea ornata (ka-LAY-thee-uh or-NAH-ta)
Calotropis gigantea (ka-LOW-troh-pis jy-GAN-tee-uh)
Chlorophytum (kloh-roh-FY-tum)
Citrus mitis (SIT-rus MIT-iss)
Clivia miniata (KLY-vee-uh or KLIH-vee-uh min-ee-AH-

tuh), *nobilis* (NO-bil-iss), *gardenii* (gar-DEN-ee-eye), *caudescens* (kawl-ESS-kens), *mirabilis* (mih-RAB-ih-liss), *robusta* (roh-BUS-tuh)

Colocasia esculenta (kol-oh-KAY-see-uh es-kew-LEN-tuh)
Croton (KROH-tun)
Cryptanthus (krip-TAN-thus)

Dieffenbachia (def-en-BAH-kee-ah)
Dizygotheca elegantissima (dizz-ih-GOTH-eh-ca el-ee-gan-TISS-ee-muh)
Dracaena (dra-SEE-nah)
Dryopteris (dry-OP-ter-iss)

Encephalartos longifolius (en-sef-uh-LAR-tos lon-jee-FOH-lee-us)
Equisetum diffusum (ek-wis-SEE-tum dy-FEW-sum)
Euphorbia tirucalli (yoo-FOR-bee-uh tee-roo-KAL-ee)

Ficus elastica (FY-kus ee-LASS-tih-kuh)
Ficus pumilla (FY-kus POO-mil-uh)
Fittonia (fit-TOH-nee-uh)

Garcinia (gar-SIN-ee-uh)

Hedera helix (HED-er-uh HEE-licks)
Helxine soleirolii (so-ley-ROH-lee-uh so-ley-ROH-lee-eye)
Hoya (HOY-a)
Hypoestes phyllostachya (hy-poh-ES-teez fy-lo-STAK-ee-hu)

Juncus spiralis (JUN-kus spir-AH-liss)

Ledebouria (le-de-BOR-ree-a)
Lithops (LY-thops)

Melastoma (mel-LAS-toh-muh)
Mesembryanthemum (mes-em-bry-ANTH-ee-mum)
Myriophyllum aquaticum (my-ree-oh-FIL-um a-KWA-ti-kum)

Neanthe bella (nee-AN-theh BELL-a)
Nematanthus (nee-ma-TAN-thus)
Nepenthes (nep-EN-theez)
Nephitis (ne-FY-tiss)
Nephrolepis exaltata (nef-roh-LEP-is eks-all-TAY-tuh)

Opuntia (op-UN-shee-a)
Oxalis variabilis (oks-AL-iss var-ee-AH-bil-iss)

Passiflora (pass-iff-FLOR-uh)
Peperomia (pep-er-ROH-mee-uh)
Pereskia aculeata (per-ESS-kee-uh ah-kew-lee-AY-tuh)
Philodendron bipinnatifidum (fil-oh-DEN-dron by-pin-uh-TIFF-ih-dum)
Pilea glauca (py-LEE-uh GLAW-kuh)
Pilea involucrata (py-LEE-uh in-vol-yoo-KRAY-tuh)
Platycerium veitchii (plat-ee-SIR-ee-um VEET-chee-eye)
Plectranthus (plek-TRAN-thus)
Plumbago auriculata (plum-BAY-go aw-rik-yoo-LAY-tuh)
Plumbago capensis (plum-BAY-go ka-PEN-sis)
Portulaca (por-tew-LAK-uh)
Pothos (PAY-thos)
Protea (PROH-tee-uh)
Pteridophyte (tch-RID-uh-fites)

Ravenala madagascariensis (ra-VEN-ah-la mad-uh-gas-KAR-ee-EN-sis)

Sansevieria (san-se-VEER-ee-uh)
Schefflera actinophylla (shef-LER-uh ak-ten-oh-FIL-uh)
Selaginella (sell-lah-gi-NEL-uh)
Spathiphyllum (spath-ee-FIL-um)
Stephanotis floribunda (stef-ah-NO-tis flor-ih-BUN-duh)
Strelitzia reginae (stre-LITZ-ee-uh ree-JIN-ay-ee)
Streptocarpus (strep-toh-KAR-pus)
Stromanthe (stroh-MAN-thee)
Syngonium (sin-GO-nee-um)

Xanthosoma (zan-tho-SO-muh)

Appendix B
HOW TO CREATE A LIVING WALL

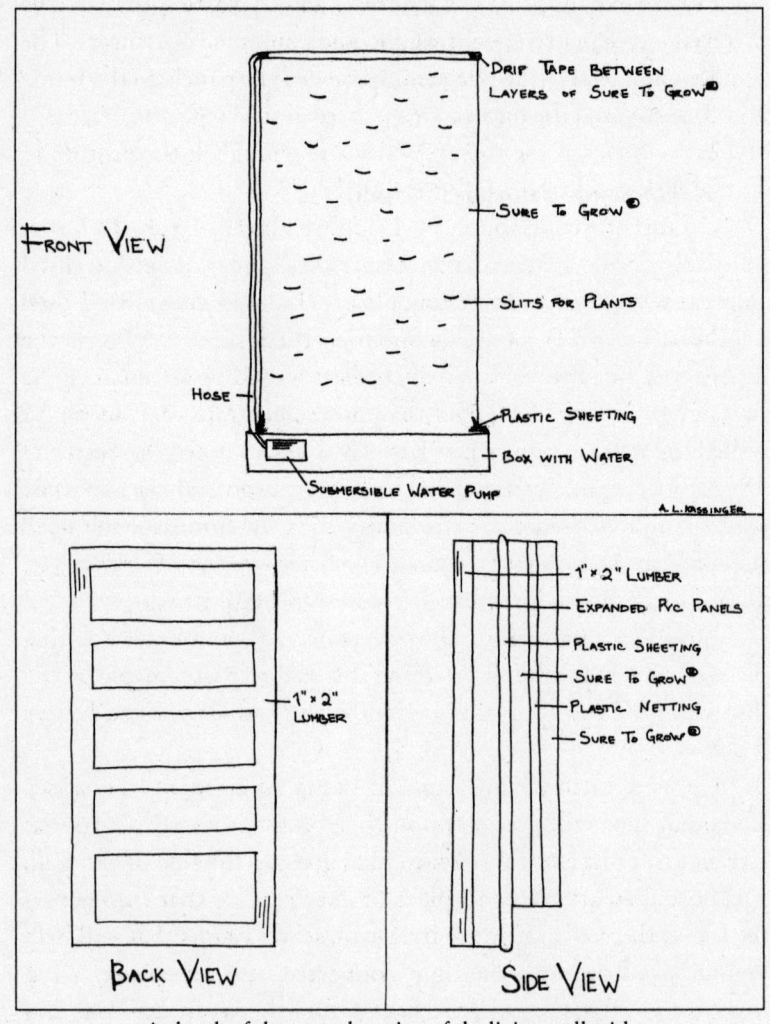

A sketch of the second version of the living wall with
Sure To Grow® and plastic netting.   *By Anna Kassinger.*

Start by constructing a frame that will hold the living wall away from the wall of your house. I used one-by-two-inch pine, screwing pieces in a framelike shape to the studs behind the wallboard. I drilled some holes in the frame to provide a little ventilation.

I found expanded PVC paneling at a local plastics retailer. The material is inexpensive, lightweight, and comes in large sheets. The retailer cut it to the size I needed. I screwed the panels to the frame and then covered the panels with a sheet of heavy plastic, leaving a few extra inches at the top and sides and enough at the bottom to extend well inside the window box.

On top of the plastic sheet, I stapled a layer of Sure To Grow (available online), then a layer of lightweight plastic netting (used to prevent children from falling off porches and decks), and then another layer of STG. I used a one-inch-thick sheet of STG on the inner layer, but I think a half-inch sheet would be adequate. (The roots grow into the STG, but they don't penetrate very deeply.) I pulled the netting tight when I attached it, but it may be better to leave a little slack. If the netting is loose, it is possible to slip some plants' roots behind the netting and thereby eliminate the need for stapling. Make sure to use stainless steel staples or, better yet, plastic staples (which require a special staple gun.)

I found a window box as wide as my wall and lined it with a piece of rubber pond liner, stapling the liner in place. Staple on the outside or the top edge of the window box, otherwise you'll have leaks!

I used a Little Giant fountain pump to circulate the water. The pump size will depend on the height of your wall. The pump attaches to a piece of garden hose that goes up the side of the wall. The hose then attaches to a piece of flat drip line that runs across the top of the wall. There are irrigation stores online that will help you choose drip tape, the right connector, and, of course, a cap for the end of the drip line. I have a filter between the hose and the drip line, which the irrigation store encouraged me to add. It's probably a good thing, but you'll have to put a hook in the side of the wall, screwed into the lumber, to support it. Wrapping the hose connections with Teflon tape prevents drips.

You can buy drip line without holes because you will need to add holes every two inches or so. I used a 9/16 drill bit, but it would be fine just to hammer (and remove) a nail through the drip line every two inches. You need to have holes on both sides of the drip line.

I ran the drip line between the two layers of STG, so the holes send water into both layers. I folded the excess plastic sheeting at the top of the wall over the two layers of STG and drip line and used a glue gun to secure the edge of the plastic sheeting to the outer layer. No doubt, there's a more elegant way to do this, but it works. Put a timer between the wall socket and the pump, so the pump cycles on for a few minutes every six hours.

The wall waters itself, but you need to pay attention to what is in the water. Use a nutrient mix designed for hydroponics. The pH of the water must be about 5.6 for the plants to access the nutrients. Litmus paper strips (for testing pool water, for example) will help you determine the pH level. You can use phosphoric acid to lower the pH, but you have to be very careful—it can burn you quickly. Measure the water at least twice a week because as the plants take up nutrients, the pH level changes.

There are many ways to deal with bacteria in the water. I started using hydrogen peroxide, but now use Physan 20. A growth hormone like SUPERthrive seems to be a good idea. I soak the bare roots of plantlets for fifteen minutes before I put them in the wall, and then add a drop per gallon of water to the window box every week.

To plant a plantlet, first wash off as much soil from the roots as you can. Make a horizontal slit in the outer layer of the STG and slip in the roots of the plantlet. I shoot one staple along the side of the plantlet to keep it from flopping over. (Once the plantlet roots, you can remove the staple if you like.) So far, I have found

Philodendron, Fittonia, Hedera (ivy), *Spathiphyllum, Cryptanthus, Chlorophytum* (spider plant), staghorn ferns, *Syngonium,* and *Pilea* the easiest to grow in the low-light conditions of my conservatory.

I learned the hard way that the water in the window box needs to be refreshed once a week. To do so, I unscrew the hose from the pump, attach another hose in its place, and turn on the pump. In two minutes, the window box is nearly empty. I pump the water into a nearby sink, but it would be easy to pump it into a bucket. Then, you can recycle the water into your garden.

Bibliography

Adanson, Michel. *A Voyage to Senegal, the Isle of Goree, and the River Gambia.* London: J. Nourse, 1759.

Allen, David Elliston. *The Victorian Fern Craze.* London: Hutchinson & Co, 1969.

Allen, Will. *The War on Bugs.* White River Junction, VT: Chelsea Green, 2008.

Alexander, Caroline. *The Bounty: The True Story of the Mutiny on the Bounty.* New York: Penguin Group, 2004.

Alling, Abigail, and Mark Nelson. *Life Under Glass.* Biosphere Press, 1993.

Aster, Jane. *The Habits of Society: A Handbook for Ladies and Gentlemen.* New York: Carleton, 1869.

Attenborough, David. *The Private Life of Plants.* Princeton, NJ: Princeton University Press, 1995.

Bellairs, Nona. *Hardy Ferns: How I Collected and Cultivated Them.* London: Smith, Elder, and Co., 1865.

Bennett, Jennifer. *Lilies of the Hearth.* Ontario, Canada: Camden House, 1991.

Blanc, Patrick. *The Vertical Garden: From Nature to the City.* New York: Norton, 2008.

Boyd, P. D. A. *The Victorian Fern Cult in South West Britain. In Fern Horticulture: Past, Present and Future Perspectives,* edited by J. M. Ide, A. C. Jermy, and A. M. Paul, 33–56. Andover: Intercept, 1992. http://www.peterboyd.com/ferncultsw.htm

Brockway, Lucile H. *Science and Colonial Expansion.* New York: Academic Press-Harcourt Brace Jovanovich, 1979.

Brown, A. C., ed. *A History of Scientific Endeavour in South Africa.* Cape Town, South Africa: Royal Society of South Africa, 1977.

Brown, Deni. *Aroids: Plants of the Arum Family.* 2nd ed. Portland, OR: Timber Press, 2000.

Campbell, Susan. *A History of Kitchen Gardening.* London: Frances Lincoln, 2005.

Carson, Rachel. *Silent Spring.* Greenwich, CT: Fawcett Crest, 1962.

Christmas, Jack. *The History of the Foliage Industry 1910–1980,* unpublished manuscript provided by the author.

Coats, Alice M. *The Plant Hunters.* New York: McGraw-Hill, 1969.

Davidson, William, Ray Bilton, and Clive Innes. *Exotic Houseplants.* London: Quantum Books, 2003.

Davis, Tony. *Starving in Bedworth.* Coventry, England: [Tony Davis], 1990.

DeBach, Paul. *Biological Control by Natural Elements.* London: Cambridge University Press, 1974.

Delumeau, Jean. *History of Paradise.* Trans. Matthew O'Connell. New York: Continuum, 1995.

Desmond, Ray. *The European Discovery of the Indian Flora.* Oxford: Oxford University Press, 1992.

De Vleeschouwer, Olivier. *Greenhouses and Conservatories.* Trans. Lisa Davidson. Paris: Flammarion, 2001.

Drayton, Richard. *Nature's Government.* New Delhi, India: Orient Longman, 2000.

Elliot, Brent. *Victorian Gardens.* London: B. T. Batsford, 1986.

Firmly Planted: A History of the Morris Arboretum. Virginia Beach: Donning Company, 2001.

Gardner, Brian. *The East India Company.* New York: Barnes & Noble Books, 1971.

Gloag, John. *Mr. Loudon's England.* Newcastle upon Tyne, England: Oriel Press, 1970.

Golby, J. M., and A. W. Purdue. *The Civilisation of the Crowd.* London: Batsford Academic and Educational, 1984.

Gribbin, Mary, and John Gribbin. *Flower Hunters.* Oxford: Oxford University Press, 2008.

Hamilton, Jill. *Thomas Cook: The Holiday-Maker.* Gloucestershire, England: N.p.: Sutton Publishing, 2005.

Hibberd, Shirley. *Rustic Adornments for Homes of Taste.* London: Century, 1856.

———. *The Fern Garden: How to Make, Keep, and Enjoy It, or, Fern Culture Made Easy.* London: Groombridge and Sons, 1869.

Hill, Arthur W. "The History and Functions of Botanic Gardens." *Annals of the Missouri Botanical Garden 2 (1915)*: 185–234.

Hix, John. *The Glass House.* Cambridge, MA: MIT Press, 1974.

Hobhouse, Henry. *Seeds of Change: Five Plants That Transformed Mankind.* New York: Harper & Row, 1986.

Hochschild, Adam. *King Leopold's Ghost.* Boston: Houghton Mifflin, 1998.

Houghton, Walter E. *The Victorian Frame of Mind, 1830–1870.* New Haven, CT: Yale University Press, 1957.

Hove, Anton Panteleone. *Tours for Scientific and Economical Research Made in Guzerat, Kattiawar and the Conkuns, in 1787–88.* Bombay, India: Bombay Education Society's Press, 1855.

Hyams, Edward. *A History of Gardens and Gardening.* New York: Praeger, 1971.

Jackson, Hazelle. "A Brief History of Regent's Park." London Parks & Gardens Trust. http://www.londongardenstrust.org/features/regents.htm (last accessed 6/15/09).

Kallet, Arthur, and F. J. Schlink. *100,000,000 Guinea Pigs.* New York: Vanguard Press, 1933.

King, Ronald. *Royal Kew.* London: Constable, 1985.

Kingsley, Charles. *Glaucus, or The Wonders of the Shore.* London: Macmillan, 1881.

Knight, Charles, ed. *London, vol. 5.* London: Charles Knight & Co., 1843.

Kohlmaier, Georg, and Barna Von Sartory. *Houses of Glass.* Trans. John C. Harvey. Cambridge, MA: MIT Press, n.d.

Koopowitz, Harold. *Clivias.* Portland, OR: Timber Press, 2002.

Koppelkamm, Stefan. *Glasshouses and Wintergardens of the Nineteenth Century.* Trans. Kathrine Talbot. New York: Rizzoli International, 1981.

Kyte, Lydiane, and John Kleyn. *Plants from Test Tubes.* Portland, OR: Timber Press, 1996.

Lawrence, George H. M., ed. Hunt Botanical Library. Adanson. Pittsburgh: Carnegie Institute of Technology, 1965.

Lees-Milne, James. *The Bachelor Duke.* London: John Murray, 1991.

Lemmon, Kenneth. *The Covered Garden.* London: Museum Press, 1962.

———. *The Golden Age of Plant Hunters.* Cranbury, NJ: A. S. Barnes, 1969.

Loudon, John Claudius. *The Different Modes of Cultivating the Pine-apple.* London: Horticultural Society of London, 1822.

Lytle, Mark Hamilton. *The Gentle Subversive.* New York: Oxford University Press, 2007.

MacGregor, Arthur, ed. *Sir Hans Sloane.* London: British Museum Press, 1994.

Mangan, J. A., ed. *A Sport-Loving Society: Victorian and Edwardian Middle-Class England at Play.* Sport in the Global Society. London: Routledge-Taylor & Francis Group, 2005.

Martin, Tovah. *Once Upon a Windowsill.* Portland, OR: Timber Press, 1988.

———. *Well-Clad Windowsills.* New York: Macmillan, 1994.

McPhee, John. *Oranges.* New York: Farrar, Straus and Giroux, 1967.

A Medieval Herbal: A Facsimilie of British Library Egerton MS 747. London: Folio Society, 2002.

Minter, Sue. *The Apothecaries' Garden.* Gloucestershire, England: Sutton Publishing, 2000.

———. *The Greatest Glass House.* London: HMSO, 1990.

Morton, A. G. *History of Botanical Science.* London: Academic Press, 1981.

New York Botanical Garden. *Glasshouses.* Bronx: New York Botanical Garden, 2005.

Pavord, Anna. *The Naming of Names.* New York: Bloomsbury, 2005.

Perkins, John H. *Insects, Experts, and the Insecticide Crisis.* New York: Plenum Press, 1982.

Phillips, Samuel. *Guide to the Crystal Palace and Its Park and Gardens.* London: Bradbury & Evans, 1858.

Piggott, J. R. *Palace of the People.* Madison: University of Wisconsin Press, 2004.

Pleasant, Barbara. *The Complete Houseplant Survival Manual.* North Adams, MA: Storey Publishing, 2005.

Plever, Herb, and Joyce L. Brehm, eds. *Bromeliads.* Torrance, CA: The Bromeliad Society International, 2003.

Poynter, Jane. *The Human Experiment: Two Years and Twenty Minutes Inside Biosphere 2.* New York: Thunder's Mouth Press, 2006.

Prudentius, Aurelius Clemens. *The Hymns of Prudentius.* Middlesex, England: Echo Library, 2008.

Rincon-Vitova Insectary, www.rinconvitova.com/history.

Sheller, Mimi. *Consuming the Caribbean.* London: Routledge-Taylor & Francis Group, 2003.

Shofner, Jerrell H. *History of Apopka.* Tallahassee, FL: Apopka Historical Society, 1982.

Short, Philip. *In Pursuit of Plants.* Portland, OR: Timber Press, 2004.

Shteir, Ann B. *Cultivating Women, Cultivating Science.* Baltimore: Johns Hopkins University Press, 1996.

Simons, Paul, and John Ruthven. *Potted Histories.* London: BBC Books, 1995.

Solomon, David. *Loddiges of Hackney.* London: Hackney Society, 1995.

St. Ephrem. *Hymns on Paradise.* Trans. Sebastian Brock. Crestwood: St. Vladimary's Seminary Press, 1990.

Swithinbank, Anne. *The Conservatory Gardener.* New York: TODTRI, 1993.

Syon House. N.p.: Syon House Estate, 1968.

Tolkowsky, Samuel. *Hesperides.* London: John Bale, Sons & Curnow, 1938.

Tresidder, Jane, and Stafford Cliff. *Living Under Glass.* New York: Clarkson N. Potter, 1986.

Van den Bosch, Robert. *The Pesticide Conspiracy.* Garden City, NY: Doubleday, 1978.

Van den Muijzenberg, E. W. B. *A History of Greenhouses.* Wageningen, Holland: Insititute for Agricultural Engineering, 1980.

Whorton, James. *Before Silent Spring.* Princeton, NJ: Princeton University Press, 1974.

Williams, Roger L. *Botanophilia in Eighteenth-Century France.* Dordrecht, Germany: Kluwer Academic Publishers, 2001.

Woods, May, and Arete Swartz Warren. *Glass Houses.* New York: Rizzoli, 1988.

Wright, Lawrence. *Home Fires Burning.* London: Routledge & Kegan Paul, 1964.

Young, Linda. *Middle-Class Culture in the Nineteenth Century.* New York: Palgrave Macmillan, 2003.